REACTION AND RECONSTRUCTION IN ENGLISH POLITICS
1832-1852

REACTION AND RECONSTRUCTION IN ENGLISH POLITICS
1832–1852

THE FORD LECTURES

DELIVERED IN
THE UNIVERSITY OF OXFORD
IN THE HILARY TERM 1964

BY

NORMAN GASH

PROFESSOR OF HISTORY IN THE
UNIVERSITY OF ST. ANDREWS

GREENWOOD PRESS, PUBLISHERS
WESTPORT, CONNECTICUT

Library of Congress Cataloging in Publication Data

Gash, Norman.
    Reaction and reconstruction in English politics,
1832-1952.

    Reprint. Originally published: Oxford : Clarendon
Press. (The Ford lectures ; 1964)
    Bibliography: p.
    Includes index.
    1. Great Britain--Politics and government--1830-
1837. 2. Great Britain--Politics and government--
1837-1901. I. Title. II. Series: Ford lectures ;
1964.
DA559.7.G35 1981   941.07'5   81-1813
ISBN 0-313-22927-9 (lib. bdg.)   AACR2

This reprint has been authorized by the Oxford University
Press.

Reprinted in 1981 by Greenwood Press
A division of Congressional Information Service, Inc.
88 Post Road West, Westport, Connecticut 06881

Printed in the United States of America

10 9 8 7 6 5 4 3 2 1

IN MEMORIAM

F.G.   1963   K.G.

A.W.

'After the result of the first general election under the Reform Bill was known, the exclamation resounded throughout the land: "The Tory party is annihilated!" The Whigs believed that they were firmly established in power for half a century, and their opponents, although they talked of "reaction", had no serious hopes of rallying during the present generation.'

LORD CAMPBELL

'Their lot was cast in the ten years of inevitable reaction, when, the Reform excitement being over, and the few legislative improvements which the public really called for having been rapidly effected, power gravitated back in its natural direction, to those who were for keeping things as they were.'

J. S. MILL

FOREWORD

THESE lectures are printed as given except for some passages, mainly in chapters V and VI, which had to be omitted in delivery because of limitations of time. I have, on the other hand, made fuller use of footnotes than I would otherwise have felt justified in doing, in order to expand and illustrate points more briefly made in the text.

I wish to express my deep gratitude to the University of Oxford and to the Board of Electors to the Ford lectureship for the honour they did me in inviting me to deliver the lectures. I take this opportunity also of thanking the President and Fellows of my own college of St. John's for the personal kindness and hospitality they showed me during the period when the lectures were being given.

My further acknowledgements are due to His Grace the Duke of Wellington, to the Earl of Clarendon, to Sir Fergus Graham, and to Major-General E. H. Goulburn for their courtesy in allowing me to quote from their family papers; and to Professor W. O. Aydelotte for assistance and information on many points connected with the Parliament of 1841–7. My friend and colleague Dr. F. A. Dreyer not only taught me much in his unpublished thesis on 'The Russell Administration, 1846–52' and in many conversations, but with great generosity put at my disposal his transcripts of the Russell, Grey, Broughton, and Clarendon MSS. for that period. One other indebtedness may be mentioned. I began systematic reading for these lectures when I was Hinkley Visiting Professor at Johns Hopkins University in 1962. If I now gratefully recall the leisure and facilities afforded me there by the staff of the history department under their chairman Dr. Charles Barker, they will know that I am only recording a small part of the sum of my obligations to them.

NORMAN GASH

St. Salvator's College
St. Andrews
July 1964

CONTENTS

I

THE END OF THE HANOVERIAN MONARCHY

'THIS', said the *Edinburgh Review* in 1831,[1] 'is the age of reform.' Yet John Stuart Mill, looking back on his early manhood among the Philosophic Radicals of the 1830's, reflected that 'their lot was cast in the ten years of inevitable reaction' after the Reform Act and the 'few legislative improvements which the public really called for' had been effected.[2] The sententious truism of the *Review* is a commonplace; Mill's observation has been less often repeated. Yet there is an undeniable truth in what he said. The truth, moreover, is considerably broadened if we interpret reaction not merely in the political sense of negative opposition but also in the physical sense: the response of men and institutions who were not eager for innovation but who under pressure were politic enough to accept and even initiate reforms of a select and modified kind. There is even a third category: men who started as reformers but were either disappointed at the results of reform or disturbed at the lengths to which others wished to carry it.

It is a melancholy thought that as soon as reforms are put into practice, disillusionment enters the political scene. The great initial reforms of the 1820's, designed to pacify and heal, seemed only to exacerbate feeling. The return to gold in 1821 and the attempts to revise the Corn Laws between 1822 and 1828 created the unease among agriculturists which flared up so memorably in 1846. The repeal of the Test and Corporations Acts in 1828 was followed by twenty years of greater bitterness between Church and Dissent than had been known since Queen Anne's reign. The passage of Catholic Emancipation was followed by twenty years of growing fear and dislike of Roman Catholicism. The Reform Act of 1832 was followed by the political alienation of the working classes, the progressive

---

[1] Vol. 53, p. 384 (June 1831), article on 'The Universities of England—Oxford'.
[2] J. S. Mill, *Autobiography* (1873), p. 195.

B

disillusionment of many of the middle classes, the decline of parliamentary radicalism, and the emergence of the two greatest extra-parliamentary political movements of the century; while the Crown and the House of Lords were more active in the succeeding five years—and more active against reform—than in the preceding twenty-five. The domestic history of the 1832–52 period can be largely construed in terms of those who wished to press forward, those who wished to compound with, and those who wished to resist 'the Movement' (in the phrase borrowed from continental politics) which had won its first successes in the great organic changes of 1828–32. By themselves those changes decided very little; they were facilitating rather than operative measures. The crucial issue was what religious equality and parliamentary reform would mean in the language of practical legislation and exercise of power. In a sense, it was only after the Reform Act had passed that the real crisis began: the post-Reform crisis of adjustment between what had been done and what men thought should be the consequences of what had been done. Many of the subsequent reforms are important; but equally significant is the phenomenon of reforms attempted and defeated, and those deflected or transformed.

There is a case then for trying to give a more general and synoptic treatment to those aspects of the period after 1832 which consisted in reaction to reform; and they can be studied most clearly in the context of the political constitution, not only because the effective test was political, but also because that constitution itself was the main object of assault. As a generalization, what gave unity and coherence to the early nineteenth-century reform movement was the attack on the eighteenth-century structure of social and political power. The 'Movement' had an undeniable air of class war. But there were many cross-currents, and it was a confused conflict which did not end in complete victory or complete defeat. If the period after 1852 is, as Professor Burn has called it, an age of equipoise, it was because the previous decades had seen a prolonged battle of interests, parties, and ideas in which most of the combatants fought themselves to a standstill. Yet there was no sudden change from reform to stagnation. The equilibrium had already begun to assert itself in the 1840's. Rival strengths had been tested at various points, and the limits of effective action more clearly marked than ever before. Much was done; a great deal abandoned as impracticable. The exaggerated hopes and fears of the reform era gave way to a more sober appraisement of the realities of social and political life; and in the end the moderate men were left in possession of the field.

II

An analysis of post-Reform Act politics from this standpoint may conveniently begin with the obvious and relatively simple problem of the monarchy. When men spoke,[1] in the conventional constitutional vocabulary of the day, of the destruction by the Reform Act of the balance of the constitution, they were not entirely unreasonable or unrealistic. If the Act enhanced the power of the Commons, it inevitably diminished that of the other two branches of the legislature: the Crown and the House of Lords. Yet the power of the Crown in this context largely meant its ability to influence the House of Commons; and this power had been declining for the previous half-century. The Reform Act added to the decline in a physical sense by diminishing the number of close constituencies. But the ability of the Crown to 'make a House' had disappeared before 1832. The general election of 1830 did not see, in any modern sense, the defeat of the Government; yet the resignation of the Wellington Ministry in November, through lack of support in the Commons, and so soon after a general election, was a clear sign of the weakness of executive influence. Any technical effect the Reform Act had in increasing this weakness operated mainly in one narrow but important sphere: the inability of a new Ministry even to be sure of getting its official House of Commons men re-elected on taking office, for sheer lack of enough safe seats in which to stow them. One primary technical reason for Peel's dissolution in 1834 was the difficulty of forming a new Ministry without it. Since, in view of the disparity of parties, a dissolution was inevitable sooner or later, any men appointed

[1] For example Sir George Clerk at the Constitutional Meeting at Edinburgh, 28 Nov. 1831: 'It was absolutely necessary for the safe working of the Constitution that both the Crown and the Aristocracy should have a direct influence in the House of Commons, to prevent the dangers that would arise if the three branches of the Legislature were to be kept quite distinct and separate from each other, according to what some persons believed to be the true theory of the Constitution' (*Report of the Speeches at* &c., Edinburgh, 1831).

with seats in the Lower House would have had to face the prospect of two elections in quick succession; and there were not many who could risk or afford that.[1] Yet if the King could not change his Ministers without a general election, this in itself was a serious limitation on his freedom of action. As Burdett wrote in November 1834,

I fear the King has made a rash move and with no apparent justification, and as by the Reform Bill he cannot in reality appoint his Ministers, as whoever he appoints must go to large bodies of constituents to be approved, and as in the present unsettled state of the public mind, they may very likely be rejected, the King and the country will be placed in a very dangerous position.[2]

The pre-existing limitations on the royal power are obscured, however, by the coincidence that 1830 saw both a Reform Ministry and a new King.

In part the contrast between the monarchy before and after

[1] Peel, *Memoirs*, ed. Lord Mahon and E. Cardwell, 1856, ii. 47. This was one of several counter-arguments against those who thought that Peel in 1834–5 should have followed the line taken by Pitt in 1783–4: that of meeting Parliament and bidding for public support before holding an election. Talking to Gladstone a couple of years later about the decision in 1834 to dissolve without meeting Parliament, Aberdeen argued that a Government could not be *made* in a reformed Parliament and dissolution was therefore necessary, although in other respects it would have been preferable to have met Parliament and explained the government's policy before going to the country (Add. MS. 44777, f. 31).

[2] M. W. Patterson, *Sir Francis Burdett*, ii. 627. From the Ministerial point of view, the statutory vacation of House of Commons seats on appointment to office was a serious handicap to manœuvre. During the Reform Bill discussions Lord Northampton brought in a Bill (subsequently abandoned) to repeal the Act of Anne (6 Anne c. 7) which Lord Grey was said to favour (A. Aspinall, *Three Early Nineteenth Century Diaries*, p. 271 and n.). In 1835 Grey was ready to consider a reduction in the maximum duration of Parliament in exchange for a measure to abolish the need for vacation of seats on appointment (*Melbourne Papers*, ed. L. C. Sanders, pp. 247–8). Examples of the embarrassment caused are plentiful. Thus in 1839 there was a strong feeling in the Government in favour of a sweeping reshuffle of offices, but both Russell and Lansdowne agreed that this could not be done without so many fresh elections that it might entail a dissolution of Parliament and a general election (Spencer Walpole, *Life of Lord John Russell* (1891), i. 335). Equal difficulties presented themselves to the Opposition. In the winter of 1839–40 Graham, discussing the situation which might arise if the Conservatives took office without a previous dissolution, pointed out that between mid February and late April no Government could dissolve because of the need to pass the Mutiny Act and vote Service supplies before 25 April, when the Act expired. A new Ministry taking office in that period could not dissolve and would have to meet Parliament with some thirty or forty members absent securing their re-election (Add. MS. 40318, f. 173). On the other hand, when Peel formed a Government in 1841 immediately after a general election, all the House of Commons Ministers were re-elected without the loss of a single seat.

the Reform Act is a personal one. George IV had been in most respects a highly constitutional King. He had never dismissed a Ministry (except Wellington's in 1829 and then only for a few agitated hours); he maintained in office the Ministers he had inherited from his father; he accepted Canning's return to the Cabinet in 1822 under pressure from Liverpool and Wellington; he accepted Catholic Emancipation in 1829 under pressure from Wellington and Peel. His one major act of choice —the appointment of Canning as Prime Minister in 1827—was the one clearly pointed out by all public and personal considerations.[1] His influence on Government policy was peripheral and not central; his intervention in administration exasperating but not critical. No doubt indolence and cowardice explained this constitutional propriety. 'George IV is the model of a constitutional King of England', remarked Campbell, the ironic Whig lawyer, in April 1830 as the King lay dying. 'And when he is missed, he may be mourned. *He has stood by and let the country govern itself.*'[2] By contrast William IV was a cauldron of energy. In his short reign of seven years, he twice dismissed a Ministry;[3] twice dissolved Parliament for political purposes before its time; three times made formal proposals to his Ministers for a coalition with their political opponents; and on one celebrated occasion allowed his name to be used, independently of his political advisers, to influence a crucial vote in the House of Lords.

Moreover, William had a recognizable policy, even if he could not enforce it; and it was a policy arising directly from the Reform crisis of 1831–2. If he is to be placed in any political category, he was an 'Old Whig'. He agreed with his Ministers that a measure of parliamentary reform was expedient, and to be useful, must be effective. But the first Reform Bill was the beginning and end of his reform career. He felt deceived, as he had certainly been misled,[4] on the chances of passing such a

---

[1] See, for example, the letter from S. R. Lushington to Knighton, 26 Mar. 1827 (*Letters of George IV*, ed. A. Aspinall, iii. 207).

[2] *Life of Lord Campbell*, ed. Mrs. Hardcastle (1881), i. 467.

[3] Technically the dismissal of Grey's Ministry in 1832, like that of Wellington's in 1829, was the resignation of Ministers in the face of royal refusal to accept their advice. The practical issue was virtually the same, however, as the monarch knew in each case that his action would involve parting with his Ministry.

[4] For example, 'Earl Grey is very sanguine in his hopes of being able to carry

Bill through the existing Parliament; and when first a dissolution of the Lower and then coercion of the Upper House became necessary, he moved rapidly into a conservative position. In a sense his was the first great defection from the Whig Ministry, preceding that of Stanley and Graham, and after a fashion that of Grey himself. Indeed, given the King's greater latitude of action as an individual unhampered by party or Cabinet loyalties, his action in 1834 in dismissing Melbourne is the equivalent of Grey's retirement from the Government or Stanley's secession and ultimate junction with the Conservatives. Like Graham, William IV could charge the Whigs with having kept the name but lost the principle; it was not that the King had altered but that the Whigs had progressed. For William the Reform Act had been the final, complete, and generous concession to a public demand. It left the country with what he described to Brougham in 1834 as its 'present admirable constitution and valuable institutions'.[1] He regarded 1832 therefore as the terminus and not the starting-point of the reform movement. The tendency apparent in the Whig party even under Grey to move with public opinion and introduce reform measures for Ireland, the Church, and municipal corporations filled him with distrust. When under Melbourne the tendency became a policy, he was driven to oppose. The considerations which impelled him were not merely narrow fears for himself and his office, but a wider if ignorant concern for the Church, to which he was sincerely and naïvely attached, the authority of government in Ireland, and the position of the aristocracy, of which (wrote his Secretary, Sir Herbert Taylor) 'he considers the existence and the maintenance with unimpaired influence, to be clearly connected with that of the monarchy, and essential to the character and the credit of the country'.[2]

The abrupt dismissal of the Whigs in 1834, though the most ostentatious, was not the only effective way in which the King's hostility manifested itself; but it did at least illustrate William's

---

this important measure successfully through Parliament' (Grey to the King, 8 Feb. 1831); and, 'I still feel assured . . . that there will be a considerable majority on Monday in favour of Reform' (Grey to Taylor, 19 Mar. 1831. *Correspondence of Earl Grey and William IV*, i. 118, 154).

[1] Lord Brougham, *Life and Times* (1871), iii. 403.

[2] Ibid. 407.

conception of the royal prerogative and throw into sharp relief the deciding forces in the political field. By 1834 the King was already deeply suspicious of the Whigs. The resignation of the Stanleyites crystallized this feeling into a determination to change the Ministry at the first opportunity. As long as Grey held office, the King had too much respect and confidence in him to dismiss the Cabinet; but when Grey in turn resigned in July 1834, the royal politician made his first move. Melbourne was summoned not to form a Whig Ministry but to engineer a conservative coalition. He was desired to communicate with Peel, Stanley, and the Duke of Wellington, 'with others of their respective parties', for the purpose of forming an alliance of moderates to resist further change. Melbourne refused; not only, he replied, had Peel, Wellington, and Stanley opposed Irish measures which Melbourne considered 'vital and essential', but there did not appear 'any ground upon which they can be brought together at present, nor any chance of such an accommodation as would be consistent with their own avowed principles, and satisfactory to the country'.[1] At the King's request he forwarded the correspondence to Stanley and the Conservative leaders; but no more support was forthcoming from the men in opposition than from those in power. Peel sent Melbourne a memorandum for the King stating that a coalition was impossible and pointing out that if Grey's Ministry had broken up on internal differences within the Whig party, how much more would members of opposed parties fail to agree.[2] The King in fact had run his head not so much against

[1] W. M. Torrens, *Memoirs of Lord Melbourne* (1890), pp. 288–90.

[2] Peel, *Memoirs*, ii. 7–11. It is clear that this was not merely a matter of bringing together men who had been formerly opposed and who might therefore consider their personal honour engaged if they consented to a coalition. Undoubtedly this personal factor played a part; but Peel rested his case on a wider basis. 'Such an union could not, in the present state of parties and the present position of public affairs, hold out the prospect of an efficient and vigorous administration. . . . The impracticability of reuniting in Your Majesty's service those who were agreed in their general views of policy, appears to exclude the hope that any selection of men from parties opposed to each other could at the present time ensure an administration united in principle and strong in the mutual confidence of its members.' Grey in retirement saw no more prospect of a workable coalition than the active politicians. 'The King wishes to bring about an union of Parties. This is simply and absolutely impossible. The only practicable alternative that I can see is the formation of a Tory Administration, under the Duke of Wellington or Sir Robert Peel' (Grey to Wellesley, 12 July 1834. G. M. Trevelyan, *Lord Grey of the Reform Bill* (1952). Appendix J, p. 392).

the Reform Parliament as against the party system; though perhaps the two were not unconnected. He now turned to direct negotiation with his Minister on matters of policy and personnel. The construction of a Whig Government could no longer be prevented, but he thought some adjustment and modification might result from the private use of royal influence. He began by putting two questions: what materials would Melbourne use to construct his Ministry, and what security could be given against the introduction of those whose principles the King 'dreads and deprecates'. Melbourne's reply was a courteous rebuke for what he clearly thought was unwarrantable interference. To answer the first question, he wrote, would also reply to the second; but in any case the principle of exclusion was 'impolitic and dangerous', and he hoped the King would allow him to reserve to himself the right of recommending Ministers.[1] It was plain that as long as Melbourne was entrusted with the government, he would carry out his own views and choose his own men. A coalition had been demonstrated to be impossible. There remained one last way of opposing the march of reform: the dismissal of the Whigs and their replacement by the Conservatives.

By any calculation it was a hazardous stroke. Nothing like the 1834 experiment had been attempted by the Crown for over a quarter of a century. George IV had never tried anything so foolhardy. Even in eighteenth-century conditions William's action would have been a rash and precipitous one; and the conditions had altered vastly since then. Nevertheless, the altered conditions had never been tested in precisely this way. William at least remedied that constitutional deficiency. There were several problems involved. Could anything be attempted while Melbourne retained his Ministerial and House of Commons solidity? It might entail an appeal to the country. Would a general election under new Ministers strengthen or diminish reforming influence? And finally, what pretext or occasion could the King use for dismissing his Ministers and how would the country react to this extraordinary use of the royal prerogative? The last question perhaps troubled the King least. The right of choosing his own Ministers was one which William undoubtedly felt he possessed, and he was not without support

[1] *Melbourne Papers*, pp. 205–6.

for that view. It is easy both to overestimate and misinterpret the indignation his action evoked. The Whigs were naturally surprised and embittered at being suddenly thrust from place and power; and the Conservatives themselves felt that the King's action had been ill-timed. But the fact that the King had been prejudiced and unwise did not make his action illegal or unconstitutional. The political opposition to a partisan act of the Crown must be distinguished from the constitutional opposition to a violation of convention. Of the latter there was remarkably little, and for some people indeed the intervention of the Crown might have been decisive in preventing opposition to the new Ministry.[1] Althorp (now Lord Spencer) and Russell might think privately that it would be a constitutional error to pass over the dismissal of the Melbourne Ministry without a formal parliamentary protest; but this pure milk of Whig principle was too heady for most parliamentarians.[2]

In the end Russell bowed to the general opinion in his party. A direct motion of censure was avoided because it could not have been carried; and the Opposition amendment to the address made the dissolution of Parliament and not the change of Government its primary object of attack. The argument in general revolved round the policy and character of the new Ministry rather than the action of the Crown. The crucial debate was on the Address, and in moving it Lord Sandon declared at the outset that, though a supporter of the Reform Bill in all its main stages, 'I was yet not inclined to put upon it that construction which it has of late been the fashion to force upon it, viz., that it was not so much intended to give to public opinion a useful and efficient control over the measures of the Ministers of the Crown, as to decide who those Ministers should be.' Morpeth, the mover of the Whig amendment, while admitting the 'undoubted prerogative' of the Crown to dismiss Ministers, argued that 'whether before or after the passing of

[1] Cf. *Greville Memoirs*, 27 Nov. 1834: 'Though the Crown is not so powerful as it was, there probably still remains a great deal of attachment and respect to it, and if the King can show a fair case to the country, there will be found both in Parliament and out of it a vast number of persons who will reflect deeply upon the consequences of coming to a serious collision with the Throne, and consider whether the exigency is such as to justify such extremities.' Melbourne thought 'the increase of Tories, though perhaps principally owing to the natural influence of the Government and of the King's name, shows to a certain degree a change of opinion in the country' (*Melbourne Papers*, p. 238).   [2] Walpole, *Russell*, i. 219, 226–7.

the Reform Bill, the power must reside with this House—and through this House, with the people of this country—of deciding who the Ministers of the Crown are to be'. But if he meant anything precise by this rather vague form of words, he received little backing in the debate. Granted the acknowledged right of the Crown to appoint and dismiss Ministers, it would have required some hardihood to claim for the House of Commons the power of nominating Ministers. Bannerman,[1] a Scottish Liberal M.P. who seconded Morpeth, declared that 'he considered it of little importance who His Majesty's Ministers were so long as they acted in accordance with the just and legitimate wishes of the people'. Even T. Gisborne, who delivered one of the most slashing speeches against the Government, said no more than that 'he would claim for the Commons of England the right to determine who should be the Minister in this country. He would claim it negatively as to persons, but positively as to principles'.[2] The ranks of the Radicals themselves were divided on the issue; either, with Attwood, because of pleasure at the fall of 'the false, perjured and cruel Whigs',[3] or from a sense that the King still had a function in politics. This latter was most strongly stated by Cobbett in an open letter to Hume. The King, he argued with his usual vehemence in one of the last great public controversies of his career, was politically right in evicting the wretched Whig crew and constitutionally justified in exercising 'the undoubted prerogative of the King which has been given for our security; and which if it be not exercised with perfect freedom, makes him a slave and totally useless to us'.[4] The electorate at large, by adding a hundred

[1] Alexander Bannerman, Liberal M.P. for Aberdeen 1833–47, shipowner, banker, and merchant at Aberdeen; later colonial governor, knighted 1851.

[2] For the quotations from the debate, see Hansard, *Parl. Deb.*, vol. 26, 151–2, 167–9, 174, 371.

[3] C. M. Wakefield, *Life of Attwood* (1885), p. 282. Cf. speech by J. Richards, M.P. for Knaresborough, *Hansard*, loc. cit. 185 and appendix (p. 1248).

[4] *Weekly Political Register*, 13 Dec. 1834. When the House of Commons met and Manners Sutton's nomination for the Speakership was challenged, Cobbett announced that his constituents had voted an address to the King, thanking him for having dismissed his late Ministers, and he would do nothing to force them back on the King. Arguments similar to those of Cobbett were of course put on the Conservative side. Cf. the Address of the Conservative Candidates for the City of London, which argued that the functions of the Crown as an element in the Constitution would be a nullity unless the King could change his Ministers if he thought it in the public interest (*Annual Register*, 1835, pp. [12, [34).

M.P.s to the party which the King called to power, did little to contradict Cobbett's thesis.

The more important problem was to gauge the moment for the effective use of the royal prerogative. The summer of 1834 saw some signs of Conservative revival;[1] on the other hand, after Grey's retirement, the Radical elements in the Ministry seemed to be gathering strength. The question of the Irish Church and the appropriation of Church property had been raised, and if the Cabinet was not entirely united, it was clear from a disclosure made by Duncannon[2] that a fresh forward step would be taken. Althorp's elevation to the Lords seemed therefore to create an admirable opportunity. The Cabinet changes it necessitated were large enough to give colour to the withdrawal of the King's confidence; while the departure of the popular leader of the House would weaken the charge that the Crown had dismissed a Ministry enjoying the full support of the Commons. There can be no doubt that, from the tone of Melbourne's preliminary letter on the loss of Althorp's services, the King nourished the hope that the Ministry would voluntarily resign. His disappointment must have been considerable when Melbourne went down to Brighton on 13 November and refrained from any suggestion that it would be impossible for him to carry on the Government. But the fruit was ripe, and if it did not fall, the tree must be shaken. The King had thought the Government would go; he now made up his mind that it should go. Melbourne did not resign; he was dismissed.[3] The motives and reasons given by the King were various but the dominant one is clear. Apart from William's general feeling against the Whigs, the ground for their dismissal in November 1834 was not the retirement of Althorp nor the behaviour of Brougham, but Lord John Russell and Irish Church policy. Russell was marked out as the most important of the reforming

[1] The installation of the Duke of Wellington as Chancellor of Oxford University had been made the occasion for a display of the recovered strength and unity of Toryism.

[2] 'Some imprudence on the part of Duncannon, who had opened to him [sc. the King] prematurely the measure which he proposed to found upon the Report of the Commission of Enquiry in Ireland' (Melbourne to Grey, 14 Nov. 1834, *Melbourne Papers*, p. 225).

[3] There seem no grounds for the old suggestion (e.g. E. Halévy, *History of the English People, 1830–1841* (1927), pp. 178–9; Patterson, *Burdett*, ii. 625) that Melbourne engineered his own fall.

Whigs; he was openly pledged to the principle of the appropriation of Irish Church funds. If he now succeeded, as Melbourne
proposed, to the posts of Leader of the House and Chancellor of the Exchequer, his authority would be immeasurably
enhanced; and the cause of the Church correspondingly
depressed.[1] The King's attitude was comprehensible and not
without logic. The departure of Stanley, Graham, Richmond,
Ripon, Grey, and Althorp had deprived the Ministry of much
of its original character and simultaneously weakened its position in Parliament. Either the Ministers would find it more
difficult to carry on the Government, or they would have to
seek Radical support by putting forward radical measures.
The proposed appointment of Russell seemed a clear indication
of what the choice would be. Melbourne pointed out that neither
he himself nor the King had pledged themselves to specific
measures and that the King could always refuse assent to anything submitted to him. But to William's uncomplicated mind
it seemed better to act before matters reached such a crisis;
and he proceeded to realize a long-cherished dream. The Whigs
left office and the Conservatives came in.[2]

[1] 'His Majesty could not have sanctioned the nomination of Lord John Russell
to the office of Chancellorship of the Exchequer, without bringing into question
the sincerity of his Declaration that He would resist the encroachments to the pro-
secution of which that Individual had pledged himself' (William IV's Memorandum, 14 Jan. 1835, Add. MS. 40302, ff. 210–11; cf. Walpole, *Russell*, i. 217–18;
Greville, 27 Nov. 1834: 'the gist of the King's objection was the nomination of Lord
John Russell to lead the Government in the House of Commons').

[2] For details of what passed between William IV and Melbourne see C. S.
Parker, *Sir Robert Peel*, ii. 252–6; *Melbourne Papers*, pp. 219–28; Stockmar, *Memoirs*,
i. 312–50 (King's Memorandum) of which a manuscript version is in Add. MS.
40302, ff. 194 seq. Lord Melbourne was formally dismissed from office by a note
handed to him on the morning of 14 Nov. As it stood, the note grounded the
King's case on the position and character of Lord John Russell—'His Majesty
does not conceive the Individuals proposed to lead in the House of Commons
have that weight and consideration with the Members of that House and with the
country at large, to be able to carry on the government.' Melbourne pointed out
that this might cause some pain, and the King therefore accepted his suggestion
that the passage quoted above should be altered to: 'His Majesty conceives that the
general weight and consideration of the present Government is so much diminished
in the House of Commons and with the country at large, as to render it impossible
that they should continue to conduct the public affairs in the Commons.' This
amended text is the one printed, e.g., in Peel, *Memoirs*, ii. 22; the original version
is given in Add. MS. 40303, f. 227. By this alteration the emphasis was shifted
from the positive objection to Russell to the negative consideration of the loss of
Althorp. But in the King's mind the retirement of Althorp was significant only
because it made room for Russell's advancement.

In the early days of the formation of Peel's short 1834–5 Ministry, a pivotal role was played by Stanley and his 'third party'; and the King did what he could to secure that junction of forces which most moderate Conservatives regarded as the only hope of success. He warmly approved Peel's original overture, and when it failed, Sir Herbert Taylor suggested that a letter to Stanley from the King might prove useful, at any rate in strengthening Stanley's general inclination to support the new Government. Peel discouraged the project;[1] but in February 1835, after Parliament had met, letters from Lady Stanley to her uncle Sir Herbert Taylor,[2] describing the strength, deliberations, and feelings of the Stanley group, were forwarded by the King's wish to Peel; and Taylor's replies to his niece, also approved by the King, were a direct encourage-ment for Stanley to show friendship to the Ministry. But in view of Stanley's known dislike of Wellington, which was a major cause of his refusal to enter the Cabinet, Peel felt some delicacy in continuing to receive and thus indirectly sanction these backstairs communications. After the second letter from Lady Stanley, Peel refused to see any more.[3] It was soon clear that the idea of a Peel–Stanley coalition had been abandoned on both sides, and the King was early faced with the prospect of losing the Ministry he had risked so much to secure. En-couragement and persuasion were now the only weapons he had left with which to avert that personal disaster. Laying down the old-fashioned principle that 'the Confidence, the Counten-ance and the Support of the Sovereign are indispensable to the Existence and the Maintenance of the Government, so long as the Constitution of the country is monarchical'[4] he sent a despairing appeal not to be abandoned to the fury of the Oppo-sition; and he asked Peel to make every endeavour to induce moderate men on both sides to lay aside party prejudices and form a Government on a firm and extended basis for the

[1] Taylor even sent the draft of a royal letter for Peel's comments, though he said he had not spoken to the King about it. However, as Peel recorded, 'I wrote in reply discouraging the letter being sent to Lord Stanley, seeing no advantage likely to result from it' (Add. MS. 40302, f. 42, 13 Dec. 1834).

[2] Sir H. Taylor's sister Elizabeth married Edward Bootle-Wilbraham of Lathom House (cr. Baron Skelmersdale 1828) and her daughter Emma Caroline married Lord Stanley in 1825.

[3] Add. MS. 40303, ff. 23, 25, 29, 33.

[4] Ibid., f. 8, printed Parker, *Peel*, ii. 287.

maintenance and defence of the Constitution, against what he described as 'Degradation, Anarchy, and Ruin'. Stanley, Grey, and Melbourne were mentioned as possible participants in this rescue operation.[1] But coalition, to which William, like most monarchs, habitually resorted in time of stress, was too impracticable even to obtain discussion. The issue to which Peel attached greater weight was the continued damage to royal authority inflicted by a House of Commons defeating on every important point the Ministers whom the King had put into office.[2] It was partly therefore to diminish the consequences of the King's rash act that Peel resigned as soon as it was clear that the majority of the House of Commons was against him and that there was no hope of any significant shift of opinion. To the end the King struggled against the inevitable. In place of Melbourne he summoned Grey to the Palace after Peel's resignation. Grey advised him to call in Melbourne and Lansdowne. When they appeared the following day, the King again brought up his coalition proposal. But both Whig leaders declared it was impossible, and at last on the third day, 11 April 1835, Melbourne was summoned alone and asked to form a Government.

The King had been defeated. He had been defeated in his coalition policy because leading politicians felt too divided from each other not only by their past record but by actual party attachments and current political problems. Party was important because it stood not merely for political connexions but also for profound disagreements on contemporary issues. It was the paradox of the King's position that the very political circumstances which impelled him to action ensured that his action would be unsuccessful. A coalition would be called on not just to govern the country but to implement policy; and it was on the implementation of policy that a coalition would break down. He had been defeated also in the attempt to find an alternative Ministry, and the reason for this was that in the mid 1830's the only kind of House of Commons that the electoral system would produce leaned preponderantly towards one party

---

[1] Add. MS. 40303, ff. 8–11, 112–25.

[2] 'The longer we protract the struggle, if that struggle shall be ultimately unavailing, the more certain will be the blow at Royal authority' (Peel to Wellington, 4 Apr. 1835. Parker, *Peel*, ii. 302).

and one set of Ministers. No mechanism that the executive by itself could employ was capable of reversing that situation. Time, public opinion, and party organization alone could achieve an alteration. Yet these were purely political factors, and not necessarily permanent. No one in 1835 could foresee that the country had witnessed the last dismissal of a Ministry by the Crown. The King had been guilty not of constitutional impropriety but at most of political ineptitude. He had failed because he had overstepped the limitations that must necessarily accompany the legal exercise of any political and constitutional power. Yet the principle of royal choice remained. Eleven years later, for example, in May 1846, Peel was urged by Ellen-borough to announce on resigning that he would give every possible assistance to the formation of a Conservative Govern-ment. Peel gave two reasons for refusing. The second was that such a Ministry would presumably be pledged to some form of protectionism. But the first reason he adduced was that 'I think the Queen ought in the event you suppose to have a perfectly unfettered choice in respect to those whom she might be disposed to select for her confidence. It clearly would not be unfettered were those who retired from her service and by retire-ment left her in great difficulty, to intimate to her that they would support only one particular set of Ministers.'[1]

The crisis of 1834–5 became in retrospect a constitutional landmark only because about seven years later the Crown began effectively to detach itself from party politics. Moreover, William's action in that crisis, though useless for its main pur-pose, was by no means futile. Its consequences, however, were political rather than constitutional; and its beneficiaries the Conservative party rather than the Crown. The King's single act had rallied the forces of the Right, established Peel as head of the party, strengthened it with a hundred new members in the Commons, and enabled it to make a classic definition of its principles in the Tamworth Manifesto. But for the Crown it was total defeat. George III had suffered humiliations but had always gained the final victory. William IV gained a tem-porary satisfaction at the cost of permanent humiliation. He had himself at the start of the crisis likened his action to that of his

[1] Ellenborough to Peel, 29 May; Peel to Ellenborough, 30 May 1846 (Add. MS. 40473, ff. 328, 331; Ellenborough Papers, P.R.O. 30/12/21/1).

father in dismissing Fox and North in 1783.[1] It was an heroic precedent and the parallel occurred to many other people. But these were no longer heroic days for the monarchy; and in the months that succeeded the fall of the Hundred Days Ministry both Peel and Sir Herbert Taylor used their joint endeavours to persuade him of the truth '(which must be apparent however obnoxious its admission) that the joint influence of the King and the House of Lords cannot maintain a Government that cannot command a majority in the House of Commons'.[2] The truth was perhaps a truism; but it was the King's action that made it demonstrably so.

But losing game though it was, there was still one rather well-worn card in the royal pack that William now produced: the King's conscience. In April 1835, when Melbourne returned to office, William told him that his objection to the Irish Church Bill was a matter not merely of politics but of conscience, arising out of his Coronation Oath, and suggested that a committee of judges should be asked to give a ruling on the question. Melbourne refused to sanction such an elaboration of scruple. The King had appointed the Ministry and must either accept their advice or call in others.[3] William then tried another way. Lyndhurst, the Lord Chancellor of Peel's Administration, still held office pending the various negotiations which delayed the final arrangements for Melbourne's second ministry. The King suggested that the issue of obligation deriving from the Coronation Oath should be referred to Lyndhurst in Melbourne's presence. This too Melbourne refused, though he told the King that there was no objection to his obtaining private advice from any quarter he chose. Taking advantage of this, the King wrote to Lyndhurst on 16 April, telling him that he

[1] Ellenborough Journal, 21 Nov. 1834, P.R.O. 30/12/28/5.

[2] Taylor to Peel, 19 July 1835 (Add. MS. 40303, f. 240). It is clear that Peel was writing confidentially to Taylor at this time, using his influence through Taylor to get the King into a sober and accommodating course of political action.

[3] This seems to be the clear implication of Melbourne's language. Reminding the King of the circumstances of the recent change of Ministry and the proceedings in the House of Commons with respect to the appropriation clause, Melbourne told him that the Whigs 'cannot . . . undertake to carry on your Majesty's government unless it is understood that they are to act without delay upon the principle of the resolution', and again, 'if Your Majesty appoints them your Ministers Your Majesty must take them pledged and bound to act upon those their recorded principles' (Melbourne Papers, pp. 274, 276, 15 Apr. 1835).

understood that over the question of the Tithes Bill 'His [sc. the King's] special consent will be required in some of the first stages of the Bill inasmuch as its provisions will affect some of the benefices which are in the gift of the Crown'; and asking Lyndhurst's opinion whether the King could consent 'without violating the obligations imposed by his Coronation Oath'. The political embarrassment of the situation was obvious. Lyndhurst passed the letter to his party leader for advice; and Peel drafted a letter which Lyndhurst copied and sent to the King the same day.

It would not be proper [ran the material part of Lyndhurst's answer] for him to advise your Majesty upon the point on which you have been pleased to require his opinion. . . . Your Majesty is aware of the relative position of your Majesty and the Lord Chancellor at this period and it is a consideration of that position which has mainly influenced the Lord Chancellor in arriving at the Conclusion before referred to. . . . The Bill to which your Majesty refers is one with the details of which the Lord Chancellor is necessarily unacquainted . . . the Ministers who propose it, must be responsible for the Advice which they might tender to your Majesty.[1]

This of course was only a statement of Peel's view of Ministerial responsibility. On the central issue of conscience, however, his position was the same as Melbourne's. In 1833, when the Irish Church Bill was first under discussion, suggestions had been made in the Tory Press that the King was bound by his Coronation Oath not to consent to it. Peel emphatically repudiated this historical interpretation of the royal oath. As he wrote to Goulburn,

I should be very sorry to have it proved to me that Kings of England now and in all time to come were bound by their oaths to refuse their consent to any law which should affect any right, or any privilege possessed by law by any class of the clergy in the year 1689. . . . It is utterly impossible, in my opinion, to carry the obligation of the oath further than this. The King should take a deliberate

---

[1] For the whole transaction see Add. MS. 40316, ff. 185–93. In writing to Lyndhurst the King had added that 'the King is quite sensible of His own and the Lord Chancellor's relative Positions at this period, and would not have called upon him if He could have possibly avoided it. . . . The King is perfectly aware that His solemn consent will be required to give the Tythe Bill the force of Law after it shall have been passed through the two Houses of Parliament and it must therefore be obvious that His scruple applies to the sanction required for *intermediate* stages.'

view of the circumstances of the times, of the condition of the Church, of the dangers threatening it from all quarters, and if he is in his conscience convinced that a particular legislative measure will, if passed, endanger the maintenance or the essential interests and rights of the Church, more than the abstaining from such a measure, he ought to reject it.

This was probably the broadest interpretation of the oath that any responsible politician of the period was likely to proffer. But even so Peel added a practical restriction which put him substantially in the same position as Melbourne.

Perhaps (he continued cautiously) he ought not to consent to its initial stage, but should remove the Ministry which insisted upon its introduction.[1]

This was the remedy Melbourne virtually prescribed in 1835; it was the one which the King actually resorted to in 1834. So far from acting unconstitutionally, William IV merely did what the leaders of the two great parties indicated was his proper line of conduct in such circumstances. But what good had it done him? In the end the issue of conscience and the issue of Ministerial responsibility were inseparable; though neither Peel nor Melbourne chose to pursue the argument to its logical conclusion. If the King's scruples could only be relieved by changing his Ministers, and he could not as a matter of practical politics change them, the Cabinet and not the King was now the keeper of the royal conscience. This was no more than the lesson of 1829. If the Crown had no alternative Government, the Crown was helpless.

Helpless, that is to say, as regards policy; it could still do a little to help itself, if by that was meant no more than annoying its Ministers. The personal relationship remained, and if the King pleaded conscientious objections, it made it more unpleasant, if no more difficult, to override him. Melbourne himself certainly shrank from the distasteful task of 'forcing the King against his conscience, which is not desirable, however that conscience may be constituted by ignorance and prejudice'.[2] Such personal friction might have little direct effect on

---

[1] Parker, *Peel*, ii. 219.

[2] Torrens, *Melbourne*, p. 433. The actual context of the remark was Melbourne's reluctance to risk a rupture with the king by appointing either Arnold or Thirlwall a bishop in 1837.

legislation, but it would at least make tenure of office less agreeable; and William was far from abandoning a personal view of
politics. Outwardly he gave his Government official support
and confidence, and Court influence at Windsor and Brighton
was impartially used on behalf of Ministerial candidates.[1] But
in Court and official circles he made it mortifyingly clear that
though the Ministers possessed his public, they lacked his
personal confidence.[2] The year 1835 was not the end of the
Crown's activity or of the Whigs' embarrassment. William possessed other means of exerting influence. He had the indisput-
able right to be informed of and to comment on the actions of
his Government. Reports of parliamentary debates enabled him
to bestow personal praise or blame; preliminary notice of legislation and discussions at all its stages enabled him to criticize
and obstruct.[3] Even with respect to popular measures proposed
by the Whig Ministry before 1835 he recorded that 'He cannot
charge himself with having hesitated to remonstrate and to
object as far as the circumstances in which he was placed would
admit'.[4] So stated perhaps, this was no more than Bagehot's
well-known triplet: consultation, encouragement, and warning.
At no time was William prepared to withhold his consent
either to a Bill approved by Parliament or to one introduced
by the Government. He did indeed object when Ministerial
legislation was brought forward in Parliament before being
submitted to his inspection, as happened in the case of the
Irish Municipal Corporation Bill in 1835.[5] But on another

[1] See my *Politics in the Age of Peel*, ch. xiv.

[2] Cf. Peel's description of a dinner party in Aug. 1835 attended by the Elder
Brethren of Trinity House, Governors of the Bank of England, Chairmen and other
leading officials of the East India Company, Custom House, Excise, &c. 'The King
was most marked in his civility to me. He made Lord Camden, who is Master of
the Trinity House, sit on his right hand. Then he called to me to take the place
next to Lord Camden. The King was by no means courteous towards his Ministers.
He drank wine with me about ten times' (*Private Letters of Sir Robert Peel*, ed. George
Peel (1920), p. 158).

[3] For example, his letter acknowledging Russell's customary account of the
debate in the Commons on 2 July 1835: 'It is impossible for him [sc. the King],
without unworthily disguising his feelings, to avoid expressing his regret that some
of the amendments proposed have met with so little attention from the House,
especially as several were in his Majesty's opinion judicious and necessary, and in
full accordance with the sentiments He had expressed to Viscount Melbourne'
(Walpole, *Russell*, i. 254).

[4] Memorandum of the Leading Events of His Reign, 14 Jan. 1835 (Add. MS.
40302, f. 203).   [5] *Melbourne Papers*, p. 307.

occasion he informed Melbourne that no previous criticism
on his part should be taken as an objection to the introduction of a Bill for Parliamentary consideration.[1] Even so, with a
difficult measure or a tired Prime Minister, the flanking fire
of royal criticism might be of some consequence. At the least,
the Crown was in a position to impose a heavy and disagreeable
burden on the Minister from which there was no appeal to
Parliament or the electorate.[2]

There was, for example, the notorious Council scene in July
1835 when the King attacked Glenelg, the Colonial Secretary,
in the course of a conversation with Sir Charles Grey on the
occasion of the latter's appointment to the Canadian Commission. Even Melbourne was stung by what he described to Russell
as this 'mass of muddle and impropriety' and a formal remonstrance to the King was invoked to mark the Cabinet's disapproval.[3] In this incident the King acknowledged that he was
at fault. But there were others in which the line between the
maintenance of the King's prerogative and the expression of the
King's spleen was more finely drawn. He claimed the right to
sanction in advance all official appointments, and two repri-
mands to two different Ministers in 1835 underlined his claim.
The first was of trifling importance except that it involved Lord
Mulgrave, the Lord-Lieutenant of Ireland, who regarded
censure on himself as far from trifling.[4] The other concerned
the more jaunty figure of Palmerston, who had sounded St.
Petersburg on the acceptability of Lord Durham as Ambassador before sounding Windsor, and received in consequence a
royal reproof of a kind which perhaps hardened him for similar
experiences in the following reign.[5] Next year William refused
to sanction a dispatch from the unhappy Colonial Secretary

[1] *Melbourne Papers*, p. 327 (over the Church Rates Bill in 1837).

[2] His known opinions are said by Spencer Walpole (*Russell*, i. 254) to have
encouraged the Lords in their resistance to the Municipal Corporations Bill in
1835; and Peel was even told in 1833 that the abandonment of the notorious clause
147 of the Irish Church Bill was due to a 'positive order from the King' (Parker,
Peel, ii. 222).

[3] *Melbourne Papers*, pp. 334–6; Walpole, *Russell*, i. 250 and n.; *Greville*, i, 15 July
1835.

[4] Lord Mulgrave had appointed an Usher of the Black Rod in the Order of St.
Patrick without the King's knowledge. The King's censure of Mulgrave became
public and Mulgrave had to be soothed down by Melbourne and Russell with the
characteristic argument that all Ministers fared alike (Walpole, *Russell*, i. 250 n.).

[5] *Melbourne Papers*, pp. 333–4.

to Lord Gosford, the Governor of Lower Canada, on the ground that it was 'his *determination* and *fixed* resolution *never* to permit any despatch to . . . Canada or any other colony . . . relative to any change in the manner of the appointment in the King's Councils in the numerous colonies'. Not until after several refusals was the offending dispatch allowed to go out.[1] But to show his dislike of the '*vacillating* and *procrastinating* Lord Glenelg', he declined to grant a Riband of St. Patrick as Melbourne wished, until Glenelg had conferred a Military Grand Cross of the Bath as the King wished.[2] It is not surprising that Melbourne grew weary. 'In his present mood', he wrote to Russell in the summer of 1836, 'having got rid of the Parliament, and having five months before him, he would not be unwilling, I think, to drive me to a resignation', and a week later, 'I feel my temper giving way. To have two or three great points to fight would be nothing; but to be fretted by opposition upon every little matter is intolerable.'[3]

But the weariness was not all on one side. Penned within the narrow triangle of Ministerial responsibility, House of Commons supremacy, and the party system, the King himself inevitably felt frustrated and impotent; and it was this, as well as his physical deterioration, which accounted for the increasing wildness of his behaviour noted in 1836. Yet even within these limitations, it was clear that there was still a sphere in which the Crown and Ministers were not agreed on their respective rights and duties; that the King was prepared to make his position felt with all the force at his disposal; and that his death in 1837 perceptibly lightened the task of the Prime Minister. There can be little doubt that Victoria prolonged and William, had he lived, would have curtailed the duration of Whig power. Rumours current in the spring of 1837 of an early dissolution at once disappeared, and with Victoria's favour the Whigs could not only expect but look forward with enjoyment to a few more years of office. Nevertheless, the King had forced one crucial dissolution of Parliament in 1834—the only general election over which the Conservatives presided in office between 1830 and 1852—and his death added yet another to the abnormally high number of general elections (1835, 1837, and

[1] Ibid., pp. 349–50; Walpole, *Russell*, i. 279.
[2] Walpole, *Russell*, i. 279–80.   [3] Ibid. 280.

1841—three in six years) which whittled away the great reform majority. It was the misfortune of the Whigs that the dissolution of Parliament which necessarily accompanied the accession of a sympathetic sovereign, saw the virtual disappearance of their working majority in the Commons. In the now delicate balance of party, however, royal influence took on a proportionately greater weight. The personal and partisan involvement of the Crown in politics continued for the first four years of the new reign as it had existed under William IV; and the state of the House of Commons gave the young Queen potentially a greater latitude of action than William had ever enjoyed, though in practice she exercised it only against one side.

The difference was that whereas William had at least till 1835 some recognizable policy, Victoria merely had predilections. She came, as Palmerston is reported to have said, 'from the nursery to the throne' and could not therefore uphold royal authority in the face of the Cabinet—and, he added, 'that is the kind of thing the nation does not like'.[1] From the point of view of the monarchy as an institution, Melbourne's decision not to appoint a Private Secretary to the Queen but to constitute himself in some sort in that capacity, was not a specially felicitous arrangement. Stockmar was not so far wrong when he spoke of the 'contradictory nature' of the two offices of Prime Minister and Private Secretary to the Crown. There were other objections. It emphasized the close tie between the Queen and the Whig party; it left her without any impartial counsellor; and it ensured that a change of Ministry would disrupt her official habits more than any loss of her Ladies could do. Indeed, it was probably because of her anger at losing her Prime Minister that she chose to make a stand over her Ladies. It is true that the appointment of Baron Stockmar, the Queen's own candidate for the post, would have been unpopular; but it would not have been difficult to find a sensible Englishman as Private Secretary. Both Sir Herbert Taylor, the Tory Secretary to William IV, and George Anson, the Whig Secretary to Prince Albert, gave their masters loyal, intelligent, and disinterested service. As it was, Victoria's adolescent attachment to Mel-

---

[1] Stockmar to Prince Albert, 5 Jan. 1854 (Sir T. Martin, *Life of the Prince Consort* (1882), Pt. II, p. 93), in the course of a long letter discussing the position of the Crown and *inter alia* the status of the monarch's Private Secretary.

bourne, and by extension her emotional though not intellectual adherence to the Whigs, created unusual difficulties for the only possible alternative Ministry. The effect of the Queen's name in the elections of 1837 and 1841 became a factor in the calculations of party electioneering experts, and her relationship with the Prime Minister in those of the party leaders. All this was a reversal to the distinctly early period. From the start Melbourne seemed to have assumed a role *vis-à-vis* the Queen of a kind which had not been known since the days of Lord Bute and the young George III. Some historical-minded observers went back even further for a parallel. Aberdeen remarked as early as August 1837 that for all Melbourne's moderation 'no Minister has ever been in such a situation since the Protector Somerset'.[1] He himself testified to the great effect on the Scottish elections of the use of the Queen's name; and Wellington's unwillingness to have the Conservative party 'forced upon the Queen' undoubtedly influenced his restraining advice on party tactics in these years.[2] Graham in 1839 was writing in his gloomiest vein of the 'hostility' of the Queen and the 'active participation of the Crown' in the dangerous policies of the Government, and expressed the fear that the Ministers would give Prince Albert a Household, as he phrased it, packed with their firmest and most crafty adherents, who would be immovable on a change of Ministry.[3]

---

[1] Add. MS. 40312, f. 290, Aberdeen to Peel, 11 Aug. 1837.

[2] Parker, *Peel*, ii. 364, Wellington to Peel, 22 Feb. 1838.

[3] Add. MS. 40318, f. 163, to Peel, 18 Dec. 1839 (passage omitted from the printed version in Parker, *Peel*, ii. 420). See also f. 131, Graham to Peel, 20 Jan. 1839. A similar view was expressed by Croker writing to Lord Hertford in May 1839: 'Our old Constitution had foreseen and provided against every disturbing cause, except the unimaginable one of a junction between the Crown and the mob.' But Croker and Graham encouraged each other. Only a week before, Graham had written to him: 'The Crown in alliance with Democracy baffles every calculation on the balance of power in our mixed form of Government. Aristocracy and Church cannot contend against Queen and people united' (*Croker Papers*, ed. L. J. Jennings (1884), ii. 346, 356). Nevertheless the feeling was widespread. As late as July 1841 Fremantle, a former Conservative Chief Whip, could write of 'the great struggle we are engaged in against the influence of the Crown and the personal feelings of the Sovereign' (Add. MS. 40476, f. 25). Graham's suspicions about Albert's Household were not as exaggerated as they sound in view of Victoria's and Melbourne's insistence that George Anson, a Whig, a former parliamentary candidate and Melbourne's Secretary, should become Private Secretary to the Prince. The initial suggestion was even that Anson should serve on Albert's staff while remaining Melbourne's Secretary. Despite Albert's protests that to take the Prime Minister's

The Bedchamber crisis of 1839 therefore was in the existing circumstances considerably more significant than later commentators have sometimes allowed. There is in fact a strong case for arguing that whereas William IV in 1834 acted constitutionally but unsuccessfully, Victoria in 1839 acted successfully but unconstitutionally. Stripped of its complications—the nervous, angry emotionalism of a girl of twenty; the ignorance of the Whig Cabinet over what precisely Peel had requested; their equivocal status when giving advice to the Queen after Peel had been asked to form a Government; the technical distinctions between Queen Regnant and Queen Consort, and between Household officials in and out of Parliament; the absence of recent precedents—three things are clear. The Queen was, and was known to be, partisan in her politics, and her Court notoriously full of Whig ladies and close relatives of Whig politicians. Secondly, both Parliament and the country at large attached at least marginal importance to open signs of royal favour. Lastly, Peel did not possess a majority in the House of Commons, and it was a resignation of the existing Ministers that obliged the Queen to send for him. If as leader of a party he asked for a symbol of confidence, it was because the Queen as a partisan had previously shown every mark of no-confidence.[1] Melbourne himself had laid it down to the King in 1835 that

At all times and in all circumstances it is necessary for the conduct of public affairs under our constitution that the Ministry should possess, and be known and felt to possess, the full confidence of the Crown [and] the advantage of all the influence which it can com-

Secretary on his staff would make him appear as a party man, he secured no more than that Anson should leave Melbourne as soon as appointed to the Court. Victoria informed Albert that 'it is also necessary that it should appear that you went with me in having some of your people who are staunch Whigs', as a politically neutral Household for the Prince would arouse comments on the contrast between his servants and those of the Queen (*Letters of Queen Victoria*, ed. A. C. Benson and Viscount Esher (1908), i. 199–200, 206; *Letters of Prince Consort*, ed. K. Jagow, trans. E. T. S. Dugdale (1938), p. 40; R. Fulford, *Prince Consort* (1949), pp. 48–49).

[1] The question of dissolving Parliament was raised but not settled between Peel and the Queen in the negotiations. She told Peel that she was against it, and it is by no means certain that in her then mood she would have granted a dissolution. To Wellington she announced that she intended to see Lord Melbourne often 'as a friend' and seemed to think that the fact that she told him this openly was a proof of her fairness to the new Government (*Victoria Letters*, i. 158–9).

mand. . . . Among these marks of confidence, Viscount Melbourne places the appointment of the officers of your Majesty's Household.[1]

And the veteran Earl Grey impartially admitted to him in May 1839 that the Whig Ladies of the Bedchamber 'must be naturally regarded with uneasiness by the Ministers called upon to succeed you'.[2]

Had the Whigs, or Melbourne, held a modern constitutional view of the detached, non-party role of the monarchy, their support for Victoria in 1839 would have been more tenable. In fact, it was by their own standards and actions that Peel's request was justified; and the naturalness of his request is shown by the fact that he never anticipated any difficulty on that score before his interview with the Queen. The clearest comment on the issue, however, is that the position maintained by Victoria in 1839 and rather confusedly supported by the Whigs, was abandoned without protest two years later.[3] Melbourne may have been a constitutional tutor to the young Queen; but the constitution he taught her was the one he had learned in his youth. He assumed that the monarch must have political partialities, and since—for a change—they were now Whiggish, he took it for granted that the party would make what profit it decently could from this rare conjuncture of circumstances. Certainly he hesitated at first at exposing the Queen's name to what he regarded as the probable outcome of the 1841 election: 'an Opposition returned smack against it'. But this in itself proved how he habitually identified Crown and Party. He took responsibility for giving Victoria's early

[1] *Melbourne Papers*, pp. 270–1. Melbourne went on to say that 'with respect to Your Majesty's household, Viscount Melbourne would be anxious not to interfere with its present constitution, provided those who compose it, and who have seats in either House of Parliament, are prepared to give your Majesty's servants a firm, unequivocal support; but Viscount Melbourne trusts that, upon occasions of future vacancies, those members of either Lords or Commons will not be selected whose principles and opinions are adverse to your Majesty's Government'. The dispute over the Ladies, who by definition could not sit in Parliament, hinged on the degree to which their close connexion with active politicians brought them under this ruling in the case of a Queen Regnant.

[2] Ibid., p. 397, Grey to Melbourne, 10 May 1839.

[3] Melbourne in fact told Anson in May 1841 that he would inform the Queen that 'she must carefully abstain from playing the same part she did, again, on Sir R. Peel's attempt to form a Ministry, for that nothing but the forbearance of the Tories had enabled himself and his colleagues to support H.M. at that time' (*Victoria Letters*, i. 268).

Court so decidedly a Whig flavour; and even on the matter of her husband, he laid it down that the Prince should be considered as 'countenancing the policy of the actual Government' and that his Household should 'have a decided leaning' to the opinions of the Government, though (contradictorily) it 'should not change upon a change of administration'.[1] When in 1841 the Cabinet decided in the end to dissolve, it was at least partly to use every ounce of executive influence in the elections; and in this the Crown was necessarily involved. Parkes, the party's chief electoral adviser, told Russell that if the Government resigned without a dissolution 'many present M.P.s representing *Liberal* Constituencies would, as always on a counter-party dissolution, retire and not recontest their counties and boroughs. . . . Moreover, the Liberal constituencies in the entire Kingdom would be correspondingly dispirited by the Court and a Peel Government making the dissolution against them.'[2] The Queen was brought down in person to prorogue Parliament, and when Anson protested, Melbourne told him that 'the Queen has committed herself too decidedly to hold back now and her opinions are well known to be with us'.[3] A sum of £15,000 from

[1] Jagow, *Letters of Prince Consort*, pp. 51–52. Albert's own reactions to this can be seen in the memorandum he had drawn up in May 1841 which laid down that 'the Head of the Prince's Household should change with every Administration, thereby giving sanction to the Queen's existing government', and that 'all other members of the House of Commons in His Royal Highness's Household should be required to give up their seats in parliament or to resign their offices' (F. Eyck, *The Prince Consort*, p. 25).

[2] See Appendix A for text of this letter. Brougham, in formally advising the Queen not to grant a dissolution, correctly stated the current constitutional theory whatever his personal motive was in doing so. 'They who advise it must needs proceed upon the supposition that a majority will be returned favourable to the continuance of the present Administration and favourable to their lately announced policy. On no other ground is it possible that any such advice should be tendered to your Majesty. For no one could ever think of such a proceeding as advising the Crown to dissolve the Parliament in order to increase the force of the Opposition to its own future Ministers, thus perverting to the mere purposes of party the exercise of by far the most eminent of the Royal prerogatives' (*Victoria Letters*, i. 293). Parkes' argument, that unless the Whigs dissolved themselves they would lose heavily in the next election, came perilously close to this perversion for the 'mere purposes of party'. At best he offered no more than the prospect of retaining the existing Liberal strength, which had already proved insufficient for purposes of the Administration.

[3] Eyck, *Prince Consort*, p. 25. The Archbishop of York, with whom the Queen stayed in June, apparently tried to dissuade her from proroguing Parliament in person. Melbourne wrote to Victoria on 16 June that 'the Archbishop is a very agreeable man; but he is not without cunning, and Lord Melbourne can easily

the Queen's Privy Purse was spent on behalf of Whig election-eering, and the Prime Minister brushed aside Albert's purist objections with the observation that this was nothing compared to what George III used to spend on elections.[1] His final advice to Victoria as outgoing Minister was that she should tell Peel that 'your Majesty's present servants possessed your Majesty's confidence, and that you only parted with them in deference to the opinion of Parliament'.[2]

Inevitably therefore the more committed Conservative poli-ticians felt after the 1839 incident that the enmity of Victoria was not only a reversal of the ordinary laws of political nature but a formidable obstacle on the road to power. 'The Crown and Democracy combined', wrote Graham to Stanley in October, 'form an impossible quantity in our political equation: the solvent is wanting. Shall we find it in a Husband?'[3] It was a prophetic question. The real starting-point for the new era in the history of the Crown, actively political but non-partisan, was 1840, the date which separates the first three Hanoverian years of Victoria's reign from its succeeding Albertine period; or to be more exact, November 1840, when in her first letter to Melbourne after the birth of the Princess Royal, Victoria arranged for Albert to have his own key to the secret dispatch boxes.[4] The serious, prematurely reflective young German Prince had his own view of the raffish atmosphere of favourites and partisans, both personal and political, in which Victoria moved with every appearance of satisfaction; and all he learned of the preceding events of the reign hardened his determination

understand his eagerness that the Queen should not prorogue Parliament in person. He knows that it will greatly assist the Tories' (*Victoria Letters*, i. 292.) It is perhaps significant that the Queen declined to open Parliament after the 1841 election. For this she had the backing of her medical advisers (her second confinement was due in November), but Court gossip attributed other reasons. Arbuthnot's son, who had a military appointment at Windsor, wrote to his father (13 Aug.) that 'in this Lord Melbourne concurred but it has annoyed the other ministers greatly, as they had hoped, that her making the speech from the Throne, would have pro-duced an effect', but 'the Baroness de Lehzen told a person with whom she is very intimate, and who being a friend of mine repeated it to me, that the Queen cannot bear being deceived, and that she is very angry at having been led to dissolve upon the positive assurances that the Whigs were sure of gaining a considerable majority in the Elections. This, it is said, will ensure to Sir R. Peel a good reception when he is sent for' (Add. MS. 40484, f. 30).

[1] Fulford, *Prince Consort*, p. 70.   [2] *Victoria Letters*, i. 307.
[3] Graham MS., 6 Oct. 1839.   [4] Fulford, *Prince Consort*, p. 66.

to make a fundamental change in the political role of the monarchy. Even before his marriage he had answered complaints by Victoria about the behaviour of the Tories by observing that it need not trouble the Queen, except for her friendship with Melbourne—'otherwise a constitutional sovereign may be indifferent to what is said against his Ministry';[1] and two months after becoming her husband, he recorded that 'I do not think it is necessary to belong to any party. Composed as party is here of two extremes, both must be wrong. . . . My endeavour will be to form my opinions quite apart from politics and party, and I believe such an attempt may succeed.'[2] These reflections of a twenty-one-year-old foreigner were not perhaps very profound, nor unreminiscent of the attitude of earlier Hanoverian kings. But they were different in that they accepted party rule as a political fact; and they were important in that Albert was better placed than any other person to instil them into the Queen. His influence was soon felt. It was Albert who initiated the private approach to Peel through his Secretary Anson in May 1841 which cleared the troublesome question of the Ladies from the threshold of the new Ministry;[3] and Albert, with his

[1] Jagow, *Letters of Prince Consort*, p. 37.
[2] Eyck, *Prince Consort*, p. 24.
[3] Fulford, *Prince Consort*, p. 67, says that this was done without the knowledge of the Queen, but Victoria told Melbourne on 5 May that she was prepared to give way on the question of the Ladies if required, and hoped that the point might be settled previously by negotiation with Peel to avoid discussion or differences. This was presumably a result of Anson's interview with Melbourne on the previous day when he told the Prime Minister of Albert's suggestion for entering on some negotiations with Peel. Melbourne thought the Prince should not do so personally but that Anson might. Anson's first interview with Peel was on 9 May when he told Peel that he came by desire of Prince Albert and that the Queen was aware of his visit and its general purport. The second was on 10 May. The third, a formal one to agree on the accuracy of Peel's written record of the talks, was on 11 May. On that day Victoria had a memorandum drawn up on the subject in which she recognized the right of the Minister to decide on (male) Court appointments whose holders were in Parliament; and agreed in principle that her appointments to the Ladies of the Bedchamber should be mentioned to the Minister in case he should deem any of them injurious to the Government 'when the Queen would probably not appoint the Lady'. On 12 May Melbourne gave Victoria copies of Anson's conversations with Peel. The essence of these was that Peel said he would be perfectly satisfied if the Ladies who held the chief offices and were immediately connected with the retiring Administration voluntarily resigned and the Queen would permit the vacancies to be filled by Ladies having other party connexions (*Victoria Letters*, i. 268–74; Parker, *Peel*, ii. 455–8). In subsequent conversations and correspondence between Peel and Anson it was settled that while the Queen would retain the right of personally announcing the appointments to the Ladies

detached Coburg view of the British party dog-fight, who weaned the Queen from her early partisan ties towards his conception of a supra-party constitutional monarchy. By April 1842 Graham, now Home Secretary, could write cheerfully to his colleague Ellenborough in India that 'the Court is reconciled to us; Albert is our friend'.[1]

Albert certainly found the Peelites more congenial than the Whigs, not merely because of a similarity of outlook but because of the high importance which Peel attached to the monarchy as an institution. The transformation, however, was not so much personal as political. For the first time the monarchy was ready to react to, and not against, the consequences of the Reform Act. The contrast between the behaviour of the Crown in 1832, 1834, and 1839 and its behaviour in December 1845, in 1846, and in 1852 is one between isolation and co-operation, between legal power and political influence, and between obstruction and mediation. It did not mean that Victoria and Albert had necessarily a less effective role to play than William IV; it did mean that their role was more harmonious and therefore less conspicuous. It was the difference between working with, and against the grain of politics.

concerned, the Prime Minister would be authorized to notify them of her intention to appoint. A provisional list of possible new Ladies was then drawn up. (Add. MS. 40303, ff. 257–85; cf. also Eyck, *Prince Consort*, pp. 26–28.)

The success of these secret negotiations in May 1841, at a time when there was a distinct probability that the Government would resign, made the question of granting a dissolution later the same month more than usually critical. It would have been constitutionally proper for Victoria to have refused a dissolution, as she now clearly had an alternative Administration on hand. There is some evidence that Albert was not in favour of a Whig dissolution unless there was in fact a real prospect of success (Interview between Anson and Melbourne, 4 May, *Victoria Letters*, i. 268; cf. Fulford, *Prince Consort*, pp. 68–69).

[1] Graham MS., 7 Apr. 1842.

II

THE PEERS AND REFORM

IN one sense the most revolutionary aspect of the Reform crisis of 1831–2 was not the Reform Bill itself but the coercion of the House of Lords. The blow to the independence of the Upper House seemed a more serious because a more immediate derangement of the theoretical balance of power in the constitution than any consequential limitation of Crown influence. In the period after Waterloo two things had characterized the activities of the House of Lords: the generally good relations between them and the Government, and the generally good-humoured acceptance of their rejections and amendments by the Commons. Though far from liberal, the Upper House had never degenerated into a reactionary chamber; and it was peculiarly amenable to executive influence. If the peers under Eldon's leadership massacred the legal reforms put up by Mackintosh's committee in 1820, they gave an easy passage under Lord Tenterden's auspices to Peel's criminal legislation between 1822 and 1830. They accepted the currency reforms; they accepted the emergency corn measure of 1826. Wellington upset Canning's Corn Bill in 1827, but this was largely due to a genuine misunderstanding between himself and Huskisson. Even in the volcanic field of religion the peers passed with only minor emendations the repeal of the Test and Corporations Acts in 1828. It was true that over Catholic Emancipation the House of Lords twice (in 1821 and 1825) rejected Bills sent up to them from the Commons; but the important fact here was that the Bills were not Government measures and that they were opposed by the Prime Minister and most of his Cabinet colleagues in the Upper House.[1] Even so, after 1825 Liverpool

---

[1] Cf., for example, the attitude of the Duke of Northumberland when accepting Wellington's invitation to go to Ireland as Lord-Lieutenant in Jan. 1829. He told the Prime Minister that though he had voted against the measures of Catholic Emancipation brought forward in the Upper House by persons not authorized by the Crown to propose them, he would welcome a final settlement of the question at the hands of the Government (*Despatches etc. of the Duke of Wellington, 1819–32*, v. 453).

thought it impossible that the peers could much longer resist the repeated sense of the Commons. When in 1829 for the first time an Emancipation Bill came before the Lords with the recommendation of the Government, they passed it. In the decade preceding the Reform Act the Lords might fairly have claimed that they were equal but not unreasonable partners in the business of legislation.

The shock of coercion was therefore great, because it concerned a reality of political power: the semi-independent function of the Upper House. Moreover, unlike the Reform Bill which was the occasion for the collision, the coercive tactic of the Government was the unpremeditated and desperate measure of a Cabinet which had gone too far not to go further.[1] The language of the Ministers themselves is sufficient. 'It is a question then which goes to the absolute destruction of the House of Lords,' wrote Grey to Burdett in November 1831,[2] 'an event which I certainly did not contemplate in endeavouring to reform the House of Commons'; and to Althorp in March 1832 he described a large peerage creation as 'a measure of extreme violence; there is no precedent for it in our history, the case of Queen Anne's peers not being in point; it is a certain evil, dangerous itself as a precedent'.[3] Campbell, the Whig Lord Chancellor, looking back at the issue across the reflective gap of ten years, put it down as his considered opinion that 'a numerous creation of peers to carry a particular measure against the opinion of the existing House, cannot in my opinion be considered a constitutional proceeding, and can only be defended as a *coup d'état* to ward off greater evils'.[4] The traumatic effect of the 1832 operation was therefore felt as keenly by the surgeons as by the patients. Whatever else was to be done, it was humanly improbable that the members of the Reform Cabinet would expose themselves to such an experience again.[5] Seven years

---

[1] The issue of the peerage creations nearly broke up Grey's Cabinet; the Reform Bill never did. Grey himself was very reluctant and Althorp's initial reaction (Oct. 1831) was that a peerage creation large enough to overcome the majority of 41 against the second reading of the Bill was out of the question (D. Le Marchant, *Memoir of Viscount Althorp* (1876), p. 354).

[2] Patterson, *Burdett*, ii. 598. Dated 1832, but this is clearly an error.

[3] Le Marchant, *Althorp*, p. 411.   [4] *Life*, ii. 12.

[5] It was of course precisely to induce this state of mind that Peel was working in his encouragement to the peers to resist to the last even though he had no doubt that the Bill would pass (see, e.g., Parker, *Peel*, ii. 201–2).

later, when rejecting any suggestion that the Whigs should support the Corn Law repeal agitation, Melbourne observed that even if the movement were strong in itself, 'we shall still only carry it by the same means as we carried the Reform Bill, and I am not for being the instrument . . . of another similar performance'.[1] Ten years later still, in 1849, Palmerston told Russell that his parliamentary reform proposals, unless very moderate, would 'meet with much opposition in the Commons and certain defeat in the Lords, and I doubt whether public opinion would support us in re-enacting in these times, and in this matter, the scenes of the Reform Bill conflict'.[2] It is not surprising that with these scarred memories the general attitude of Whig Cabinets in the 1830's towards obstruction in the Lords was one of scriptural patience relieved by occasional mutters of resignation.[3]

Yet, after all, the crisis of the House of Lords had been psychological rather than physical. There had been in fact no mass creation of new peers, and the House of Lords remained after the Reform Act much as it had been before. In the eyes of Radicals and Radical-Whigs, the Upper House was still a reactionary Pittite chamber, and its conduct during the crisis had only put it more evidently in need of reform. At the start of the struggle Whigs of advanced views and little responsibility could talk in aggressive terms of doing something about the peers. Colonel Torrens, in September 1831, spoke of putting the House of Lords in Schedule A if they persisted in rejecting reform.[4] Charles Western, another M.P., privately argued with Graham on the even greater need to reform the Upper House

[1] *Melbourne Papers*, p. 389, Melbourne to Russell, 18 Jan. 1839.

[2] Russell MS., Palmerston to Russell, 23 Oct. 1849, P.R.O. 30/22/8 pt. I.

[3] For example, Althorp thought in July 1833 that the Government could not carry on in the teeth of the majority in the House of Lords. His remedy was resignation, though with the ulterior prospect of the formation of a Tory Ministry, its defeat in the Commons, and recourse by the King once again to the Whigs—'and no Whig in his senses can attempt to form a Government unless the King will secure to him a majority in the House of Lords' (Althorp to his father, 12 July 1833. Le Marchant, *Althorp*, pp. 473–4).

[4] For this language, held both at a meeting in the City and in the House of Commons, William IV wanted to dismiss 'an Individual who has thus committed himself and shown the cloven foot'. As an officer in the Royal Marines, Torrens came under Government jurisdiction; but Lord Grey, while deprecating Torrens's 'indecent, violent and indefensible' language, advised firmly against any disciplinary action (C. S. Parker, *Life of Sir James Graham* (1907), i. 125–6).

than the Lower, and declared that no Whig or Liberal Ministry
could stand unless after sixty years of Tory creations there was
an infusion of fresh blood into the peerage.[1] For a brief interval
after the collapse of resistance in the Lords, there was room for
optimistic hope among Radical politicians that the morale of
the peers had been broken. At the start of the first session of the
reformed Parliament, Robert Ingham (M.P. for South Shields
and, according to James Wortley, 'a frightened Whig') said
that when he spoke to the wild men of the Reform majority on
the danger of opposition to Government Church reforms in the
House of Lords, they merely laughed and said, 'Let them! Lord
Grey settled that for us last year'.[2] But Lord Grey had not
settled it, and three months later he was being warned by
Brougham, now sitting among their lordships, how much they
had recovered their courage and how ready they were for
mischief.[3] The Government's Irish Church Bill provided an
admirable vantage ground for a move to unseat the Ministry,
and by July 1833 it seemed as if Wellington (himself wavering
on the issue) was losing control of the Opposition peers. Cumberland and Buckingham were running in effect a separatist
group, holding private meetings of ultra-Tory supporters; and
even ex-Ministers like Ellenborough and Lyndhurst leaned towards a rejection of the Bill on the second reading. In the end
the tactical restraint of the Duke of Wellington, aided by the
private influence of the Crown,[4] carried the day. Nevertheless,

[1] Ibid. 127. By Mar. 1832 Graham himself was persuaded that 'a large infusion
of popular spirit and feeling is wanted in the House of Lords; and that the Government of this country can never be conducted on Liberal principles in accordance
with public opinion, which every day acquires fresh power in the House of Commons, unless a counterpoise be established in the House of Lords to the weight of
Tory influence created there by Mr. Pitt and his successors' (Graham to Lord
Grey, 9 Mar. 1832, ibid., p. 140).

[2] C. Grosvenor, *Lady Wharncliffe and Her Family* (1927), ii. 177. James Wortley
to Lady Wharncliffe, 24 Feb. 1833.

[3] Brougham, *Life and Times*, iii. 269.

[4] For the King's letter of 6 June 1833 to the Archbishop of Canterbury, urging
the bishops not to obstruct the Administration or help to undermine the stability
of government at a time when there was no practical alternative Ministry, see
Brougham, *Life and Times*, iii. 275. Cf. Littleton's Diary for 20 July printed in
Aspinall, *Three Early Nineteenth Century Diaries*, p. 349. The intervention of the
Crown caused a flutter in official circles and Lord Winchilsea raised the issue in the
House of Lords on the grounds that it infringed the independence of the legislature.
But the King had acted on his own responsibility (though possibly encouraged by
Brougham through the intermediacy of Sir H. Taylor) and no reproach could be

the Government was beaten on the clause for suspending moribund benefices and for a time seriously considered resignation.[1] By the end of the 1833 session it was clear that the hostile and potentially obstructive majority in the Lords,[2] combined with the instability of Government support in the Commons, already made the continuation of a Reform Ministry a doubtful proposition. Though Grey was not disinclined to a token creation of five or six peers as a demonstration of royal confidence, any notion of creating enough peers to counterbalance the hostile majority was put out of the question by the Cabinet.[3] Everything depended therefore on the self-restraint of the peers, or conceivably on the mobilization of a strong public opinion against them.

The session of 1834, which saw the successive resignations of nearly half the Cabinet,[4] inevitably distracted attention from the quarrel with the Lords to the quarrels within the Government. Even so, the successful opposition in the Upper House to the Irish Tithe Bill at the end of the session moved the extreme Dissenting periodical, the *Christian Advocate*, to prophesy that among the measures that would be forced on the House of Commons the following year would be one for the reconstruction of the Lords. 'We shall inevitably have a second Parliamentary Reform bill.'[5] In the light of all that happened since 1832, therefore, it was possible for many Radicals to interpret the King's dismissal of Melbourne in November as an attempt to avert a collision between the two branches of the legislature, not by reforming the Lords but by dissolving the Commons.

---

levelled against the Ministers. The Bishop of London, replying to Winchilsea's attack, argued that the King had a perfect right to communicate his sentiments to the bishops and it would obviously be inconvenient for them to be obliged to repeat in the House such expressions of opinion. Wellington came to the relief of the Ecclesiastical Bench with a few tactful words, and the discussion ended (*Hansard*, vol. 19, 916–18; cf. *Greville*, 26, 28 June, 20 July 1833; Brougham, *Life and Times*, iii. 280 seq.).

[1] Aspinall, *Three Diaries*, xliii, pp. 347–50, 352–3, 364–6. In the Cabinet the strongest advocate of resignation was Althorp.

[2] There had been other set-backs for the Government in the House of Lords, notably a virtual vote of censure on foreign affairs (June) and the defeat of Brougham's Local Courts Bill (July).

[3] Brougham, *Life and Times*, iii. 294–5.

[4] Stanley, Graham, Richmond, Ripon, Grey, and Althorp (later withdrawn) out of a Cabinet of fourteen.

[5] 11 Aug. 1834, quoted in the *British Magazine*, vi. 318 (Sept. 1834).

This was the argument of E. Lytton Bulwer's *Letter to a late Cabinet Minister*, one of the ablest and probably the most widely read of the Radical-Whig pamphlets evoked by the crisis,[1] which declared roundly that 'England has two prominent causes of trouble: the one is the state of Ireland, the other is her House of Lords' and that 'in the next election this question is to be tried, "ARE THE PEOPLE OF ENGLAND TO BE GOVERNED ACCORDING TO THE OPINION OF THE HOUSE OF LORDS, OR ACCORDING TO THE PRINCIPLES OF THEIR OWN REFORM" '. The *Appendix to the Black Book*, which appeared in December 1834, by the original editor of that well-known Radical piece of propaganda, headed its chapter on the peers, the 'Catastrophe of the House of Lords', and declared that the Constitution was still unsettled —'we are still in the *course of revolution*',[2] and that the work of reform was still unfinished as long as the peers could veto the policy of a liberal ministry and a liberal House of Commons. 'Up, then, Britons! One victory more and you have done.'

The fright administered by the King's action, the return of a Liberal Cabinet in April 1835, and the continued obduracy of the Lords, ushered in the real period of crisis for the Upper House in the years 1835-6. The end of the 1835 session, which had seen the rejection by the Lords of a new Irish Tithe Bill (armed now with an appropriation clause) and only the last-minute salvage of the Municipal Corporations Act from Lyndhurst's wrecking squad, made the question raised by the Radical pamphleteers the previous winter the subject of widespread and passionate debate. O'Connell made an oratorical pilgrimage to Scotland and the north of England to 'rouse the public mind to the necessity of reforming the House of Lords';[3] and put forward a scheme for an elective chamber of 120 peers, chosen

[1] It sold out on the day of publication and for the next fortnight a fresh issue appeared each day. Twenty editions were disposed of at the relatively high price of 3s. 6d. and it was generally recognized as one of the major literary strokes on behalf of the evicted Whig Ministry (T. H. S. Prescott, *Edward Bulwer, 1st Baron Lytton* (1910), p. 216).

[2] The editor outlined a scheme for reform of the Lords, comprising the exclusion of (1) the bishops, (2) the representative peers of Scotland and Ireland, (3) all 'pauper peers', and (4) if necessary, sons of Pittite peers created after 1792. For quotations in the text see pp. 49, 53-54, 75.

[3] For a description of O'Connell's campaign (he spoke at Manchester, Newcastle, Edinburgh, and Glasgow), see the *Annual Register*, pp. [367 seq.]

by constituencies each with a population of 200,000.[1] Abercromby reported to Melbourne after a visit to Yorkshire that
'everywhere I find that the House of Lords is a general topic of
discussion. Their present safety consists in the absence of any
practicable plan capable of being carried out without a violent
struggle.'[2] Place, the veteran, and Roebuck, the apprentice
Radical reformer, both thought the Government had missed an
opportunity over the Municipal Corporations Bill of turning on
their opponents. 'The Lords will not be reformed, not they,'
wrote Place, 'but it is good to make every one see that they
must either be reformed or abolished.'[3] Greville's contempt for
the reckless folly of the peers in running headlong into danger
is well known;[4] but even he was anxious at the prospect of a
direct clash with the House of Commons, which would bring
both sides to the 'brink of the precipice'. More responsible
politicians in private were subject to similar fears. Peel, writing
to Aberdeen from the autumnal peace of Drayton in September
1835, showed himself seriously concerned at the political threat
to the independence of the House of Lords and the risk of a
remodelling of their chamber either by the creation of fresh
peers or by a reduction of their constitutional powers, or both.[5]
The tension lasted for another eighteen months. In the 1836
session the Lords amended the Irish Tithes, the Irish Corporations, and the English Municipal Corporations Amendment
Bills so drastically that the Government abandoned all three;
and at the same time the peers had the satisfaction of receiving
addresses from Belfast, Leeds, and London in support of their
rights as an independent branch of the legislature.[6]

The Radicals, on their side, continued their agitation for a

---

[1] In his Edinburgh speech.

[2] *Melbourne Papers*, p. 291 (Oct. 1835).

[3] G. Wallas, *Life of Francis Place* (1918), p. 346 (30 Sept. 1835). Roebuck in his
pamphlet *The Crisis* argued not only for rejecting all the Lords' amendments to
the Corporations Bill but for taking up the wider task of depriving the Upper House
of its powers to work such mischief (R. E. Leader, *Life of J. A. Roebuck* (1897),
p. 69).

[4] He made the point that the House of Lords was exhibiting itself not so much as
an independent branch of the legislature as 'a dominant party-faction which is too
numerous to be affected by any constitutional process and too obstinate to be turned
from its fixed purpose of opposing all the measures which have a tendency to
diminish the influence of the Conservative party in the country' (15, 19 Aug. 1835).

[5] Add. MS. 43061, f. 177, 19 Sept. 1835.

[6] *Annual Register*, 1836, p. [63.

reform of the Lords, and the theme was pursued for party propaganda purposes by the Liberal Press in general.[1] Surveying the acrimonious scene with the large views engendered by a distance of 11,000 miles and a delay of four months in his English mail, Macaulay wrote to Spring Rice (Melbourne's new Chancellor of the Exchequer) that 'there is, in my opinion, a question compared with which the Ballot and everything else sinks into insignificance, I mean the question of a hereditary peerage. I do not see how it is possible to avoid a final collision between the two Houses.' Even the hypothetical notion of doubling the peerage by making 400 Whig lords he thought both a bad and impermanent remedy, and preferred something which would go to 'the seat of the evil'.[2] What was perhaps invisible at Ootacamund, however, was that by 1836 a note of desperation was creeping into the Radical attitude towards the peers, and the real fear was that if the House of Lords continued successfully to obstruct the Government's reform legislation, a split would open up between the Whigs and their more intransigent supporters.[3] Henry Lytton Bulwer devoted most of his 1836 pamphlet on *The Lords, the Government and the Country*[4] to the argument that the Lords would in time infallibly cut their own throats provided the Liberal party in politics kept solidly together; and Parkes, whose talent lay in pulling strings rather than in writing pamphlets, told Durham in St. Petersburg that

[1] Cf. *Blackwood's Magazine* in Nov. 1835 (vol. 38, p. 575). 'Government journals now openly advocate such an alteration in the constitution of the Upper House by a creation of Peers, an infusion of representative Peers, or otherwise, as may put it "in harmony", as it is called, with the Commons; in other words subject it altogether to its authority.' That organ of cautious Whiggery, the *Edinburgh Review*, was, however, an exception. Apart from its own nostrum of 'free conference' (see below, p. 43, n. 1), it steadfastly rejected all plans for remodelling or restricting the powers of the Upper House, and emphasized the fact that everything depended on the House of Commons. The peers could only be influential if they had the support of a strong minority in the Lower House; the Government could only deal effectively with legislation if it had a strong majority there. The moral for reformers therefore was to improve the position of the Ministers at the next election (cf. vol. 62, pp. 201–2, Oct. 1835).

[2] Torrens, *Melbourne*, pp. 406–7.

[3] As early as Jan. 1837 the *Edinburgh Review* was complaining that 'radical newspapers have joined Lord Lyndhurst in the sneer on the ministers' (vol. 64, p. 537).

[4] Henry Lytton Bulwer, better known as Sir Henry Bulwer, brother of Edward Lytton Bulwer, was at this time M.P. for Marylebone, one of the wealthiest and most populous of the metropolitan constituencies.

if the King lived another three or four years, the only way for the
Liberals to get on as a party would be 'by an attack on the
constitution of the House of Lords'.[1] The following session there
were motions by Lushington and Buller to exclude bishops from
the House of Lords, and by Duncombe to abolish proxy voting;
and part of the Radical support for Canada was occasioned by
the insistence of the Canadians on an elective Upper House.
All this was small beer; but even small beer would have been
a welcome refreshment to the Radicals at this stage.

The real problem was what the Government could or would
do, both to meet the challenge of the peers and to satisfy the
discontent of their extreme supporters; and the Ministers were
in no mood for Macaulayesque heroics. Lord Holland in 1836
doubted the propriety of going on much longer against the
House of Lords, and when the Cabinet discussed the issue after
the defeat of the Irish Corporations Bill in June, Melbourne
pacifically argued that though normally resignation was the
answer, no new situation had been created. The opposition of
the Lords was known beforehand, and it would be best therefore to go quietly on and introduce a new Bill the following
session.[2] Yet if the situation was no different, it was no better.
'It is the first time', remarked the *Annual Register* for 1837, not
without a degree of satisfaction, '. . . that any men have consented to administer the government without the means of
generally commanding the success of those measures which they
thought it their duty to bring forward in either branch of the
legislature' and concluded, after a review of rival strengths,
that 'under these circumstances of equipoise, the movement of
the government, as far as concerned all general measures, had
come to what in mechanics is called a *deadlock*. The ordinary
detail of administration was suffered to take its course; but
beyond that, the ministers could do nothing, either for public
or party purposes.'[3] This was an exaggeration; but it was
sufficiently near the bone to be painful.

The dilemma for the Ministry was acute, for the deadlock
could not be broken by mechanical means, since this postulated

---

[1] S. J. Reid, *Life of Durham* (1906), ii. 90 (7 Aug. 1836). A couple of months
earlier the Grotes dined with Hume, and Mrs. Grote recorded, 'Hume very resolute
about reforming the House of Lords' (*Life of Grote* (1873), by Mrs. Grote, p. 108).

[2] Lord Broughton, *Recollections*, ed. Lady Dorchester (1910–11), v. 57.

[3] pp. [7–8.

a political strength which they did not possess. Russell, characteristically responsive to movements in the party and equally characteristically unreliable in his judgement of what workable conclusions should be drawn from them, fretted for some kind of action; though his varying moods indicated his own uncertainty on the issue. In October 1835 he pressed Melbourne to make the King realize that the Lords could not go on regarding themselves as without any check or control, but admitted that the precedent of Queen Anne[1] was more to their purpose than that of 1832, and was doubtful even if this was a remedy which would serve any purpose. Then in June 1836 he prepared a memorandum for the Cabinet, pointing out the obvious fact that the majority of the peers were combining to veto all measures obnoxious to them, and that the Government confessed the evil without consenting to a remedy. As between the conservative principle which aimed at the maintenance unimpaired of the powers of the Upper House, and the radical one which aimed at an elective chamber, the Government was caught without a principle at all. Russell's proposal was to begin immediately with the creation of some eight or twelve peers and be prepared to repeat the dose whenever provoked. Dread of large creations had coerced the Lords in 1832; if they thought the Government was in earnest, they might be disposed to yield once more. But Melbourne thought little of the proposal, except indeed that it would undoubtedly lead to the resignation of the Government; and Russell therefore withdrew his memorandum stillborn.[2] He was still unconvinced, however, that nothing should be done; but when, on the third reading of the Irish Municipal Corporations Bill in April 1837, he declared it was a vital question to the Administration, the threat was not taken very seriously by the politicians in either House.[3] Melbourne was certainly against resignation at this point, partly because of the difficulty of finding any Government to

---

[1] When twelve peers were created to pass the Treaty of Utrecht.
[2] Russell, *Early Correspondence*, ed. R. Russell (1913), ii. 144–5; 185–7.
[3] Walpole, *Russell*, i. 291–2, perhaps overemphasizes this aspect of Russell's speech. Peel met the threat very coolly. 'He knew not what was the nature of the vague intimation on the part of His Majesty's government of their intention of relinquishing office, he knew nothing about it; he viewed it with great indifference, and he was not at all surprised at their desire to relinquish office' (*Speeches*, iii. 395 (11 Apr. 1837) in debate on Municipal Corporations (Ireland)).

succeed them, and, more characteristically, because it would seem like abandoning their own friends and supporters.[1] Both arguments were soon given strong adventitious force by the illness of the King in May and his death in June.

But the truth was that the crisis was already over and the balance of victory lay with the Lords. The Government's abandonment of the appropriation clause, foreshadowed by Russell's remarks in the 1837 session, removed the sting from its Irish legislation; and Russell's own election speech at Stroud contained an impeccable declaration against 'altering the ancient constitution of this country' and for the maintenance of the 'Crown, Lords and Commons' at the outset of what he prophesied would be 'a female reign illustrious in its deeds of peace'.[2] At the same time, the results of the elections, by diminishing still further the Liberal majority in the Commons, destroyed the last ground for an attack on the Lords. The years from 1838 to 1841 saw a growing relaxation in the relations of the Ministry with the Upper House. Over the Hansard privilege case, the Union of the two Canadas, and the Canadian clergy reserve, the peers allowed the Government Bills through; and on Irish tithe, Poor Law, municipal corporations and Church measures, the broad Peel–Wellington compromises were at last accepted by the Government. When in the spring of 1839 Lord Roden carried a hostile motion of inquiry in the Upper House against the Government's Irish administration, Lord Normanby[3] showed signs of temper and some Whigs again suggested a token creation of some half-dozen peers. The Cabinet, however, contented itself with a counter-demonstration in the House of Commons.[4] After the Bedchamber episode Melbourne's repudiation of Radical policy, and Wellington's assurances of support for moderate Whig principles as long as they were moderate,[5] indicated indeed a degree of harmony in

---

[1] Walpole, *Russell*, i. 292 n. (3).

[2] Ibid., p. 296.

[3] Who had been Lord-Lieutenant in the period covered by the inquiry, 1835–9. He was succeeded in the latter year by Lord Ebrington.

[4] Russell moved a resolution approving the Government's Irish policy, which was carried by 318–296. According to Greville, Lord Normanby wanted 'resignation or reparation'; and the Cabinet did in fact have a long discussion on the issue (*Melbourne Papers*, pp. 395–6; *Greville*, 25 Mar. 1839).

[5] This was the general interpretation put on the more parliamentary language of the two leaders. On 31 May a debate on the adjournment was brought on by

the Upper House sufficient to alarm more partisan Conservative politicians in the Lower.[1] In fact, since 1836 the steam had gone out of the Lords Reform locomotive. In that year, if in any, had been presented the best chance of intimidating the Upper House and of either forcing through the Government's Irish legislation or placing some effective restrictions on the powers of the Lords. The chance—if it was a chance—had been let slip. Reformers fell to quarrelling among themselves; and public interest waned. Back from India in June 1838, Macaulay found such a general lack of enthusiasm for a reform of the Lords that he told Greville in an unmistakable phrase that it no more occurred to him to agitate the question in the existing state of the public mind than it would to advocate representative government in Turkey or monarchy and the hereditary peerage in the U.S.A.[2]

The House of Lords had survived the crisis; and, as could be seen in retrospect, with a greater margin of safety than was apparent at the time. It had done so for a number of reasons. In the first place the storm that blew round their heads between 1835 and 1837 had reflected more anger at their political actions than a permanent alienation of interest from them as an institution. The aristocracy was too deeply rooted in English life and covered too wide an area of society for a class division to open up between the peerage on one side and the rest of the community on the other. As Lord Morley, the cheerful aristocratic Whig uncle of George Villiers,[3] wrote at the height of the agitation in July 1836,

the talk about the reform of the House of Lords is all nothing at all. The House of Lords is supported by the great mass of the property

Lord Winchilsea, who pressed for further clarification of the Government's intentions. In the course of a speech which conveyed the impression that he was not going to make concessions to the Radicals, Melbourne said, 'I am not prepared to adopt measures contrary to my feelings, contrary to my opinions, contrary to my conscience, for the sake of obtaining any support which they might obtain.' Wellington, who observed in passing that he did not think that the Government had had good reason for resignation anyhow, warmly approved Melbourne's declaration and added, 'I earnestly recommend him to persevere in the intentions which he has announced in the course of the discussion this night' and 'trust to the good sense of Parliament and the country for his support' (*Hansard*, vol. 47, 1162, 1187).

[1] Cf. Graham's letter to Arbuthnot of 1 June 1839 (Parker, *Graham*, i. 283)
[2] *Greville*, 14 July 1838.
[3] Later 4th Earl of Clarendon.

and intelligence of the country, and was never in greater strength than at present. . . . There is no disturbance, no agitation whatever, no hostility in private society. The whole virulence which is felt is exhibited by the newspaper writers. The *Times*, the *Morning Herald*, the *Morning Post*, brawl on one side, and the *Chronicle*, *Spectator* and *Examiner* on the other, but without producing the slightest effect.[1]

This was perhaps a shade complacent; but it was a good deal nearer the truth than the acid remark of his Radical nephew, C. P. Villiers (of Corn Law fame), who asserted a few months later that 'the Lords Forester and Chesterfield et *hoc genus omne* are regarded now just as Gatton and Sarum were a few years before their destruction'.[2] Melbourne, who had a shrewder sense of realities than C. P. Villiers or even John Russell, made a pertinent observation in 1835 on the differences between the institutions which were criticized politically and those which were in real danger of reconstruction as a consequence of the Reform Act. In 1835 the Lords had after all eventually passed the Municipal Corporations Act. That seemed to him the essential political fact, not the rhodomontades of Lyndhurst, the clamour of electoral mobs, or the logic of the Radical theorists. The real interest threatened was elsewhere. 'Depend upon it, it is the Established Church, not the hereditary peerage, that has need to set its house in order.'[3]

---

[1] H. Maxwell, *Life of 4th Earl of Clarendon* (1913), i. 122. Morley said that the only two real grievances against the House of Lords were that they had rejected the Irish Tithe Bill in 1834, although it had no appropriation clause, and that they had rejected the Irish Municipal Corporations Bill in 1836. But, he added, the latter had come before them for the first time and had a strong minority against it (200–300) in the House of Commons; and would probably pass next year in any case.   [2] Ibid., p. 127.

[3] Torrens, *Melbourne*, pp. 386–7. That acute foreign critic, Alexis de Tocqueville, on his visit to England in 1833, had made similar observations on the strength of the aristocracy in English society. 'Talk with a man of the people or with a member of the middle classes and you will see that he has a vague feeling of discomfort. He will complain of such-and-such a Lord, or the course which the House of Lords has adopted, but it does not seem to have entered his head that one could do without Lords. His anger will be brought to bear against some individual, but you will only very rarely notice in him that violent feeling, full of hatred and envy, which incites the lower classes in France against all those who are above them. These feelings, it is true, are germinating among the English, but they are not yet developed and perhaps it will be a long time before they are so if the aristocracy avoids a head-on collision with the people. . . . So, too, if you speak to a member of the middle classes; you will find he hates some aristocrats but not the aristocracy. On the contrary, he is himself full of aristocratic prejudices' (*Journeys to England and Ireland*, ed. J. P. Mayer (1958), p. 70).

Even if the principle of reforming the Lords were conceded, the Liberal party was completely split on the mode of reform.[1] Essentially the difference was between a constitutional reconstruction designed to ensure harmony between the two branches of the legislature—or, more precisely, the subordination of the Upper to the Lower House[2]—and a political revolution designed to produce a Reform majority in the Lords. Yet if the real quarrel with the peers was not that they were an hereditary chamber but that they were an anti-reform chamber, it followed that the solution of creating an elective Upper House was hardly a practical possibility. The fact that O'Connell made himself the spokesman for that species of reform was in itself enough to ruin its chances. 'The question is not now brought to a contest between the Peers and the Commons', declared *Blackwood's Magazine* with a certain arrogance in November 1835, 'but between the Peers of England, with the Commons of England, against a motley band of Scotch and Irish revolutionists.'[3] Even O'Connell's prescription left many questions unanswered. 'I see some persons propose electing the House of Lords', wrote Durham to Parkes in November 1836. 'If so, by whom, by what classes, and in what manner? Are all the peers to be elected at once by the whole constituent body throughout the empire, or are they to represent districts as in the House of Commons. . . . If a second or upper house of assembly is necessary in a state, it is for the purpose of checking or auditing, as it were, the acts of the lower.'[4] Yet an Upper House produced by the same machinery as the Lower seemed to him merely designed to reproduce the special interests and blemishes of the Lower.

[1] The *Edinburgh Review* catalogued the current prescriptions in Apr. 1835 and dismissed them all from practical consideration. The creation of more peers was 'full of difficulty'. To abolish the Upper House was 'too desperate to be thought of'. Life peers would make the House entirely dependent on the Crown, or rather the Ministers of the day. An elective House of Lords, if elected by the peers themselves or any select or high-property qualification electorate, would produce an even more illiberal chamber than the existing one. Its own pet remedy was a system of 'free conference' between the two Houses to decide on disputed legislation by a joint vote of 900 members (550 from the House of Commons and 350 from the House of Lords). (See vol. 61, pp. 1 seq.)

[2] The *Appendix to the Black Book* (1835) asserted that 'the peerage must be brought into that position of subserviency to the other branches of the legislature which the Commons, previously to the Reform Act, occupied' (p. 55).

[3] Vol. 38, p. 584.

[4] C. W. New, *Life of Durham* (1929), p. 305.

Speaking to the Durham Reform Society shortly after the 1837 election, he affirmed stoutly that 'an elective House of Lords is an absurdity and a moral impossibility'.[1]

To any reflective critic, indeed, it was clear (as the *Edinburgh Review* pointed out in April 1835) that an Upper House elected by either the peers or any limited electorate, would be an even more conservative assembly than the existing chamber. It was already a constant complaint of Liberals that the system of elective peers for Scotland and Ireland produced a solid mass of Tory votes in the Upper House from those two kingdoms. On the other hand, an Upper House elected by the same constituencies as the Lower would nullify the revisionary and delaying functions of the peers, and in fact deprive it of any reason for existence.[2] The more practicable alternative was the creation, either on an hereditary or life basis, of enough Liberal peers to constitute a reform majority, facilitated possibly by the elimination of bishops, elective peers, and other species particularly obnoxious to reformers. The first would involve sweeping the highways and byways of the Whig connexion to make, as Russell accused Pitt of having made to his own detriment, 'dull country gentlemen duller Lords', and with no guarantee of perpetual loyalty to liberal views;[3] the second a constitutional struggle which the Ministry lacked both strength and resolution to carry through. In view of the small majority on which the Government could rely in the Commons, the cry for reform of the Lords, as the *Edinburgh Review* sensibly observed,[4] 'means dissolution or it means nothing' and dissolution at such a time and on such an issue was an incalculable risk. Other devices, such as Roebuck's plan for allowing the Lords a suspensory veto only, involved the same difficulty.[5] Fundamentally there was no strong body of opinion in favour either of destroying the hereditary basis of the Upper House or of abrogating its powers.

---

[1] C. W. New, *Life of Durham* (1929), p. 317.

[2] See also the article in the *Edinburgh Review* of Oct. 1835 (vol. 62, pp. 185 seq.).

[3] Russell, *Early Corr.* ii. 144. The *Edinburgh Review* estimated (Apr. 1835) that even 60 or 70 new Liberal peers would barely secure a majority in the Upper House, and pointed out that if other parties followed this dangerous precedent when they came to power, it would completely destroy the character of the peerage (vol. 61, p. 18).

[4] Oct. 1835 (vol. 62, p. 203).

[5] For the contemporary discussion on various schemes of reform of the House of Lords, see A. S. Turberville, *House of Lords in the Age of Reform* (1958), ch. xiv.

For the House of Lords to retain its dignity and status—and not many wished otherwise—it must also have a degree of independence; and independence was a fiction if the Lords could not on occasion disagree with the Commons.

Exploration of constitutional remedies led therefore only to difficulties, disagreements, and deadlock. The solution when it came was not constitutional but political; and it grew naturally out of the same soil that had produced the problem. The essence of the dispute was that it was one, not between two Houses, but between two parties, each with control of one chamber; and where party issues were at stake, there was always room for restraint, concession, and a *modus vivendi*. The constitution would work if politicians were in the last resort ready to make it work; and here at least Melbourne, Russell, Peel, and Wellington were in agreement. That the House of Lords should retain a measure of independence and a real legislative function was clearly a Conservative interest; but it was the constant argument of Peel that the peers were more likely to retain their influence if they followed a moderate line rather than that of refusing any concession. Similarly the Duke of Wellington was always sensitive to the consideration that if a strong Conservative Government were ever to be formed again, it would only be done by keeping together a united party drawn from both Houses.[1] In 1833 and 1834 co-ordination, both political and personal, between Peel and Wellington had been negligible; and this was reflected in the wayward and sometimes extreme actions of the Tory majority in the Lords.[2]

[1] When Peel wrote to Wellington in Apr. 1835 on the desirability of concerting their actions over the Municipal Corporations Bill, the Duke replied, 'That which is in my opinion most necessary in the Country is *a Government*. The most trifling accident would destroy the Power and Influence of this Country throughout the World; and we are exposed to such a one at every moment . . . because there is *no Government* with strength to prevent the Evil or apply an early Remedy.' Hence, he continued, he was not indisposed to make sacrifices of opinion on some of the Corporations questions if necessary 'to keep a Party together or to form a Party which should be strong enough to have a chance of governing' (Add. MS. 40310, f. 101). Peel's letter of 24 Apr., to which this is the reply, is partly printed in Parker, *Peel*, ii. 313.

[2] Over the Irish Church Bill in 1833 Wellington's wavering course indicated the various pressures brought to bear on him. His support for the rejection of the Irish Tithes Bill in 1834 was probably a political error and certainly in contradiction to Peel's line; though the difficulties of the Government gave a clear tactical opening for successful resistance in that session.

The following session, Lyndhurst's behaviour over the Municipal Corporations Bill strained the relations between the two
wings of the party to breaking-point. It was not a coincidence
that the years when the Conservative peers were most independent of the House of Commons Conservatives were also
the years of their greatest danger and unpopularity. Yet it had
been Wellington, after all, who at the crucial meeting at Apsley
House on 3 September 1835 advised the Conservative peers to
yield over municipal reform; and even more remarkably
Lyndhurst who consented to take the lead in proposing the new
conciliatory concessions.[1] From 1836 onwards party ties between
the two Houses grew closer, and the tactics of the Lords in
consequence more subtle. In May 1837, at a party meeting of
peers, Wellington emphasized the dangers of an isolated position
unsupported by the King and the Opposition in the House of
Commons and argued for the expediency of agreeing with the
Commons whenever possible.[2] The Irish Municipal Bill was
not rejected, but postponed until more was known of the
Government's policy on tithe and Poor Law; and in 1840, over
Canada and the Hansard privilege case, though Wellington
disagreed with Peel and had a majority behind him in the
Lords, he refused to split the party by taking the tactical victory
that was within his grasp.[3] Indeed, if Peel (as Russell suggested
in 1850) was responsible more than any other one man for
making the House of Commons work after 1832, Wellington
performed the same office for the House of Lords after 1834.
Behind Wellington was the steady pull of party, and the pre-
cedence he attached to party considerations over isolated details
of legislation in the end proved more effective than the influence
of the ultras or the personal views and ambitions of men like
Lyndhurst and Ellenborough. In so doing he helped not only
to preserve the unity of the Conservative party, but to extricate
the Peers from the crisis of 1835–6 without loss of power or
dignity.

The years 1841–5, with a Conservative Ministry in power,
saw a general passivity in the House of Lords.[4] Even Maynooth

[1] Add. MS. 40312, f. 250, Aberdeen to Peel, 4 Sept. 1835. Cf. Turberville,
op. cit., pp. 357–8.
[2] Ellenborough Journal, P.R.O. 30/12/28/6, 4 May 1837.
[3] Cf. Parker, *Graham*, i. 294–7.
[4] Campbell, who became a peer on his appointment as Irish Lord Chancellor

in 1845, though it angered the permanently dissident Orange peers and provoked the resignation of the Conservative Chief Whip in the Upper House (Lord Redesdale), did little to disturb the harmony. Roden's delaying motion for an inquiry attracted only 69 supporters and the Bill passed its second and third readings by majorities of 157 and 131—as large as those in the House of Commons.[1] What proved, significantly, more dangerous to the Government's control of the Upper House was the Irish Tenant's Compensation Bill, a first-fruit of the Devon Commission, which produced a coalition of peers with Irish estates irrespective of party. The obnoxious principle of interference between landlord and tenant brought the Ministerial majority down to 14 in a thin House on the second reading of the Bill, until it was put into the cold storage of a Select Committee.[2] But Stanley's Tenant Bill never reached the Commons, and it was not until the Corn Law crisis of 1846 that any serious likelihood of disagreement between the Upper and Lower Houses emerged.

On the face of it one of the most surprising aspects of the crisis was the unobtrusive part played by the House of Lords. For an assembly composed predominantly of large landowners, with no responsibilities to constituents, to pass the repeal of the Corn Laws with less debate and difficulty than the Lower House, was a phenomenon which has received less attention than it deserves. The argument (used by Halévy, for example) that the peers sacrificed the most valuable of their economic privileges

---

in the summer of 1841, commented bitterly on the inactivity in his new chamber after the change of Government. The feebleness (in his view) of the Ministerial front bench was only equalled by the 'extreme listlessness of our own friends' and he complained that 'the House was at all times more like a club chatting upon the news of the day than a deliberative assembly met to make laws for a mighty empire' (*Life*, ii. 163–5).

[1] The voting on the second reading was: *for the Bill*, 144 present, 82 proxies, total 226; *against*, 55 present, 14 proxies, total 69; *majority* 157 (*Hansard*, vol. 81, 116–19, 4 June 1845). Mr. D. Large, in his article on 'The House of Lords and Ireland in the age of Peel, 1832–50' (*Irish Historical Studies*, ix. 387–8) adds four pairs, making the total opposition 73. He estimates that nearly a hundred Whig peers voted for the Bill; but his statement that without these the Government would have been outnumbered is only true if the Whigs had not merely abstained but voted against.

[2] The voting was 48–34 (24 June 1845). In the course of the debate Lord Londonderry produced a remonstrance signed by 36 peers with property in Ireland. The importance of the Irish interest in the House of Lords in this period (i.e. Irish peers or peers with Irish estates) is discussed by Mr. Large, *ut supra*, pp. 367 seq.

in order to retain what was left of their political privileges is not
merely an over-simplified generalization but one that fits rather
awkwardly the role played by the peers since 1832. It is true,
no doubt, that there were underlying social and economic
motives; but they were more mixed than Halévy suggested,
extremely hard to disentangle, and not all on the side of agriculture. A number of peers had sizeable industrial and commercial interests (some twenty-odd at least in coal and minerals
alone); a few, extensive and lucrative urban property. The railway boom indirectly assisted many other landowners and perhaps was more important financially (it has been suggested)
than improved methods of farming and estate management.
Moreover, the peers as a class had contacts over a wider area
of early Victorian economic society than the squirearchy; and
those who still maintained electoral influence in industrial
counties like Yorkshire and Durham or in the middling
boroughs, were obliged to consider interests other than agricultural. Yet it would be easy to overestimate this element in
the peerage. Men like Portland, Grosvenor, Bedford, Cleve-
land, Sidmouth, and Fitzwilliam, with anything from a fifth to
a half of their income drawn from urban and industrial sources,
were an exception; and it was to be another generation before
fortunes directly derived from industry were to be represented
among the peers. In the mid 1840's they were not even beginning to be directors of railway companies.[1] The great majority
of the members of the Upper House lived on agricultural rents;
and if the 'economic man' of the theorists had been any more
real than the 'pains and pleasures man' of the Utilitarians, there
could have been little doubt which way the peers would have
leaned.

Even the agricultural interest, however, was far from being
a single and uniform block. Landowners and farmers alike
exhibited different opinions and shades of emphasis on the
question of protection. In the north of England and in Scotland,
in areas with large mixed farms with light soils suitable for
barley and sheep, as opposed to cold clay districts with smaller
and more specialized corn farms, in grazing as distinct from
arable districts, there was no united support for the Corn

[1] See generally F. M. L. Thompson, *English Landed Society in the Nineteenth
Century* (1963), chs. vii–ix, esp. pp. 266–8.

Laws; and the long violent agitation against them had succeeded in producing among some farmers and landowners, if
not an intellectual conviction, at least a readiness to accept
some solution which would remove the issue from the public
stage.[1] Men of accessible capital and prosperous estates could
afford to look on repeal with greater detachment than small
freeholders, old-fashioned farmers, impoverished squires, or
debt-ridden owners of large mortgaged estates. The development of scientific farming offered to some a fairer and firmer
prospect than legislative protection, even though its appeal
depended very much on the amount of individual capital that
could be directed to the improvement of soil, husbandry, and
stock. An intellectual scepticism as to the real value of protection
had been making some headway among the landed interest;
and there were rational converts to Free Trade among the
peers long before the Corn Law crisis blew up in the winter of
1845–6.[2]

An attempt therefore to find a logical pattern of economic
interest in the votes of the Upper House would not be easy;

[1] Lord Londonderry in the debate on the second reading of the Bill said that
'he believed that the general feeling in the north of England was in favour of this
measure, and that the farmers there entertained very different views from what
were entertained in the south'. He added that the Corn Law was not a question
of high policy. 'In fact it was not a question of party at all, or of one on which
were ranged on one side those connected with the interests of agriculture, and those
connected with commerce and manufactures on the other' (*Hansard*, vol. 86,
1124–5). Lord Haddington in the same debate said he did not think that the landed
interest would be injured if protection were abolished. The Earl of Aberdeen was
told by his agent in Jan. 1846 that in the Buchan district he found divisions of
opinion among farmers. Some favoured ending the agitation by immediate repeal;
some a permanent small duty of 1s.; some a gradual reduction to 1s. But there was
a general desire to see the question settled and no great apprehension of a catastrophic fall in grain prices (Add. MS. 40455, f. 314). Similarly Sidney Herbert
received a letter from a large farmer in his constituency of South Wiltshire approving Peel's measure but regretting that it was not immediate. Greville indeed noted
by Mar. 1846 that farmers in many places were becoming anxious for a settlement;
they did not dread repeal of the Corn Laws but wanted it settled (*Greville*, 2 Feb.,
18 Mar., 14 Apr. 1846).

[2] Including that unpredictable character, the Duke of Wellington. Although he
had told Lord Mahon in Dec. 1838 that 'if there is one thing in the world of which
I know positively nothing, it is agriculture', a year later Mahon found him of the
opinion that at some time in the future, as a result of reforms and capital outlay,
English agriculture would become independent of the Corn Laws. He told Mahon
that for some years he had been devoting the whole of his income from his estate
to its better cultivation and improvement (Stanhope, *Conversations with the Duke of
Wellington* (1889), pp. 133, 159).

to diagnose all the individual motives among nearly four hundred peers would be impossible. Yet it is probable that intellectual and political considerations weighed at least as heavily as economic in deciding the attitudes of the Upper House. Certainly it is unrealistic to detach the actions of the Lords from party and personal influences. For some it was decisive that the measures came to them armed with the prestige and authority of Peel. They had watched the general recovery of the country since 1841; they respected, without attempting to rival, his knowledge and judgement. 'I was among that number of your friends, who viewing your corn measures with alarm, could not vote for them', wrote Dunraven in April 1846, 'yet the confidence I still felt in your judgement led me to examine the whole subject as fully as I could—certainly dispassionately—and I frankly own the result has been my conversion and conviction that your measures are not only expedient at the present moment but contain principles on which alone the constitution and greatness of England can rest securely.'[1] For the Opposition this deferential attitude was one of their major difficulties. 'We never vote against the Government, other noble lords say,' observed Richmond satirically in leading the attack on the second reading of the Corn Bill, 'we don't like to vote against the Bill, we have always supported Sir Robert Peel, we don't like to abandon our party.'[2] The fact that the measure would be laid before the House as the recommendation of a Conservative Ministry was a consideration not only in influencing particular peers but in deciding Peel's general strategy. He was determined not to fight a general election on the question of repeal—not merely because he thought it the duty of the Government as an executive to carry it through—but also because an election would have taken the form and something of the substance of a social conflict, 'the issue of which', as he wrote later to Goulburn, 'would have been a disgraceful submission on the part of the House of Lords as the least of the evils to be encountered'.[3]

[1] Apsley House MS., Peel to Wellington, 9 Apr. 1846, enclosing a letter from Dunraven to Peel of 7 Apr., putting his proxy at the Government's disposal. See the speech of the Earl of Essex in the debate on the second reading for his avowal of similar conversion and confidence in Peel.

[2] *Hansard*, vol. 86, 1108.

[3] Goulburn MS., Peel to Goulburn, 20 Dec. (1846).

This contingency was also clear to some of the peers. Being a money Bill, the repeal of the Corn Laws could only be accepted or rejected by the Upper House.[1] Rejection would entail a delay of at least a year, and it would probably return to the House after a general election, at the hands of a different Ministry, and with overwhelming popular support.[2] It was substantially this which Wellington made the staple of his argument in winding up the debate on the second reading of the Bill.

We know that, if we should reject this Bill, it is a Bill which has been agreed to by the other two branches of the Legislature; and that the House of Lords stands alone in rejecting this measure. Now, that, my Lords, is a situation in which . . . you ought not to stand; it is a position in which you cannot stand, because you are entirely powerless; without the House of Commons and the Crown, the House of Lords can do nothing. You have vast influence on public opinion . . . but without the Crown or the House of Commons you can do nothing, till the connexion with the Crown and the House of Commons is revived. . . . I conclude that another Government will be formed; but whether another Government is formed or not, let me ask, do your Lordships suppose that you will not have this very same measure brought before you by the next Administration which can be formed? And do your Lordships mean to reject the measure a second time?[3]

[1] This would not necessarily have debarred the House of Lords from amending the Bill; but it did mean that if amended by the Lords, the Bill would not have been accepted by the Commons, because (to use Wellington's words) 'such alteration would be on the part of the House of Lords an usurpation of power not admitted by the other branches of the Constitution'. (Peel, *Memoirs*, ii. 276.) In effect therefore amendment was equivalent to rejection. Peel's main anxiety in the first week of June was not the fate of the Coercion Bill but the safe passage of the Corn and Tariff Bills through the House of Lords committee stage. He wrote to Arbuthnot on 8 June: 'The point on which I am far more anxious than any other is the safety of the Corn bill and the Tariff bill. I see nothing but confusion from the failure of those bills. I have done everything in my power to ensure personal attendance in Committee' (Add. MS. 40484, f. 327).

[2] Cf. the speeches of Earl Fitzwilliam and Lord Haddington (who appealed to the House not to lose the opportunity of graceful concession to public feeling).

[3] *Hansard*, vol. 86, 1404. Cf. Wellington to Peel, 19 May 1846: 'The course which I can take in the House of Lords, and in which I can really be of service to the Government, is in urging the House to avoid to separate itself from the House of Commons and the Crown, which is the course that I have successfully taken upon former occasions' (Peel, *Memoirs*, ii. 284). Cf. also Peel to the Queen, 15 Dec. 1845: 'Sir Robert Peel concurs in the opinion expressed by Lord Lansdowne, that collision between the House of Lords and Commons on this particular question would be most injurious to the country. Sir Robert Peel cannot of course give any assurances as to the

Yet if party and Government influence was at work in the Upper House, it was not by a party vote that the Bill passed. Over half the majority for the second reading was composed of Whig peers, and only a handful of them voted against.[1]

The attitude of the Whig party was therefore crucial; and it was by no means certain at the start of the crisis whether all or even most of the Whig peers favoured outright repeal. The Whig party line had, after all, been a fixed duty and not all the great Whig landowners liked the prospect either of outright repeal or of repeal unaccompanied by substantial financial assistance to agriculture. Though Russell in February had got the general assent of his House of Commons followers to support for Peel's policy, the Whig peers were less manageable. Indeed, there was a small but influential group of Whig peers with large Irish estates—Lansdowne, Clanricarde, Bessborough, and Ponsonby—who were ironically at first favourable to Peel's Coercion Bill but opposed to total and immediate repeal of the Corn Laws. Bessborough in fact at one stage even toyed with the notion of a coalition with Bentinck and the Protectionists on the basis of concessions to Ireland[2] and presumably a small fixed duty on corn.[3] Palmerston in the Commons was personally in

course which the House of Lords might take, but it is his impression that many peers of great authority who might not assent to the necessity or the advantage of a particular measure, would exercise their influence in the House of Lords to prevent its rejection after it had passed the House of Commons' (Parker, *Peel*, iii. 249).

[1] D. Southgate, *Passing of the Whigs* (1962), p. 131, gives the figures 115 Whig peers out of a total majority of 211; only 15 Whigs in the minority of 164.

[2] *Greville*, 23 and 26 Apr. 1846; Arbuthnot to Peel, 5 Apr. 1846 (Parker, *Peel*, iii. 345). Cf. the reference by Disraeli in *Lord George Bentinck* (1872), p. 167 to this potential Whig–Protectionist alliance. Dr. Dreyer is of the opinion that the Whig 'nobleman' mentioned by Disraeli is Bessborough; and it is in fact clear that Bessborough raised the possibility with Russell, Hobhouse, and doubtless others (Walpole, *Russell*, i. 439, n. 1; Broughton Diaries, 18 Mar. 1846, Add. MS. 43748). He seems to have been supported by Normanby and Ponsonby. The Duke of Bedford told Arbuthnot at the beginning of Apr. that the great body of Whigs supported Peel's measure only with great reluctance, and Arbuthnot, in relating this to Peel, added that he was quite sure that the Whigs were ill at ease. 'They have a hankering after a connection with part of the Protectionists; but they feel that should this be accomplished, they must disconnect themselves from the Radicals. They have been led, as the Duke of Bedford told me, to look to the Protectionists in consequence of what Lord G. Bentinck has said to a Whig friend of his. Lord George told his friend that a considerable portion of the persons with whom he acted would be glad to see a moderate Whig government formed, and that their demands would be very moderate and could easily bes atisfied' (Add. MS. 40484, f. 292).

[3] The Duke of Bedford told Hobhouse on 7 May that the House of Lords would

favour of a compromise low duty, and, though he was not prepared to separate from Russell on the issue, there was always
the chance that a successful amendment in the House of Lords
might make the Whig leaders in the Commons alter their
policy. What with the Irish Bill and the Corn Bill, and the
two discordant wings of the party in either House, there was
for a time considerable hesitation in Whig tactics. But by the
end of April Bessborough and Clanricarde had changed their
minds about coercion and the only real problem was to secure
unanimity over corn.[1] It was at this point that Russell, with his
characteristic courage and something more than his characteristic sagacity, displayed one of the most important and decisive acts of leadership in the whole history of his connexion with
the Whig party. On 23 May he summoned a meeting of all the
Whig peers at Lansdowne House.[2] When they met, Lansdowne
announced that though abstractly he still believed a fixed duty
was best, he advised the acceptance of Peel's Bill without
amendment. The issue, however, was clinched by Russell, who
told the Whig peers flatly that he could be no party to any
alteration or mutilation of the Bill, and that if the Government
resigned as the result of a hostile amendment, he could not
undertake a Government to carry a fixed duty[3] and 'they must

probably substitute a fixed duty when they went into committee (Broughton,
Recollections, vi. 169). The Earl of Wicklow in fact moved an amendment for the
imposition of a duty of 5s. in place of 1s. on foreign wheat which was defeated by
107–140. Cf. *Greville*, 7 and 21 May 1846, for general reports of overtures by the
Protectionists to dissident Protectionist Whigs and Russell's repudiation of them,
and also for the sentiments of the Palmerston circle on the desirability of a compromise settlement in conjunction with the Protectionists.

[1] Arbuthnot, who had private sources of information on the manœuvres within
the Whig party, told Peel on 8 June that Russell 'had at one time meant to support
it (i.e. the Coercion Bill), as the Duke of Bedford told me, but he changed his mind
when the Whig peers, who had voted for the bill, informed him that they no longer
wished for the measure. The Duke of Bedford carried the message to his brother
from Lord Bessborough as he himself informed me' (Add. MS. 40484, f. 317).

[2] Fifty-three attended, together with Russell, Palmerston, and Labouchere.
Clarendon told the meeting that he had been informed by the Lord Chancellor
that any amendment in committee would be struck out when reported back to the
House (when the Government could use their proxies) and though Normanby
and Clanricarde protested at acquiescence in such a procedure, the two Whig
law lords, Cottenham and Campbell, both supported the principle and precedent
of such an action. Clarendon's information was of course quite correct. The
Cabinet had closely examined the question of use of proxies to reject amendments
in committee and were unanimous in deciding to do so if necessary. (Peel, *Memoirs*,
ii. 271–81.)

[3] Lord Grey's Diary, 23 May 1846 (Grey MS.) gives a full description of the

choose another leader'.[1] This was conclusive, and two days later party discipline, and the imminent prospect of a Whig Ministry, swung the Whig peers almost to a man behind the Bill.[2] The House of Lords in fact had been caught by the two most powerful single influences that could have been brought to bear on them—a Peelite executive supported by Wellington and the Crown, the Government *de facto*, and the solidarity of the Whig party, the Government *in posse*. The twin pressures were irresistible and the Corn Laws were repealed.

In the years between 1846 and 1852 the relative quiescence of the House of Lords resulted primarily from the circumstances in which the Whig Ministry came into office. Superficially, the disappearance of a cohesive Conservative party in the Commons might have been expected to result in the loosening of restraint over the peers and the emergence of guerrilla activity by diehard Tories against an ostensibly Liberal Ministry led now not by the sceptical Melbourne but by radical John Russell. It did not happen, if only because the uneasy position of the Government in the Commons prevented any great liberal reforming programme on the model of the 1830's. There were, however, moments when the attitude of the Lords seemed crucial. One was over the repeal of the Navigation Act in 1849, which was widely regarded as the coping stone to the Free Trade edifice and to some extent therefore resurrected the passions of 1846.[3]

meeting and confirms the remarkable accuracy of the account given by Greville second-hand (1 June 1846). It is clear from Grey's account that some peers (de Mauley and Vivian) remained obdurately opposed to repeal, and that Normanby and Clanricarde had still been hoping to defeat the Government on the issue of a fixed duty.

[1] The quoted phrase is Russell's own description of what he said (Broughton Diary, 25 May 1846, Add. MS. 43748).

[2] Cf. Hobhouse: 'The conclusion from this unanimity was that the Bill would pass, a great change from yesterday.' Palmerston told Hobhouse, in his usual jaunty fashion, that the Whig peers had been 'all unanimous against the Bill, and all unanimous not to oppose it'. This was gross exaggeration, but it at least indicated the importance of the decision taken at the meeting in securing party unity. As one of the dissentients said, 'What could we do? Lord John Russell told us that if we took any other line, we should break up the party' (Broughton, *Recollections*, vi. 173). Of the rebellious Whig peers, Ponsonby voted against the Bill, but Clanricarde, Bessborough, Anglesey, and de Mauley followed the party line.

[3] Brougham, speaking on 12 June, said that many peers supported the measure because 'they thought that the throwing out of this Bill would tend to the throwing out of Her Majesty's Government, and that if the Government were thrown out, an appeal would be made to the country by a dissolution of Parliament . . . that a dissolution, at this moment, would lead to a contention fatal to the internal peace

The Government made it a question of confidence in the Upper House[1] and unusual efforts were made on both sides to whip up attendance, a personal appeal being made by Charles Wood (the Whig Chancellor of the Exchequer) to Peel for his aid in influencing the Peelite and Wellingtonian group in the Lords.[2] The Government won a victory on the second reading, but only by ten votes; and the narrow majority provoked Russell to consider once more the old question of a reform of the House. In a memorandum of June 1849[3] he argued that though the creation of peers by Grey and Melbourne[4] and the appointment of new bishops had given the Liberal Ministry a casual and transient majority of 8 to 10 votes in the Upper House, it was desirable to bring that body more into harmony with the Commons. One method was the advancement of men of distinction and adequate income; another the creation of life peers from the ranks of the Liberal Irish and Scots peers virtually debarred because of their Liberalism from becoming representative peers, or from judges and lawyers who for lack of substantial means would not wish to become hereditary peers. Lansdowne, the Leader of the House, whose views on such matters naturally carried much weight, agreed that some

of the country—that it would lead to a war of free-traders against protectionists —setting class against class, and arraying the manufacturing and commercial against the agricultural interests' (*Hansard*, vol. 106, 24.)

[1] The Cabinet had actually decided on 18 Apr. to resign if defeated on the Bill (Grey Diaries, same date).

[2] Parker, *Peel*, iii. 504–5. The Peelites took little part in the debate, but Wellington, Argyll, Aberdeen, Devon, de Grey, Ellesmere, Ripon, St. Germans, Hardinge, Ashburton, and Wharncliffe all voted for the Government on the second reading. In effect, therefore, the Peelites gave the Government its majority. Alternatively this credit can go to the Archbishops of Canterbury, York, and Dublin, and the eleven other bishops who voted for repeal—and were threatened in consequence by Lord Winchilsea with the prospect of a revival of Convocation and a limitation of episcopal representation in the Upper House. The opposition to the Bill included such diverse politicians as Stanley, Brougham, Ellenborough, Londonderry, and Harrowby. Greville (11 May 1849) said that 'the greatest whip-up was made on both sides that ever was known'; and the Government apparently brought back their ambassadors from Paris and Vienna (Normanby and Ponsonby) to be present at the committee stage, where proxies could not be used (see Brougham's speech of 12 June, *Hansard*, vol. 106, 23).

[3] Russell MS. 19 June (1849), P.R.O. 30/22/7.

[4] Between 1830 and 1837 there had been 59 creations, of which 40 were due to Grey and Melbourne. Four of these were eldest sons of peers called up in their father's baronies (Turberville, *House of Lords in the Age of Reform*, p. 367). Melbourne made 19 new creations, Russell 9, and Peel 4 in the 1837–52 period.

additions should be made to the Liberal benches in the Lords, but doubted whether the innovation of life peerages would not arouse more opposition than it was worth. Russell's arguments, he thought, justified sufficient new creations of the conventional style, even though the Prime Minister seemed reluctant to pursue the example of his party predecessors.[1]

The question was renewed the following year in consequence of the weakness of the Government in the Commons and the difficulties the Ministry encountered there over Palmerston's Greek policy. In June Lord Stanley in the Upper House, supported by the Peelite Aberdeen,[2] carried a motion of censure against the Government's foreign policy by 37 votes, and the Cabinet seriously considered resignation.[3] Lansdowne was clearly mortified at his position. He complained to Russell that Stanley was the real Leader of the House of Lords, and though he did not think that the Government should resign on a vote of the peers, he was unwilling to carry on without some unequivocal vote of confidence from the Commons.[4] The Don Pacifico debate was therefore primarily brought on to strengthen the Government's position in the Lords. Though it

[1] Lansdowne's memorandum of 19 Oct. 1849 in the Russell MS., P.R.O. 30/22/8, Pt. 1. If life peers were to be introduced, however, Lansdowne thought that preference should be given to Liberal Scots and Irish peers because of the practical working of the elective system to which Russell had referred.

[2] Peel and Graham agreed with Aberdeen's view of the dangers implicit in Palmerston's conduct of foreign affairs, but refrained from attack because they did not wish to bring down the Ministry by a defeat in the Commons and so let in the Protectionists. Aberdeen was primarily concerned with a demonstration in Parliament that would have some effect both in Europe generally and in restraining the Cabinet; and he pressed Peel to join in the demonstration. 'I care very little for the House of Commons', he wrote to Peel in Apr., 'and am only anxious that a policy which in fact you think mischievous should not appear to receive your sanction' (Parker, *Peel*, iii, 540). But Peel in fact only joined the opposition to Palmerston in the House of Commons over Roebuck's motion when it was clear that the Government would not be defeated.

[3] A third of the Cabinet (Grey, Wood, Labouchere, and Hobhouse) were in favour of resigning, but eight of their colleagues voted against and Russell said that if he resigned, he would announce that he personally had been ready to go on, but had been deserted by his colleagues. This ended the talk of resignation although, curiously, it was also decided not to originate a counter-motion in the Commons (Broughton Diaries, Add. MS. 43754, pp. 70-72).

[4] Lansdowne to Russell, 1850, undated but clearly written soon after the defeat in the Lords (17 June) and the Cabinet meeting of 18 June when it was decided not to resign and not to move a motion in the Commons. It was Lansdowne's attitude presumably that made Russell change his mind (Russell MS., P.R.O. 30/22/8, Pt. 2).

produced the required (and expected) vote for the Government, it did not end Russell's restlessness about the peers. At the end of the session he again raised the issue in the Cabinet. Pursuing Lansdowne's line, he argued that Stanley was turning the Upper House into a Tory stronghold and said he already had nearly all the Scots and Irish representative peers behind him. But once more he showed his personal antipathy to large additions to the hereditary peerage, and declared that almost anything was preferable to what William IV had sanctioned in 1832: the creation of a mass of peers or the use of Crown influence to dissuade the Opposition. His remedy was again the elevation to life peerages of eminent judicial, military, and professional men. The Cabinet were dubious of such a revolutionary device to counteract what most of them thought was merely Stanley's hotheadedness, and on this as on many other issues the Prime Minister received no support from his Laodicean colleagues.[1] At the end of the year Lansdowne was able to greet with relief his leader's abandonment of the life peerage scheme.

Russell's attempt to reconcile Whig aristocratic exclusiveness with a judicious infiltration of Liberalism into the House of Lords had a certain curiosity value; but it lacked any real prospect of success because the danger it sought to avert was largely illusory. The fundamental weakness of the Government after 1847 lay in the fractured state of the Commons and Russell's own increasing loss of control over his own party. In any case the Whig creations since 1830—nearly seventy between 1830 and 1852 as against Peel's nine in his own Ministries of the period—had already done much to redress the balance of parties in the Upper House. What had been threatened as a single act of coercion in 1832 had been done by degrees over the next twenty years, even though the effects were piecemeal and impermanent. Stanley in fact was never able to create and hold together a strong party in the House of Lords between 1846 and 1852. At the moment when the Prime Minister was embarrassing his Cabinet colleagues with fancy schemes of reform, Stanley was complaining to Croker of the pernicious existence of 'a body of professed neutrals in the Lords, always ready to

[1] Broughton Diaries, Add. MSS. 43754, pp. 125–7; cf. also 43756, pp. 36–37; Broughton, *Recollections*, vi. 262–4.

impede our otherwise successful opposition'.[1] To Lord Ashley, succeeding to his father's earldom in 1851, the Upper House was a 'dormitory', a 'statue-gallery'; and in 1853 he mournfully recorded that 'unless something be done, and that speedily, to give activity and vigour to the House of Lords, it will sink into a mere registration office for the decrees of the House of Commons'.[2] With the gradual lowering of political temperature after 1846 it was inevitable that the House of Lords should become more quiescent than the Commons. The absence of a strong party system in the Lower House deprived the Upper House of direction; the absence of controversial policies deprived it of energy. The detached social position of the peers made their House increasingly ineffective as an institution when divorced from wider forces in society; and both Peel and Russell would have agreed that the Lords were out of the main stream of national political life.[3] Their cushioned and luxurious existence made it difficult for their chamber to function as an efficient part of the legislature. Even if the peers attended debates, they dined out, ended their discussions early, and then were faced with a rush of Bills towards the end of session which they had no time adequately to examine.[4]

But this was in a sense their protection. There could be no political campaign against an institution so inoffensive. The House of Lords had survived the stormy thirties and the isolated

[1] 18 Aug. 1850 (*Croker Papers*, iii. 219). The *Quarterly Review* had already declared in the previous year that 'the House of Lords, in its present temper and practice, is no effectual barrier to the encroachments of democracy' (vol. lxxxv, p. 302, June 1849, quoted but with wrong reference in Turberville, *House of Lords in the Age of Reform*, p. 416.

[2] E. Hodder, *Life of Shaftesbury* (1890), pp. 445, 484.

[3] Peel had said as early as 1837 that 'whatever party is in, the ministers who sit in the House of Lords will be very different men from those in the House of Commons; will live exclusively among gentlemen, will dine out every day, and will pass their time in abusing the House of Commons' (conversation reported by Gladstone, 9 Dec. 1837). And in Mar. 1844, in a discussion in Cabinet on the strength of the Anti-Corn Law movement, as witnessed in the cowed and timid temper of the majority in the House of Commons, and the reluctance of the country gentlemen to intervene in debate, Peel said that 'he wished a deputation of Lords could always be present during the debates in the Commons, for he believed it impossible for that House in any other way to know the movement of public opinion' (19 Mar. 1844, Add. MS. 44777, ff. 40, 149).

[4] 'Bills come up in a cloud in the month of August; 70 or 80 to be discussed and passed in a week. How can we do anything but simply inspect and register them?' (Shaftesbury, 10 Aug. 1853; Hodder, op. cit., p. 484).

perils of the forties by a show of activity which had been in effect
both strong enough to win victories and restrained enough to
save it from driving still deeper into peril. But essentially this
had been, so to speak, derivative. The activity would have been
useless without a strong parallel effort in the Commons;[1] and
the restraint more often than not had been imposed by influences outside their walls. It was a curious footnote to the
stirring role of the Lords in the days of Grey and Melbourne
that when Lord Lansdowne made his valedictory speech in
February 1852, on the retirement of the Whig Ministry, he
complimented the peers on the absence of acrimony and violence
in their proceedings (whereby, he observed, 'your Lordships
will best maintain that authority in the country which you
derive from its constitution; an authority which . . . it ought to
be the wish of all the sane part of this country you should continue to enjoy') and concluded by saying that 'I entertain the
most ardent hope that under whatever Government this country
is placed, your Lordships will continue to maintain a course
which entitles you to the respect of the country. I am confident
that by deserving that respect you will continue to obtain it.'[2]
Yet if the Lords by 1852 had taken on such a degree of protec-
tive colouring that they were politically almost invisible, they
had at least survived a testing period with no technical loss of
power; and survivors could always live to fight another day.

[1] It was a significant development of post-1832 politics that the old eighteenth-
century function of the House of Lords as a convenient mechanism for blocking
legislation unwanted by the Government but allowed for reasons of expediency
to pass the Commons became virtually extinct. Lord Ashburton, criticizing the
severity of Peel's discipline in the Commons over the Factory Bill in 1844, harked
back to an old tradition when he observed that there were other means of defeating
bad measures. 'What is our Lordships' House good for?' (*Croker Papers*, iii. 17–18).
But it was precisely because of the dominant role of the Commons that Peel
insisted on such discipline rather than putting the onus on the House of Lords.

[2] *Hansard*, vol. 119, 884. Lord Campbell derived a rather different and even
more emphatic impression from this speech. 'He (i.e. Lansdowne) gave some good
advice to the Peers', he noted in his journal the next day, '—that, besides being
mild and courteous, they must be more energetic and enterprising, so as to fill a
larger space in the public eye, or they will soon be superseded and forgotten' (*Life*,
ii. 302), *The Times*, however (24 Feb. 1852), confirms the *Hansard* text.

III

CHURCH AND DISSENT:
THE CONFLICT

IT is arguable, on the evidence of public agitation in the post-Waterloo period, that by 1830 it was the Church rather than the Crown or the aristocracy which was in danger. The criticism and abuse directed against it by the Liberal, Radical, and popular press ranged from didactic and admonitory articles in the *Edinburgh Review*[1] to Cruikshank's savage caricature of the clerical magistrate—a two-faced beast shown on the pulpit side in surplice and bands, with Bible and upraised cross; on the Bench side grasping blunderbuss, cat-o'-nine-tails, and felon's fetters, and holding aloft an image of the gibbet.[2] Lower still in the social scale was the persistent element of proletarian anti-clerical and anti-religious feeling, seen for example in the Sunday gutter Press[3] and the London park orators[4] of the late Georgian and early Victorian era. In the

[1] For example, 'Church Establishments' (1823), and 'The Church of England' (1826) in vols. 38 and 44.

[2] It appeared in Hone's well-known satirical poem *The Political House that Jack Built*, published in 1819.

[3] An excerpt from the self-styled *Weekly Police Gazette*, reproduced with horror in the *British Magazine*, vol. 7, p. 193 (Feb. 1835), ran as follows: 'The clergy, as a body, are, in despite of their gowns, and bands, and oaths, a swarm of detected, blasted infidels. The living is their God, Toryism is their creed, knowledge is their aversion, and libertinism is their practice. The return of the Tories to office—for we cannot say to power—and this general election, has called them publicly forth, like the return of spring calls forth wild animals out of their holes.' The *British Magazine* commented that this was the common style of these newspapers, of which 50,000 were alleged to circulate among the lower orders every Sunday, characterized by lewdness, indecency, and blasphemy.

[4] In 1842 Lord Lincoln, the new Commissioner for Woods and Forests, who had the superintendence of the royal parks, was horrified at the 'disgusting and demoralizing exhibitions' of socialist and infidel lecturers who regularly gave anti-religious speeches in Regent's Park. He wanted to stop them, but Graham, the Home Secretary, and Rowan, the Chief Commissioner of the Metropolitan Police, did not think it was practicable to proceed against them by law. But when Peel drew Graham's attention to the public exhibition of 'revolting infidel publications and placards' in print shops in 'Hollowell Street' (probably Holywell St., Strand),

long run this popular anti-clericalism, which formed a perceptible strand in Chartist literature, was as dangerous to Dissent[1] as to the Establishment. But the exposed and vulnerable position of the Church attracted a seething flood of attack in which it was not easy to distinguish the anti-Establishment, anti-clerical, or outright anti-Christian elements. To the outward view the Church of England was politically unpopular, socially exclusive, and administratively corrupt. It shared the discredit into which all the organs of the State had fallen, while lacking the autonomy of the executive and the legislature. It was a profession which could not impose its own training, discipline, or promotion; a monopoly bitterly resented by its professional rivals; a national institution identified with a class. It lacked neither piety nor vigour, as the evangelical revival and the great church-building programme launched in 1818 had demonstrated.[2] But there had been no fundamental change in the system; and it was the system rather than individuals that was the point of attack. As Cobbett not unkindly observed in 1831, 'the Establishment has failed of its object. . . . The fault is not, generally speaking, with those who do the work of the Church; but with those who receive its revenues. The working clergy of the Church of England are, perhaps, taking them as a body, as good men as any in the world; but those who have the benefices, it is, who have destroyed the respect and veneration for the Church.'[3]

To the Church in this situation the events of 1828–32 came

the Home Secretary did get the police to move in the matter (Add. MSS. 40481, ff. 25–39; 40448, ff. 88 seq.).

[1] The Scottish *Chartist Circular*, for example, regarded Dissent as only a degree less obnoxious than the Established Church. If they did not tyrannize or extort, 'this state of things arises far more from want of ability to persecute, than from want of inclination. Every scheme compatible with their continued existence is put into requisition to induce the deluded people to part with their money. . . . Above and beyond all, the patrimony of the poor is invaded, nay, entirely eaten up by the dissenting clergy' (8 Jan. 1842).

[2] See M. H. Port, *Six Hundred New Churches* (1961), a study of the Church Building Commission 1818–56, which dates the real revival in this sphere from the founding of the National School Society in 1811 and the Church Building Society in 1818, mainly as a result of the efforts of Joshua Watson and the Hackney Phalanx group of churchmen. The legal difficulties in the way of parochial reorganization and church extension without parliamentary authority, had put the Church at a grave disadvantage compared with the dissenting sects in the first phase of the population shifts connected with the Industrial Revolution.

[3] *Manchester Lectures* (pub. 1832), p. 62.

as a peculiar threat. The whole constitutional revolution of these years could be represented in religious terms. Two of the three main legislative changes had directly affected Church–State relations; the third did so indirectly. The repeal of the Test and Corporations Acts destroyed the formal principle of Anglican monopoly in offices of State and municipalities; Catholic Emancipation admitted Romanists to the legislature; the Reform Act gave greater political strength to the intellectual and sectarian enemies of the Establishment. In the words of a perfervid Anglican,

three of the great embankments of our constitution have recently been cut through—one in 1828, another in 1829, and a third in 1831. The first broke down the long-established qualification for office in our Christian state; the second *let in*, as *legislators*, men implacably hostile to the great living principle of all our institutions; the third, as a natural consequence of the two former, poured into the House of Commons . . . the turbid waters of sheer *mammonry*, democracy and republicanism.[1]

Even for Anglicans who did not see matters in quite so lurid a light, the tendencies implicit in the Reform movement could augur no good to the Establishment; and their fears were sharper because they were conscious of the defective state of their institution. 'In times like the present', wrote a liberal Cornish vicar in November 1830, 'I feel the trial of being connected with a system (I mean in the Church) which might have been and ought to have been amended long since. . . . Much of the good in our establishment is paralyzed; and the evil stands, ashamed because it is naked.'[2] Few thinking members of the Church could deny the need for reform; what they feared was reform at the hand of their enemies. An attack on the Church seemed a logical extension of the 'Movement'.

No perspicacity was needed to see this. The *Extraordinary Black Book*, that secular bible of radical reformers, whose subtitle was 'An Exposition of Abuses in Church and State', devoted its first three chapters to the Church in England and Ireland, and only in chapter four moved on to the revenues of the

---

[1] A correspondent of the *British Magazine*, vol. 6, p. 273 (Sept. 1834).
[2] Fisher, the Vicar of Roche, to Thomas Acland (*Memoir of Sir Thomas Dyke Acland*, ed. A. H. D. Acland (1902), p. 8).

Crown.[1] It was plain to all that not only would the actual Establishment of the Church be brought under review along with other State institutions, but that in itself it was an offence to many devout Dissenters who held that Establishment and a Church were incompatible. There was, of course, much misunderstanding about the meaning of 'Establishment'. The original concept of the Anglican Church as the English nation in its religious aspect had never quite squared with the facts and since the Revolution no longer squared with the law. By the nineteenth century it had been overlaid with the vulgar Radical notion of the Establishment as a State institution whose wealth and property were public possessions.[2] Historically this was an even grosser inaccuracy. Henry Lytton Bulwer was on safer if somewhat antiquated grounds when he argued in 1836 that Parliament, the body representing the congregation of the Church, which was in fact *the* Church, had 'a right, and the only right to deal with its property or consult for its interests'.[3] But the question of historical theory was not very important. What mattered was the competence of Parliament to legislate for the Church, and the widespread opinion that the Establishment was an expensive and unjustifiable monopoly. At its crudest the argument against the Establishment was that all churches should be put on level terms and compete in the

[1] For the general tone of its comments, the following is typical: 'Solemn pledges will be demanded from a reformed parliament that tithe shall be abolished, and that haughty prelates shall cease to haunt the chambers of legislation. A terrible storm is impending over the Church, and nothing can avert its destructive ravages save a timely abandonment of all that has long excited popular indignation—its enormous wealth—its avarice, pride and self-seeking—its insolent and oppressive power' (p. 95, 1832 edn.).

[2] Cf., for example, the pamphlet by the Revd. C. Stovel, a London Dissenting minister, entitled *A Letter to the Rt. Hon. Lord Henley* (1832), which suggested that 'the property now held by Government for the support of a State Religion, may be disposed of for the relief of the poor and the liquidating of the National Debt' (quoted in the *Eclectic Review*, 3 ser., vol. 8, p. 528, Dec. 1832). Stovel did not ask for the abolition of the Established Church or of its connexion with the State, but merely for the appropriation of its property and withdrawal of State support! Some of the literature put out by the *Society for Promoting Ecclesiastical Knowledge* (a Dissenting organization founded in 1829 to disseminate information on the principles of Dissent) argued the case for the secular origin and national ownership of Church property, although the national conference called by the United Committee in May 1834 by inference accepted the right of the Church to its own property (H. S. Skeats and C. S. Miall, *History of the Free Churches of England* (1891), pp. 481–3).

[3] In his pamphlet *The Lords, the Government and the Country* (1836), p. 43.

open market for congregations and subscriptions. Free Trade
in religion happily echoed the catchword popularized in trade
and commerce.[1]

This last, however, was an extreme as well as a nakedly
utilitarian view, and would not have been supported either by
all Radicals or by all Dissenters. 'Dissent' was not an organized
or unified body of opinion. Dissenters differed widely in doctrine
and government; and they differed even on the question of the
established Church. As a leading Dissenting periodical dryly
and accurately put it in 1832, the Dissenters were 'a very large
portion of the English nation, including several distinct denominations, among whom is to be found a very wide difference
of opinion on all subjects, political as well as ecclesiastical'.[2] On
the specific question of the Church of England, some criticized
certain aspects while accepting the principle of the Establishment. These included the majority of Presbyterians, who disliked episcopacy but not State recognition; most Wesleyan
Methodists and Unitarians; and a minority of the other Dissenting sects. The opponents of the Establishment, who laid
differing degrees of emphasis on the iniquity of the State connexion *per se*, and on the concomitant irritants of tithe, Church
rates, and legal privileges, comprised the Quakers, the Baptists,
and most Congregationalists. But nobody knew, and that great
Dissenting periodical, the *Eclectic Review*, in 1832 doubted,
whether the bulk of Dissenters were hostile to the actual existence
of the Establishment.[3] As far as State support was concerned,

---

[1] As early as 1820 J. E. Taylor, later first editor of the *Manchester Guardian*,
was asserting at Manchester that religion should be a 'marketable commodity'
(D. Read, *Press and People* (1961), p. 35). Twelve years later the editor of the
Extraordinary Black Book argued in moderate terms: 'We are not the partizans of a
free trade in religion, and think a worship patronised by the state is best, provided
it be cheap. Our reason for this preference may be somewhat peculiar, and not shared
by our readers. We prefer an established worship, not less as a means of maintaining
a rational piety, than as a counterpoise to fanaticism' (p. 93).

[2] *Eclectic Review*, in an article on Church Reform, Dec. 1832 (3 ser., vol. 8,
p. 527).

[3] The main divisions among the Dissenters in this period were as follows: the
English Presbyterians (mainly Unitarian by the early nineteenth century and
declining in numbers); the Independents or Congregationalists; the Baptists,
divided into Particular (Calvinistic, holding the doctrine of particular redemption)
and General (Armininian, holding the doctrine of general redemption); the
Quakers (rarely intervening in politics, though opposed to tithe and Church
rates); and, in a special position midway between Dissent and Establishment, the
Methodists, divided into Wesleyans, Primitive Methodists, and the New Connection,

the purity of the extreme Dissenting position was itself compromised by the acceptance of the *Regium Donum,* begun in
the reign of George I, originally as a royal gift, but since 1804
a parliamentary grant; and though Congregationalists and
Baptists, in contrast to the Presbyterians, showed increasing
embarrassment at receiving it during the 1830's, it was not
until 1851 that, at the request of the Dissenting churches, it was
finally removed from the Civil List.[1] All that could safely be
said in 1832 was that the Reform crisis had produced an expectation of further reforms; and that pressure would be exerted
on the Whig Ministry to carry out changes in the finances and
structure of the Church. Events had given a tone and confidence
to Dissent never known before;[2] and the volume of opinion
critical of the Establishment was not only vocal but potentially
effectual. Nevertheless the immediate situation was both fluid
and pragmatic; and one of the most pragmatic points of all was
the question of Church revenues.

Equally pragmatic was the programme of reform put forward
by the official representatives of Dissent. Reorganization of the
Church would take a long time and in a sense was a secondary
question; but the long-advertised grievances of Dissenters could
be met at once. It was expected that they would be met as a
natural consequence of the Reform Act, and the Dissenters did

but probably equal in numbers to all the other Dissenting churches. A quarrel
between the Congregationalists and Baptists on one side, and the anti-Trinitarian
English Presbyterians on the other, over the doctrinal issue, led in 1836 to the
separation of the latter and their gradual replacement as the Presbyterian Church
in England by the orthodox (Scottish) Presbyterians. In general, Dissent unquali-
fied normally implied the Three Denominations, i.e. Congregationalists, Baptists,
and Presbyterians. The Unitarians and Quakers were usually individualistic in their
actions; the Wesleyan Methodists apt to disclaim the title of Dissenter.

[1] The Congregational Board in 1834 made an effort to end the grant, but though
opposition to such State support was widespread among its members, it was not
unanimous. It was significant that Dr. Pye Smith, a leading London Congregationalist minister, who distributed the share of the *Regium Donum* allotted to the
independent churches, was against any violent attack on the established Church.
'To break its manifest connexion with our civil institutions', he observed in a sermon
published in 1834, 'in any other way than by the gentle operation of conviction in
the minds of its own members, would be venturing upon a dark and very perilous
course' (J. Stoughton, *Religion in England, 1800–1850* (1884), ii. 215, 273–4).

[2] George Hodson, Archdeacon of Stafford, in *Two Charges addressed to the Clergy
of the Archdeaconry of Stafford, 1831 and 1833,* spoke of the 'altered tone and conduct,
in respect to our Church, of the great body of Dissenters', and the moderate
Anglican *Christian Observer,* in reviewing the pamphlet in Feb. 1834, agreed that
this was indeed a fact.

not at first concern themselves unduly with the means of applying pressure on the Government. There was in fact a remarkably
small direct Dissenting interest in the first reformed House of
Commons. In so far as it counted politically, it was through
the constituencies and the electorate.[1] This, however, seemed
sufficient in the glow of optimism induced by the triumph of
Reform. In March 1833 the Dissenting Deputies in London[2]
resolved on the formation of a United Committee 'to consider
the grievances under which Dissenters now labour, with a view
to their Redress'.[3] In May the Committee issued a statement to
the effect that the state of public opinion presented a favourable
opportunity for action and that they would press the Government to redress Dissenting grievances before carrying any
measures for Church reform. A list of six specific grievances was
drawn up; they were all factual and limited—the compulsory
Anglican marriage ceremony, Church rates, liability of Dissenting chapels to the poor rate, absence of legal registration for
births and deaths, denial of burial rights in parochial church-
yards, and exclusion from the universities. Of these, the first
three were declared the most pressing and important.[4]

This, of course, was the voice of the official London head-
quarters of Dissent; cautious, moderate, and supremely practical. In the provinces the accents were a little shriller. Even so,
the Committee received little comfort from Lord Grey when
a deputation interviewed him in May 1833, and it was clear
that something more than a formal rehearsal of grievances
would be needed if results were to be obtained the following

[1] The only orthodox Dissenter in the first reformed Parliament, until he was
joined by Edward Baines of Leeds in 1834 as the result of a by-election consequent
on Macaulay's departure to India, was J. Wilks of Boston. The other Dissenting
M.P.s were said to be 'Socinians or Arians', i.e. anti-Trinitarians of one kind
or another: a circumstance which emphasized the constant complaint among
ordinary Evangelical Dissenters that the Unitarians had a political and social
influence in London far outweighing their real following in the country.

[2] For the general history and organization of the Deputies of the Three Denominations see B. L. Manning, *The Protestant Dissenting Deputies* (1952).

[3] A similar committee was formed in 1827 to secure the repeal of the Test and
Corporations Acts and dissolved in Dec. 1828. The 1833 Committee consisted of
the Committee of Deputies, 12 delegates from the Body of Ministers, 3 from the
United Secession Presbytery, and 3 from the Protestant Society. The Wesleyan
Conference and the Society of Friends were invited to send delegates but declined
to participate (*British Magazine*, vol. 5, p. 589 (May 1834), quoting *The Patriot*).

[4] *Baptist Magazine*, vol. 25, pp. 279–80 (June 1833); *Eclectic Review*, article on
'Proceedings and Position of the Dissenters', Jan. 1839 (N.S., vol. 5, pp. 1 seq.).

session. Meanwhile the publicity given to the United Committee, and the controversy on the whole issue of the Establishment arising out of the Irish Church debates, roused tempers on both sides.[1] In the face of mounting feeling the Whig Government in the 1834 session made various gestures of appeasement; but they remained gestures. A Universities Bill was defeated in the House of Lords; a measure for relief from marriage laws was abandoned as an unsatisfactory compromise; a Church Rates Bill which transferred the burden to the land tax was opposed by both Dissenters and Radicals.[2] Dissenters were now deeply stirred. A series of protest meetings in the great towns[3] spoke in ambiguous but disturbing language of the need for

[1] A letter from George Hadfield (the Radical politician, later M.P. for Sheffield 1852–74) printed in the *Baptist Magazine* (vol. 25, p. 597), Dec. 1833, complained that the Dissenters had misled the Government by asking for trifles when they should have been contending for great principles. 'The real points at issue between the Government and us are very few, and may soon be stated.' They were (1) entire separation of Church and State, (2) exclusion of bishops from the House of Lords, (3) abolition of all taxes for the support of any Church, (4) abolition of all religious tests in universities, (5) reform of marriage, burial, and baptismal laws. The editor of the *Magazine* observed that he could not adopt all the sentiments of this letter, but the subject itself had now become a practical one, on which all genuine Christians must decide for themselves. An extract from Hadfield's letter will illustrate the passions and resentments of the more radical Dissenters. 'We are required to submit to the domination of a corrupt state church; to be governed by bishops; to see £3,500,000 at the least (but more likely £5,000,000) annually expended in the maintenance of a clergy, of whom a vast majority do not preach the gospel; to see the cure of souls bought and sold in the open market; to have the Universities closed against us, and all the inequalities of those degraded places continued; to be taxed, tithed, and rated to the support of a system which we abjure; to be compelled to submit to objectionable rites and ceremonies at marriage, baptisms and burials;—in one word, to be left out of the social compact, and degraded.'

[2] Althorp's Church Rates Bill provided for the abolition of Church rates and an appropriation of £250,000 from the land tax for the upkeep of church fabrics. Some Liberals and Dissenters who were consulted promised support, but Radicals and extreme Dissenters threatened an opposition that would have delayed the Poor Law Amendment Bill, which the Cabinet thought a more urgent problem and one more ripe for solution (Le Marchant, *Althorp*, p. 482). The disappointment over the Bill was all the greater since a resolution moved by Divett, a liberal Anglican, earlier in the session in favour of total abolition of compulsory Church rates had been withdrawn at Althorp's request on the grounds that he proposed to bring forward a specific Bill to deal with the question.

[3] Including Bristol, Birmingham, Nottingham, Liverpool, Manchester, Edinburgh, and Glasgow. As early as Mar. 1834 a meeting of delegates at Manchester had declared that though the grievances must soon be redressed in a reformed Parliament, yet 'so long as the great question of alliance in Church and State remains untouched, the branches of the tree may be lopped off, but the root of bitterness will remain' (Stoughton, *Religion in England*, ii. 15).

separating Church and State; and there was growing Dissenting restiveness at the undue caution of the United Committee in London. *The Patriot*, an organ of the moderate Dissenters, called on Lord Grey 'to choose between the Church, as the patrimony of the oligarchy, and the people', and a delegation which interviewed Althorp under the parliamentary leadership of John Wilks and Edward Baines told him that they were so dissatisfied with the Whig relief measures that they preferred the existing situation.[1] Even more significantly, a joint meeting of the United Committee and country deputies in May agreed on the formal principle of entire separation of Church and State as a basis for action. The resolution was academic compared with the practical grievances urged on the Government by the Committee; and moderate Dissenters continued to protest that they had been forced into it by the opposition to their just claims, and that 'it was avowed as a principle, rather than asserted as a demand'.[2] But few things are so dangerous in politics as the enunciation of principles. As far as the Church was concerned, the challenge had been uttered and even moderate Anglicans (and there were many immoderate ones) could feel with justice that open war had been declared on the Establishment.[3] A flood of accompanying pamphlet literature

---

[1] *British Magazine*, vol. 5, pp. 589–90, 711–13 (May and June, 1834); *Baptist Magazine*, vol. 26, pp. 255–6 (June 1834). Even at this stage, however, the Quakers and Wesleyan Methodists refused to join in the anti-disestablishment agitation; and J. R. Stephens, a Wesleyan minister at Ashton under Lyne, was suspended for his activity in promoting the movement in his district.

[2] *Eclectic Review*, Jan. 1839, article on 'Proceedings and Position of the Dissenters' (N.S., vol. 5, p. 21). The text of the resolution was: 'This Meeting recognizes the great and leading principle of full and complete separation of Church and State, as the true basis on which equal rights and justice can be secured to all classes of His Majesty's subjects' (*Baptist Magazine*, vol. 26, p. 255 (June 1834). The formula was probably designed to soothe the country delegates, who were clearly dissatisfied at the moderation of the United Committee. The *Eclectic Review*, pp. 11–12 (*ut supra*), criticized the influence of the Unitarians in London on the Committee—rich, socially respectable, and politically ambitious, merely wanting changes in the marriage laws and abolition of university tests—who gave an unrepresentative character to the official demands of organized Dissent. The agitation over disestablishment, and the disputes over Presbyterian chapels and charitable funds which had passed under Unitarian control, was the background to the separation of the Unitarians in 1836.

[3] When assured by a Dissenting minister that many moderate Dissenters disapproved of the 'violent and pugnacious procedures which a few vehement partisans now adopt and pursue', Bishop Blomfield replied in effect: yes, no doubt, but why do not these moderate men repudiate what is said in their name? He

on both sides served still further to heighten the emotional atmosphere and darken counsel.

It was inevitable in these circumstances that the dismissal of the Whigs and the formation of a Conservative Government in November 1834 should evoke a passionate sectarian reaction which in turn powerfully influenced the political situation. The Dissenters were angry and alarmed at the strength of Anglican opposition to their claims; they had lost some of their confidence in the inevitability of reform under a paternal Whig Government; and the agitation of 1834 had shown them how to exploit their newly won electoral influence.[1] The leading Dissenting periodicals not only came out strongly against the new Ministry but called upon their readers to record their opposition at the polling booths. The United Committee publicly deplored the change of Government and asked Protestant Dissenters throughout the kingdom to show 'the most decided and uncompromising opposition to that political party who have avowed themselves the unflinching opponents of their interests'.[2] Even more effective, perhaps, for electoral purposes was the central Dissenters Parliamentary Committee, hastily formed to meet the emergency, which corresponded with local committees in the provinces.[3] With the Conservatives

added, 'I am very much afraid, that a war is beginning between the Dissenters and the Church, into which the latter will have been driven by measures of which it is impossible that the Christian public should approve.' See the exchange of letters between Blomfield and the Revd. John Clayton, Jan. 1834 (*Memoir of C. J. Blomfield, Bishop of London*, ed. A. Blomfield (1863), i. 200–2).

[1] Cf. *The Christian Advocate* (which represented the more extreme Dissenting position as compared with the milder *Patriot*): 'The gift of the elective franchise by the Reform Bill . . . took the Dissenters by surprise. They were not aware of the extent of power which it placed in their hands. . . . Now, however, the Dissenters are quite well acquainted with their means of influence. . . . If their experience of the Reformed Parliament and the Reform Ministers leads them to consolidate, and as far as possible, extend their Parliamentary strength in the new House of Commons, they will have little reason to regret the failure of the old to do them any service' (quoted in the *British Magazine*, vol. 6, p. 193 (Aug. 1834)).

[2] *Baptist Magazine*, vol. 26, pp. 572–3 (Dec. 1834); *British Magazine*, vol. 6, p. 694 (Dec. 1834).

[3] The *Eclectic Review* (Jan. 1839, N.S., vol. 5, p. 23) claimed that 'the chief merit of the well-organized exertions which had so important an influence upon the subsequent elections, is due to the "Dissenters' Parliamentary Committee", formed on the spur of the exigency, by whom a correspondence was opened with local Committees throughout the country. Dissatisfied as the Dissenters had reason to be with the Whigs, they did not hesitate for a moment to declare themselves the determined

precariously in office, and the discomfited Whigs struggling to prevent the disintegration of the great Reform majority, the situation could hardly have been more favourable for the Dissenters as an electoral interest. Indeed, from start to finish, Peel's first Ministry revolved round the issue of Dissenting grievances. He spoke at a Cabinet dinner of the need to make every possible concession to the Dissenters consistent with the maintenance of the Establishment;[1] Goulburn was commissioned to make discreet inquiries at Cambridge for university views on Dissenters' marriages and Church reforms,[2] the Duke of Wellington to try (but in vain) to persuade Oxford to do away with the matriculation subscription to the Thirty-Nine Articles;[3] and conciliatory references to Dissenting grievances were inserted in the Tamworth Manifesto.[4] The major measures the Prime Minister proposed to Parliament were all ecclesiastical: English and Irish tithes, English Church reform, and a Dissenters' Marriage Bill; and he was driven from office by defeat on the appropriation clause.

There could be no better demonstration of the contemporary dominance of religious issues in English political life; and the ultimate victory of the Opposition for a time cemented the Whig–Dissenting alliance which had cracked so ominously in 1834. The passage of the Municipal Corporations Act the same session further enhanced Dissenting political self-consciousness, and provided tangible assurance of the continuing will to reform in the Whig Administration. Yet it was not easy

opponents of the Tory restoration; and they united heartily with the Liberal party in returning candidates of popular principles'.

[1] 24 Dec. 1834, Ellenborough Journal, P.R.O. 30/12/28/5. Specific points mentioned were marriage registrations, a transfer of Church rates to the consolidated fund, burials, free admission to law and medicine.

[2] Peel to Goulburn, 1 Jan. 1835 (Goulburn MS.).

[3] Ellenborough Journal, 27 Dec. 1834. Even before the dismissal of the Melbourne Ministry, the parliamentary Conservatives had been anxious for some concession from Oxford on this point and the Heads of Houses had agreed, by a majority of one, on a measure for freeing undergraduates from the subscription. It was subsequently defeated in Convocation in May 1835 by a large majority. See Letters of Lord Blachford, ed. G. E. Marinden (1896), pp. 21, 23.

[4] In the Manifesto Peel referred to his support for Althorp's Church Rates measure and Russell's Dissenters' Marriage Bill; and though declaring his unchanged opposition to the admission of Dissenters 'as a claim of right' to the universities, he indicated that they should be put in a position of equality with university graduates as regards admission to the professions of law and medicine.

to regard Lord Melbourne as a friend to Dissent,[1] even though political necessity made him a reluctant ally; and the tardiness with which the alliance bore its fruits made the United Committee warn the Prime Minister in June 1835 that further delay 'might be attended with serious consequences in the event of a general election'.[2] In September therefore Melbourne commissioned his departmental heads to prepare legislation on Dissenting grievances for Cabinet consideration[3] and the 1836 session saw the passage of the Dissenters' Marriage Bill, provision for legal registration of births, deaths, and marriages, and the Tithe Commutation Bill. The ticklish problem of admission to the older universities was laid aside, but a charter was given to the University of London to enable it to grant degrees. There was, however, considerable Dissenting dissatisfaction over the details of these measures;[4] the secession of the influential Unitarians the same year[5] weakened the influence of the Deputies of the Three Denominations while destroying one of the closer links between official Dissent and the politicians; and the apparent subserviency of the Whigs to the new Ecclesiastical Commission raised much distrust.[6]

[1] In replying to an address from Derby at the beginning of Dec. 1834, Melbourne had somewhat tactlessly mentioned that one of the difficulties of his late Administration had been 'the violent and subversive opinions which have been declared, and particularly the bitter hostility and ulterior designs against the Established Church, which have been openly avowed by several classes and bodies of the Dissenters' (Torrens, *Melbourne*, p. 325).

[2] Manning, *Dissenting Deputies*, p. 276.

[3] Torrens, *Melbourne*, p. 388.

[4] Notably the high fees for marriage celebrations and the use of the Poor Law machinery for registration of marriages.

[5] Over the long-standing dispute between the Congregationalists and the Unitarians on the terms of Lady Hewley's Trust, which together with the contested possession of the church at Wolverhampton led not only to the withdrawal of the English Unitarian Presbyterians from the Board of Dissenting Deputies, but eventually to the passing of the Dissenters Chapels Bill during Peel's Administration in 1844 as the only means of protecting the legal status of Unitarians in the chapels they had long occupied. Though the legal dispute was over property, the fundamental breach was doctrinal. Evangelical Dissenters could not ultimately accept spiritual kinship with the bulk of Old English Presbyterians who had become Unitarian; and after the rupture of 1836 regarded them as 'particular non-Conformists', i.e. as dissenting from the Established Church not in principle but by an accident of one particular point of doctrine (see H. W. Clark, *History of English Nonconformity* (1913), ii. 311–13, 387–9).

[6] The Whig proposal in 1836 to carry into law some of the Ecclesiastical Commission's recommendations was strongly opposed by Dissenters on the grounds that it would prejudice a settlement of the Church Rates question. Russell, while

The crucial test of the Government's will and ability to secure substantial concessions for the Dissenters came in 1837 over the Church Rates Bill. The measure was in a sense a test case. Had it passed, it would have constituted, in one important respect, a denial of the national character of the Anglican Church. The responsibility of the parishioners for the maintenance of the fabric of the parish church was an ancient common law obligation; it was also a major Dissenting grievance. Althorp's abortive Bill of 1834, transferring the charge to the general land tax, merely meant that Dissenters, from being parochial, would have become national contributors to the upkeep of Anglican churches. The Bill brought forward in 1837 —not, significantly, by Lord John Russell but by Spring Rice —would have thrown this financial burden on the Church itself. The method proposed by the Government was the assumption by a special Commission of the administration of the property of bishops, deans, and chapters, which by improved management was calculated to yield, together with pew rents, a disposable surplus of a quarter of a million for church fabrics —the same sum as that envisaged by Althorp's Bill. That the estimated surplus was problematical; that its use for this purpose had been considered and rejected by the Ecclesiastical Commission; and that any sum so resulting might be more usefully employed in augmenting small livings and in church extension, were all additional debating arguments for the Opposition. The real issue, however, was whether the Church of England was to continue to rely for this purpose on a national system of local rates, or be thrown back on its own resources. Hume declared in the House of Commons that the Dissenters had agreed to concentrate exclusively on this objective and forgo all other agitation.[1] But the attempt to conciliate Dissent in this particular manner evoked what the Radical *Westminster Review* tartly described as 'an outbreak of Episcopal fury almost unparalleled in the modern annals of Ecclesiastical turbulence'.[2] Fifteen bishops meeting at Lambeth on 9 March,

postponing the more objectionable items, refused to give a guarantee that Church rates would be settled first. In consequence the Church Rates Abolition Society was formed in Oct., and in Feb. 1837 a general meeting of 400 delegates was held in London, preceded by active lobbying of the Government and M.P.s by the United Committee.   [1] *Hansard*, vol. 36, 1267 (3 Mar. 1837).
  [2] *Westminster Review*, vol. 27, p. 126 (Apr. 1837).

six days after the Government's plan was outlined in the Commons, declared unanimously against the Bill, and the same evening there was an angry clash between the Primate and Lord Melbourne on the issue in the House of Lords. In private the King argued vigorously with the Prime Minister against the plan, and it was clear that the Bill had little hope of passing the Lords.

What killed the measure, however, was the Anglican sympathies of the Whig gentry in the House of Commons. Some of them spoke against it; many protested in private; and J. E. Denison told Melbourne that 'no one likes it'.[1] The majority for going into committee was only twenty-three; and on the second reading in May it dropped to five. The death of the King and the premature end to the session enabled the Government to retire with some shreds of dignity from an impossible position; but in essence the direct attack on the Anglican Church had collapsed.[2] Its failure, followed in 1838 by the dropping of the appropriation clause from the Irish Tithe Bill, marked the end of the effective Whig–Dissenting alliance. Though the 1837 general election in many constituencies had a strong religious temper,[3] there was no attempt by the Dissenting Deputies to organize the Dissenting vote behind the Government, or on any national basis; and local Dissenting activity in the constituencies was largely aimed at securing the return of candidates pledged to their own special programme.[4] Church versus Dissent was a potent election cry, but it was not one that was of any significant assistance to the Whig party. They could offer political leadership only if Dissenting demands remained modest and practical. A feature of the closing

[1] *Melbourne Papers*, p. 331.

[2] For details in Parliament see *Hansard*, vol. 36, 1207 seq.; vol. 37, 298 seq.; vol. 38, 929 seq. See also, *Melbourne Papers*, pp. 323–32; Walpole, *Russell*, i. 290–3. Russell in 1836 still adhered to the principle of Althorp's Bill and to the opinion he had then expressed that all classes should contribute to the support of the Church. But the Cabinet did not wish to risk a renewal of the 1834 measure until all Dissenting grievances were satisfied, and thought that if on inquiry there seemed a probability of a surplus revenue of the Church, this should be used for fabric maintenance.

[3] 'The contest', said the *Eclectic Review*, 'was almost as much ecclesiastical as political', n.s., vol. 5, p. 30 (Jan. 1839).

[4] Cf. R. G. Cowherd, *Politics of English Dissent* (1956), pp. 95–96. The only step taken by the United Committee was to issue an address to Protestant Dissenters in England and Wales.

years of the decade, however, was the steady drift of Dissenting opinion away from the moderation which had generally characterized it in the years between 1828 and 1834.

After the 1837 general election the compromise and tolerance of the early Reform years tended to disappear. It was replaced by a more dogmatic approach by Dissenters, especially to the question of Church–State relationship and the ultimate issue of disestablishment. The process had started during the 1834–5 crisis. The *Extraordinary Black Book* in 1832 had not opposed the principle of the Establishment; the *Appendix to the Extraordinary Black Book* by the same editor which appeared at the end of 1834 confessed that on grounds of utility, equality, and social harmony there was no case for an Establishment any longer.[1] Similarly the *Eclectic Review*, which though opposed to compulsory financial contributions from non-Anglicans was content in 1832 to see a reformed Establishment continue, showed a steadily deepening hostility to the Church which was particularly marked in 1834–5. Price,[2] who took over the editorship from Conder[3] in 1837, did not so much alter the direction as the tone and temper of the magazine. In his first number he spoke of 'that happy consummation which Dissenters so devoutly desire—the dissolution of the disgraceful connexion between Church and State', and the same year described 'a State Church' as 'a monstrous departure from the institutions of Christ, and a fearful engine of spiritual delusion and death'.[4] When in April 1839 young Mr. Gladstone's book *The State in its Relations with the Church* was reviewed in Price's magazine, the article opened with the startling words 'Englishmen! the battle of the Reformation is to be fought over again'.[5] Denied satisfaction

---

[1] It argued that the only remedy for the existing unsatisfactory position was 'the state ceasing to patronize any sect of religionists, any more than any sect of philosophers' (p. 26).

[2] Dr. Thomas Price, Baptist minister of a congregation in Devonshire Square, London, and the historian of Nonconformity. He held the editorship of the *Eclectic Review* until the end of 1849. (See his introductory note to vol. 26 (N.S.) announcing his retirement on medical grounds after holding the office for thirteen years. The reference in Halévy, *Age of Peel and Cobden* (1947), p. 339 seems an error.)

[3] Josiah Conder, editor of the *Eclectic Review*, 1814–36, was a prominent Dissenter who also edited *The Patriot*, another Dissenting periodical, from its foundation in 1832 until 1855.

[4] *Eclectic Review*, N.S., vol. 1 (Jan. 1837) preface; vol. 2, p. 208 (Aug. 1837).

[5] The reviewer went on to argue that the work, left unfinished in the sixteenth

by the Whig Government, these pent-up feelings found various outlets. The Church Rates Abolition Society of 1836 was followed by the Religious Freedom Society formed in 1839 for the separation of Church and State. In 1841 Miall[1] started *The Nonconformist* weekly to promote the cause of disestablishment and in 1844 secured the founding of the Anti-State Church Association.[2]

It was natural that the failure to obtain redress from the Government should lead to a deepening feeling among Dissenters that all relations between Church and State should cease; and it was patent that voluntaryism and disestablishment received wider support in the 1840's than in the 1830's. Yet the proliferation of Dissenting public activity which marked the opening of Victoria's reign was not a sign of greater but of less political influence. The effort was fragmented rather than concentrated and the ties of the extremists with Radicalism, Sturges's Complete Suffrage Union, and the Anti-Corn-Law League brought no tangible reward. The limits of futility perhaps were reached in Miall's efforts in the early 1840's to run in harness disestablishment, repeal of the Corn Laws, and universal suffrage.[3] The aristocracy of Dissent stood aloof from this contact with extreme political Radicalism and even over the issue

century, must now be completed. 'The friends of the Bible and religious liberty must now stand forth for the entire emancipation of their cause from the shackles of the civil power—the severance of the Church from the State' and roundly stated that 'at the present moment it (i.e. the Church of England) is the most prolific source of our national contentions' (ibid. N.S., vol. 5, pp. 265–8).

[1] Edward Miall, Congregationalist minister at Leicester, later M.P. for Rochdale 1852–7 and Bradford 1869–74, a life-long disestablishmentarian and democratic Radical. Even before the well-known incident of the imprisonment of one of his congregation at Leicester for non-payment of Church rates, he and his friends had been planning a campaign against Church establishments (see A. Miall, *Life of Edward Miall* (1884), p. 28).

[2] Formed with the backing of the Dissenting periodicals and many provincial Religious Freedom Societies, it was the most comprehensive and formidable of the Dissenting political bodies. After 1853 it was known by the less aggressive title of the Liberation Society. Nevertheless, at the preliminary conference held in Apr.–May 1844 the delegates were mainly drawn from the Midlands and Scotland, and many prominent Nonconformists, especially in London, held aloof (Stoughton, *Religion in England*, ii. 272–3; Manning, *Dissenting Deputies*, p. 392; Cowherd, *English Dissent*, p. 158).

[3] Efforts which culminated in the meeting at Birmingham in Apr. 1842 when Sturge, Miall, Bright, Sharman Crawford, Lovett, O'Brien, Vincent, and Collins all sat on the same platform. For Miall's attitude at this period and the general tone of *The Nonconformist* see *Life of Miall*, chs. iv and v.

of disestablishment there was disagreement on tactics. The not uninfluential Evangelical Association, founded in 1839, worked to convert the Church of England from within rather than take it by assault from without.[1] Moreover, though voluntaryism fitted Dissenting theory, it was not a necessary consequence of the historical tradition of English Nonconformity, and it was only slowly and with reluctance that the parting of ways was found. Retreat into voluntaryism in fact was a retreat from politics.

The great landmark here was the Whig educational scheme of 1839. In 1833 the decision of the Government to assist education by grants to the two great societies—the Anglican National Society and the Dissenters' British and Foreign Society —had neatly avoided the twin dangers of confessional monopoly and State secularism. But its defects became increasingly prominent, especially the unequal distribution of funds between the two bodies and the large areas of illiteracy still left untouched; and a powerful movement led by Brougham, Wyse,[2] Slaney,[3] and Roebuck, supported by the political Radicals in general, pressed for a national system of State-directed lay education.[4] The Whig proposal in 1839 was threefold: to place the supervision of education and the distribution of educational grants under a committee of the Privy Council; to equalize the allotment of funds to the two main societies, and also to

[1] At Birmingham, for example, where Church rates had been abolished by a local arrangement in 1832, there were cordial relations between the Anglicans and the evangelical Congregationalists led by Mr. James, the pastor of Carr's Lane Church, who distrusted and disliked Miall and the activities of the Anti-State Church Association, and was himself a leading figure in the Evangelical Alliance formed in 1845 (see A. W. W. Dale, *Dale of Birmingham* (1905), pp. 71–73, 139–40). Miall wrote in *The Nonconformist*, soon after the founding of the Anti-State Church Association, of 'the strange shyness and suspicion with which many men, sincere Dissenters in the main, regard the Anti-State Church movement' (*Life of Miall*, p. 98). But in view of the intemperate language of his newspaper, this shyness was not altogether surprising.

[2] Sir Thomas Wyse, M.P. for Waterford, introduced a Bill for National Education in Ireland in 1835 and published a pamphlet on educational reform in 1837.

[3] Robert Aglionby Slaney, M.P. for Shrewsbury, was chairman of the Educational Committee of 1838.

[4] The Central Society of Education, founded in 1836 with Wyse as its chairman, advocated a national system of schools with democratic control and State inspectors. In June 1838 Wyse's motion in the House of Commons for the appointment of a mixed board of commissioners for education to administer parliamentary grants attracted considerable support and was almost carried against the Government (70–74).

make grants according to the needs of populous districts and not merely *pari passu* with voluntary local contributions; and to initiate a system of Normal Schools for teacher-training on a nonconfessional basis with elaborate provisions for 'general' and 'special' religious instruction.[1] The first part of the plan introduced the principle of State control; the second redressed the balance between the Church and Dissent; the third was a move towards more secular education. Except for the Wesleyan Methodists, the Dissenters in general, with some misgivings over accepting State aid and even more over the details of the provisions for religious teaching, supported the plan.[2] The Dissenting Deputies in London indeed greeted it in warm terms as 'the most unexceptionable measure for national instruction, as regards the rights of conscience, which has ever been suggested by any body of advisers of the Crown'.[3] The attitude of the Anglicans on the other hand was not merely hostile but explosive.

Long before the Whig measure was matured, the activities of the Radical-inspired Society of Education, and the intense advocacy for schemes of State education on the Government side of both Houses, had produced a strong reaction among churchmen. It took, however, the significant Peelite shape of offering not negative resistance but alternative reform. As Peel himself had said as early as November 1837, 'it won't suffice to abuse the Government plan'. Even at that date he had foreseen that with the failure of agitation over Church Rates and the Appropriation Clause, the next great battle would come over education. But, as he told Croker, there was no ground on which the Church could better defy its enemies; since it had it in its power to construct a system of education from its own resources. What was essential, however, was 'cordial concert between the clergy and the laity'.[4] That concert was in fact a marked feature

---

[1] The 'general' religious instruction was to be given collectively as part of the ordinary curriculum; the 'special' at fixed times by the permanent Anglican chaplain and by Dissenting ministers specially admitted for that purpose.

[2] Edward Baines, jun., gave the support of the influential *Leeds Mercury* to the Government scheme, though as he wrote to Kay, 'I, as a Dissenter, object to the principle of making a *certain* provision for the religious education of Churchmen in the normal school, and leaving that of the Dissenters (in your own words) "contingent" ' (F. Smith, *Life of Sir James Kay-Shuttleworth* (1923), p. 83).

[3] Manning, *Dissenting Deputies*, p. 339.

[4] *Croker Papers*, ii. 323.

of the Anglican effort. A distinguished group of young Conservatives, including Acland, Gladstone, S. F. Wood, Praed,
Sandon, and Ashley, inspired behind the scenes by G. F.
Mathison of the Mint,[1] early in 1838 pressed on the leaders of
the Church a scheme of diocesan education, including training
colleges for teachers and a system of middle-class schools, in
conjunction with the National Society; and a start on the work
had been made even before the end of the year.[2] But though the
enemy had been forestalled, it was clear that the real crisis
had not yet arrived. Gladstone could write in March 1838 of
the 'safe and precious interval, perhaps the last to those who
are desirous of placing the education of the people under the
efficient control of the clergy'[3] and Acland in January 1839 of
'the hairsbreadth escapes of last sesssion'.[4] In that year, under
the threat of imminent Government action, their efforts inten-
sified, culminating in the great public meeting of the National
Society in May, stage-managed by Acland and his friends, and
presided over by the Archbishop of Canterbury and a phalanx
of bishops.[5] Though the details of the Government scheme were
known in the spring, it was not until June that the parliamentary
battle took place. It was a test not only of the rival strengths
of Anglicans and Dissenters, but even more perhaps of rival
principles of education. The Church assumed the right, or at
least the duty, of superintending national education. The
Government, as Kay-Shuttleworth, the first Secretary of the
Education Committee, put it in 1843, was determined 'to assert
the claims of the civil power to the control of the education of the
country'.[6] While the victory of the Church was not complete,
the essential fact of 1839 was that the Government was defeated.

---

[1] 'I believe', wrote Acland in 1839, 'we are nicknamed "the young gentlemen"
among the Bishops' (Sir Thomas Acland, p. 109).

[2] The first diocesan training college opened at Chester in 1839, and by 1845
twenty-two were in existence.

[3] J. Morley, Life of Gladstone (1912), i. 109.

[4] In his pamphlet National Education, The present state of the Question Elucidated
(Sir Thomas Acland, p. 87).

[5] The meeting passed a resolution that 'it is an object of the highest national
importance to provide that instruction in the truths and precepts of Christianity
should form an essential part of every system of education intended for the people
at large, and that such instruction should be under the superintendence of the
clergy and in conformity with the doctrines of the Church of this realm as the
recognised teacher of religion' (ibid., p. 91 n.).

[6] Smith, Life of Kay-Shuttleworth, p. 148.

Even though the Ministers dropped the unpopular Normal School project before the parliamentary debate took place, they were beaten down to a majority of five on going into a Committee of Supply and of only two on the education grant itself.[1] In the House of Lords an address to the Crown, containing a series of resolutions against the scheme, was carried on the motion of the Archbishop of Canterbury by a massive majority. A prolonged controversy ensued[2] and in the following year the Government capitulated. The plan of State inspectors was abandoned; existing inspectors were to report to the diocesan bishops as well as to the Education Committee of the Council; any new inspectors were to be appointed only after consultation with and the concurrence of the bishop of the diocese; and there was a reversion, favourable to the Church, to the old system of allotting grants in proportion to the amount of private subscriptions.[3] The coming to power of a Conservative Ministry in 1841 seemed the final endorsement of the victory of the Church in 1839–40.

II

What is striking about the 1839 episode is the strength and self-confidence of the Anglican Church[4] in contrast to its

[1] The satisfaction of the Opposition may be gauged from the fact that Graham could speculate whether they should go on to press for the revocation of the Education Committee of the Privy Council or be content with the concessions already won from the Government (Graham MS., Graham to Stanley, 5 June 1839).

[2] The Archbishop of Canterbury (Howley) and Blomfield of London recommended their clergy to refuse Government grants until the plan of inspectors unsanctioned by the bishops was given up (*Memoir of Bishop Blomfield*, i. 266–72).

[3] For Russell's brief account of Blomfield's mediation and the conference at Lansdowne House between himself, Lansdowne, the Archbishop of Canterbury, and the Bishops of London and Salisbury, see *Recollections and Suggestions* (1875), p. 375. Brougham, in a published *Letter to the Duke of Bedford* admitted that 'a controversy of thirty years, with all the reason and almost all the skill, and until very lately, all the zeal on our side, has ended in an overthrow somewhat more complete than we should in all probability have sustained at the commencement of our long and well-fought campaign' (quoted in *Life of Kay-Shuttleworth*, p. 86). For details of the 'concordat' of May 1840 see ibid., pp. 95–96.

[4] It was seen not only within the Church but outside, in the change of public opinion. For example, when the Archbishop of Canterbury and Bishop Blomfield took the resolutions of the House of Lords to the Queen in July, they were (according to Lady Wharncliffe) 'loudly cheer'd' while the Ministers were 'unmercifully hiss'd and groan'd at by an immense body of people assembled about the Palace' (*Lady Wharncliffe and Her Family*, ii. 297). A few years later Greville noted, as a symptom of the intense public interest in religious issues, that the more interesting

weakness and self-consciousness in 1832. Between the Reform
Act and the accession of Victoria the position and morale of the
Church had in fact been revolutionized. As Cobbett had recognized, it was the system and not the men at fault. The Church
was sound enough, if only its structure could be modernized.
But since the suspension of Convocation in the early eighteenth century, the Church had been a Church disarmed. Its
vulnerability had been concealed by its politico-confessional
alliance with Parliament; but this was finally exposed by the
1828–32 changes. Reform meant legislation; legislation meant
parliamentary scrutiny; and after 1830 it was not clear that the
friends of the Church were in a parliamentary majority. It was
that, rather than the simple issue of reform, which perturbed
the active leaders of the Church. Had Wellington's Ministry
continued, a start might have been made on the work of renova-
tion.[1] But the coming of a Reform Ministry sharpened the
tension. Referring in January 1831 to Hume's intention to move
for a committee of inquiry into Church property, Bishop Blomfield commented crisply 'and enquired into it must be, and
most safely by a commission properly appointed. But surely the
application for a commission ought to proceed from ourselves'.[2]
Under the goad of the Whig Cabinet there were consultations
within the hierarchy towards the end of 1832; and though
many bishops were lukewarm, the genesis of the reform movement was already present in the personal alliance between the
Primate and Bishop Blomfield of London, and in the notion of
a mixed commission of clergy and laity to prepare suitable
measures.[3] 'We have a right to demand', argued Blomfield in
December, 'either a convocation (which we do not wish for)
or something which shall possess all the advantages of a convocation without the evils which were found to result from it
under its old constitution.'[4] Though both the anti-Church and

bishops' charges were read with avidity and were among the most popular
pamphlet literature of the day (*Greville*, 16 Jan. 1843).

[1] Archbishop Howley said in 1836 that he had long been aware of the need for
reform in the Church and when made Primate (Aug. 1828) he had as his first
step had an interview with the Prime Minister (Wellington) on the subject; but
a Bill prepared for the purpose was laid aside with the change of Government
(*Memoir of Bishop Blomfield*, i. 209).

[2] Ibid. 163.

[3] W. L. Mathieson, *English Church Reform 1815–40* (1923), pp. 171–3.

[4] *Memoir of Bishop Blomfield*, i. 206–7. In Sept. 1832 Whately, the new

the Church-reform movements preceded the Reform Act, therefore, the Reform crisis brought matters to a head. At the moment of its greatest unpopularity, the Church began slowly to move its great bulk along the path of recovery. Lord Henley's startling pamphlet, *A Plan for Church Reform*, appearing in 1832 just before the Reform measure became law, gave warning that one of the first problems before a reformed Parliament would be the character and application of Church revenues. Henley's plan[1] attracted more support from Dissenters than from Anglicans; but it was a bold and imaginative effort. Coming from a good churchman and a brother-in-law of Peel, it made an immense sensation, and probably widened the effective area of discussion within Anglican circles. If Anglicans as a body did not go the whole way with him, at least they were now ready to go further than even two years earlier.

The grand debate on Church property, and implicitly on the nature of the Establishment, which grew out of the 1833 proposals for the Irish Church, found therefore the lay and clerical defenders of the Church intellectually prepared. Moreover, nothing the Whig Government did in 1833 and 1834 either settled or even prejudiced the issue. Grey's Royal Commission of 1832 to inquire into ecclesiastical revenues was a conservative body of bishops, judges, and politicians of both parties; and its fact-finding terms of reference were as necessary a preliminary to reform of the Establishment as to its destruction. Once granted the readiness, sharpened by fear, of Church leaders to admit reform, it was natural that they should supply the creative ideas, since they alone were interested in strengthening the Church. The Whigs were divided, and their Dissenting and

Archbishop of Dublin, had been pressing Lord Grey for 'the appointment of Commissioners, to devise, digest, and submit to Parliament some form of government. . . . If we do not begin within the Establishment, a beginning will be made for us from without.' But what Whately had in mind by 'government' was clearly the establishment of a mixed assembly of clergy and laity, something after the model of the Kirk of Scotland, to legislate on ecclesiastical matters, or at least to declare that changes were or were not needed. Cf. O. J. Brose, *Church and Parliament* (1959), pp. 124–5.

[1] It proposed the equitable redivision of Church property and salaries; abolition of pluralities; creation of two new bishoprics; removal of bishops from the House of Lords; vesting of Crown patronage in a Board of Commissioners composed of bishops and laymen; and commutation of tithe. In the Anglican *British Magazine* Henley's pamphlet was reviewed (Oct. 1832) in sorrow rather than anger; but it was highly approved by the *Eclectic Review* (June 1832).

Radical allies more concerned with the partial or even total dismantling of the edifice.

On this crowded but balanced scene arrived Peel's Ecclesiastical Commission of 1835. It was important for three things: timing, objective, and machinery. It came, first, after several years of public controversy and attack, but with a Ministry friendly to the Church in office for the first time since November 1830. Now or never was the opportunity for the Church to show a willingness to amend its structure. Archbishop Howley told the Speaker privately that the Church could make more concessions to the new Government than its predecessor; and Peel said in Cabinet that the Church leaders were ready to go to the limit in view of their confidence in the Ministry.[1] The declared object of the Commission was not merely to inquire, but to suggest reforms: positive action, that is to say, which would turn the edge of popular criticism. The machinery was a small mixed body with strong ecclesiastical representation (two archbishops and three bishops as against seven laymen) to prepare bills for parliament and administer them when law. In this way was solved the technical problem of legislating for the Church through a secular assembly, in a manner best calculated to allay the fears of the doubtful within the Church itself. That Peel and his ecclesiastical counterpart, Bishop Blomfield, did more than any other two men of their generation to save the Church is almost incontrovertible. Yet it was an essential part of Peel's purpose not so much to secure the passage through Parliament of Church Reform measures (that was

[1] Ellenborough Journal, 11 and 27 Dec. 1834, P.R.O. 30/12/28/5. Two rank-and-file opinions reflect the mixed attitude of the party to the Commission. Croker, the instinctive Tory made Conservative reformer *malgré lui*, thought Peel's action a bad precedent in good hands, but inevitable and tactically wise. 'From the temper of the elections, I doubt whether without this the property of the Church would not have been in danger of spoliation for secular, or even Dissenting purposes' (*Croker Papers*, ii. 263). A younger Peelite, who never lived to demonstrate in the 1840's the promise of the 1830's, W. M. Praed, declared, 'Most unfortunate shall we be, if a scheme so wise and so honest for the advancement of sound religion shall be overthrown by the mere operation of party spirit. . . . What a tale it will be for history to tell, if Church Reform, thus boldly and yet temperately commenced, shall be taken from the hands of the Archbishops and Bishops of the Church, to be handed over to the Humes and O'Connells who are so ready to begin upon the task' (D. Hudson, *A Poet in Parliament* (1939), p. 213). Praed, a Cambridge graduate and barrister, poet and journalist, was M.P. for St. Germans 1830, Gt. Yarmouth 1834, Aylesbury 1837; Secretary to the Board of Control in Peel's 1834–5 Ministry; died of consumption in 1839 at the age of 37.

inevitable anyhow) but to secure acceptance by the Church of parliamentary legislation. It was as an intermediary between Church and State, and not merely as a Church politician that he acted. The prime object of his Ecclesiastical Commission was to reconcile the Church as a body to reform. With his unfailing and almost cynical realism he judged that when concrete changes were proposed to Parliament and the Church, many abstract clerical reformers would have second thoughts and many clerical opponents redouble their energies. He feared reaction inside the Church as much as Radical clamour without[1] and if he was protecting the Establishment in 1835 it was by the oblique Peelite strategy of forcing it to put its house in order.

What he did, however, was to win the initiative for Church reformers; and the importance of this can scarcely be overestimated. The Whig Ministry which succeeded him were presented with a *fait accompli* which they did not altogether like but which they could not afford to repudiate. For the semi-Erastian, instinctively anti-clerical minds of Melbourne and Russell it was not a comfortable situation. 'The majority of the Commission being opposed to us in politics, their proposals are naturally viewed with jealousy by the whole body of our supporters', observed Russell to his Leader in July 1836; but though it was clear that no extreme measures of reform (that is to say, measures popular with the Ministerialist rank-and-file) could be expected from such a body, Russell's own opinion at the time was against any separate initiative by the Government.[2] The bishops indeed had shown their mettle at the start of the new régime. When Melbourne on taking office in 1835 had proposed quite properly to replace the Conservative Ministerial members by himself, Russell, and Lansdowne, the Commissioners had exacted a pledge that they should be allowed to proceed on the same principles as before and that no Government measures should

---

[1] Cf. Peel, *Memoirs*, ii. 69–71 and his letter to the Bishop of Durham, Van Mildert, one of the reactionaries on the Episcopal Bench, ibid., p. 77.

[2] Russell, *Early Corr*. ii. 189–90. Melbourne's Erastianism was probably even more deep-seated than Russell's; but both men had a common dislike of extreme religious claims, a factor which worked (though less obviously) against Dissent as well as Anglicanism. 'I do not know', observed Melbourne in 1841, 'how I could reconcile it to my conscience to take the part of any Church or of anything ecclesiastical anywhere in opposition to the law, which is and ought to be the supreme government of every country' (*Melbourne Papers*, p. 416).

be introduced into Parliament affecting Church property that were not consonant with their recommendations. Without that pledge, recorded Blomfield afterwards, the Commission would 'certainly have declined continuing to act'.[1] In 1836 came the first legislative proposals based on the Commission's recommendations. They included a Bill to make the Commission a permanent corporate body which, despite misgivings by Melbourne at perpetuating ecclesiastical at the expense of political influence,[2] passed into law. Opposition came from the Right and the Left, from Radicals and High Churchmen; but this, if anything, was a symptom of the strong central position the Commission had already attained and a guarantee of its dominance.

Episcopal influence in the Commission not only continued in fact but was enlarged: from five bishops as against eight laymen in 1836 to thirty clerical members including the whole English and Welsh hierarchy as against twenty laymen in 1840. There were strained relations with the Government at times, notably in 1837 over the Church Rates Bill which the Church leaders regarded with some justification as a breach of Melbourne's pledge and nearly broke up the Commission's activities.[3] But the friction was mainly behind the scenes. Essentially

[1] *Memoir of Bishop Blomfield*, i. 211.

[2] Cf. his letter to the Archbishop of Canterbury in June 1836, pointing out that the Ministerial members of the Commission might be removed at any time, and probably would be before the Commission ended its labours, leaving the permanent members 'entirely of one cast and colour of opinion and character' (*Melbourne Papers*, pp. 311–12). Strictly speaking there were three Ecclesiastical Commissions in the 1830's which need to be distinguished: (1) the Church Revenues Commission (Grey) 1832; (2) Ecclesiastical Commission (Peel) Feb. 1835, renewed (Melbourne) June 1835; (3) Ecclesiastical Commission (statutory and permanent) 1836. Though Peel's Commission was smaller, some of its twelve members were also members of Grey's Commission, which was still pursuing its labours. In June 1835 Melbourne issued a new Commission in identical terms and comprising the same persons with the exception of the Ministerial changes. In 1836 the Ecclesiastical Commissions Act incorporated as a body the 'Ecclesiastical Commissioners for England' (see Mathieson, *English Church Reform*, pp. 115, 136–7; and for lists of Commissioners, Brose, *Church and Parliament*, Appendix I).

[3] *Melbourne Papers*, pp. 325–32; Torrens, *Melbourne*, p. 429. Blomfield in Jan. 1837 was anticipating a break-up of the Commission over the issue raised by the Bill and in Mar. all the episcopal members of the Commission, together with Lord Harrowby, Sir H. Jenner, and H. Hobhouse, sent a letter of protest to the Minister. The majority of Commissioners declined to act while the Bill was pending (*Memoir of Bishop Blomfield*, i. 213–14). The charge against Melbourne of breach of faith was not without some basis. The original pledge of the new Whig Ministry in 1835, 'to

the Church and State co-operation established by Peel was maintained under the Whig Government, and a steady flow of reports and amending legislation convinced the public that action was being taken. It was a mark of the degree of Church recovery that over the Deans and Chapters Bill of 1840 (much delayed and revised since its introduction in 1836) the main argument used by Melbourne, Peel, Blomfield, and other parliamentary defenders of the measure, was that it would be in the highest degree imprudent for the Church 'in a moment of returning security' (the phrase was Melbourne's) to refuse concessions promised in a moment of danger. Even so, twelve bishops voted against the Bill in the Lords and only ten in favour.[1] Eighteen months earlier Gladstone's book on Church and State had been an attempt, not to stem the slackening current of Erastianism, infidelity, and dissent, but to catch the

resist the introduction of ecclesiastical matters into either House of Parliament' not founded on the Commissioners' recommendation, specifically excluded the question of Church rates. Archbishop Howley understood this reservation to apply only to a Government measure framed on the principle of Althorp's Bill of 1834, i.e. one which did not involve the diversion of Church funds. To make the position clear, however, he wrote to Melbourne in May 1835 asking that a form of words should be added to Melbourne's communication, specifically laying down that no part of Church property should be applied to make good any deficiency caused by the abolition of Church rates. Melbourne replied that he had only raised the question of Church rates in case the matter was pressed so strongly in the House of Commons as to make some legislation unavoidable: but he added that public business, the difficulties of the question, and the inquiries of the Ecclesiastical Commission itself, were sufficient grounds for postponement and it was not the intention of the Government to depart from the principles of Althorp's measure, which were understood by the episcopal members of the Commission to mean 'that it is the duty of the State to provide that the Churches of the Establishment be kept in decent and sufficient repair'. When taxed with this by the Archbishop in January 1838, Melbourne somewhat nonchalantly replied that the passage in his letter of 26 May 1835 had escaped his mind when he decided on the measure for the abolition of Church rates in 1836, but the only difference it would have made to his conduct was that he would have felt obliged to inform the Archbishop of the change which had taken place in his opinion (see the letters from Howley to Melbourne, 9 Jan., and Melbourne to Howley, 15 Jan. 1838, in the Russell MS. P.R.O. 30/22/3 A. This is clearly the correspondence referred to in Walpole, *Russell*, i. 291 n.).

[1] Mathieson, *English Church Reform*, pp. 149–52. The vexed history of the sees of Bangor and St. Asaph afforded another example of the Anglican reaction which Peel had feared in 1835. The union of the two sees had been agreed to by Parliament in 1836 with the general assent of the bishops, the intention being to create a new bishopric at Manchester. The plan was to come into effect on the death of the Bishop of St. Asaph. But later the feeling against the amalgamation grew in intensity and when the Bishop of St. Asaph finally died in 1846, the Whig Government gave way and the union did not take place.

high tide of the Tory Anglican revival with a timely exposition of the true principles of the Establishment.[1] 'Noting the many symptoms of revival and reform within her [sc. the Church's] borders', he recorded in later life under the characteristic heading of 'Some of my Errors', 'I dreamed that she was capable of recovering lost ground, and of bringing back the nation to unity in her communion.'[2]

It was this flood of Anglican confidence that explains not only the vigorous reaction to the Whig secular education scheme of 1839 but the miscalculation and failure of Graham's Factory Education Bill of 1843. What Graham hoped for was an educational system for factory children that 'the Church might reasonably concede, and the Dissenters adopt'.[3] The emphasis was everything. He consulted the bishops but took too lightly assurances that there would be no opposition from the Dis-

[1] As compared, for example, with what Gladstone regarded as the improper ones of Dr. Chalmers, the great Scottish Presbyterian, who had attracted princes, prelates, nobility, and politicians to his fashionable series of lectures in London in 1838 on 'the establishment and extension of national Churches as affording the only adequate machinery for the moral and Christian instruction of the people'. Nevertheless, the popularity of Chalmers's lectures so far impressed the Dissenting Deputies that the following year they invited down Dr. Wardlaw, a Scottish Independent minister from Glasgow, to deliver a counterblast for the voluntary principle in a course of lectures entitled 'National Church Establishments Examined' (Stoughton, *Religion in England*, ii. 266–7; Manning, *Dissenting Deputies*, pp. 389–90; *Eclectic Review*, N.S., vol. 5, p. 695 (June 1839)). The controversies in the Church of Scotland over establishment which ultimately led to the Disruption of 1843 had an important influence on the growth of voluntaryism in England from 1834 onwards. (See Skeats and Miall, *History of the Free Churches*, pp. 474–7, 495–6.)

[2] Morley, *Gladstone*, i. 134.

[3] See his letter to the Bishop of London, 27 Dec. 1842 (Parker, *Graham*, i. 343). Graham's original idea was to allow the schoolmasters to be chosen by mixed school boards, even though this involved the risk that a body of Dissenting mill-owners might choose a Dissenting schoolmaster (see Graham's letter to Bishop of London, 21 Jan. 1842, Graham MS.). This was subsequently amended to the plan to appoint Anglican schoolmasters but admit licensed Dissenting ministers to give instruction once a week if parents applied for it. It is fair to add that at the start of his work he was encouraged by Brougham to think that the educationists on the Liberal side would accept a larger measure of Anglican control than they would have proposed themselves for the sake of getting something done in this neglected field. Graham's own advisers were unduly optimistic. Kay thought that a Conservative Ministry could achieve more than a Whig Ministry if they so desired; and R. J. Saunders, the factory inspector for the north of England, who played a leading part in the formulation of the Bill, seems to have been responsible for the fatal suggestion that the schoolmasters should be required to be Anglicans (Parker, *Graham*, i. 337–45; Smith, *Life of Kay-Shuttleworth*, pp. 141–2. Further letters on this subject are to be found in the Graham MS., esp. from Graham to the Bishop of Chester, 19 Jan. 1843; and to the Bishop of London, 20 Apr. 1843).

senters. After the great educational conflict of 1839 the essential
guarantee of success seemed to be the approval of the Establishment; and it was in deference to Church criticism that he made
various amendments to his original Bill and postponed its introduction until 1843. The draft of his new clauses was submitted to the Primate and the Bishops of London, Chester, and
Ripon, before it was seen by the Cabinet; and both Graham and
Kay, the Secretary of the Education Committee, found themselves in the defensive position of trying to meet the views of
the bishops without sacrificing 'tolerant principles'. When the
Bill was brought forward in 1843 all contingencies seemed to have
been provided for, and the great interests satisfied; consequently
the storm that broke over Graham's head took him completely
off balance. Hasty concessions—arrangements for separate
Anglican instruction in separate classrooms, general provision
for admittance of Dissenting ministers one day a week, an
elective element on the school management boards—enabled
the Bill to struggle past a second reading.[1] The essential grievances, however, remained: the permanent Anglican schoolmaster nominated by the diocesan bishop, and the practical
majority of Anglicans on the school boards.

The concessions merely cooled Anglican enthusiasm without
removing Dissenting hostility. It was viewed by them as a
Church question and a Church question only; all other arguments were insignificant. 'The real scheme', said one Dissenting
journal, 'is other than what appears, and it is therefore idle to
talk about the evils of ignorance, and the necessity for education,
when the object sought is a *preparatory ecclesiastical establishment*,
a sort of Church of England Junior'.[2] The Wesleyan Methodists,
who had supported the Church in 1839, now threw their great
weight behind their Dissenting brethren together with the
Roman Catholics; and even the Quakers were moved from their
customary other-worldliness to join the agitation. Not since
1828–9 had the non-Anglican religious world been so united.
Overwhelmed by a mass of public meetings and a volume of

[1] Strictly speaking, the second reading only determined whether State funds
should be used to extend education; the details of the scheme were still open to
further consideration.
[2] *Eclectic Review*, n.s., vol. 13, p. 593 (May 1843). Similarly, Miall in the *Nonconformist* denounced the scheme as one 'in which the State schoolmaster was to do
the work which the State priest was unable to effect' (*Life of Miall*, p. 90).

petitions which, said the *Annual Register*, 'exceeded all modern precedent'[1] and which were trundled down to the House of Commons in bales by cabs and carriages, Graham gave way and withdrew his bill. It was a victory for Dissent over what seemed a threatened invasion of Anglican-dominated State education into the industrial areas; and a victory for public opinion over the executive and the politicians. The Whig parliamentary Opposition, though critical in detail, contained too many Anglicans and educationists to make the Bill a party issue; but Parliament as a whole was helpless in the face of the outraged sentiment of those whose continued hostility would have made the Bill inoperative even if it had passed. It marked the point beyond which the Anglican revival, in its Church–State relationship, could not go.[2] 'The Dissenters and the Church', wrote Ashley valedictorily, 'have each laid down their limits which they will not pass, and there is no power that can either force, persuade, or delude them.'[3]

[1] By the time Graham introduced the amended educational clauses on 1 May 1843, over 11,000 petitions with 1¾ million signatures, mainly from Dissenters, had been sent in against the Bill. In the end over 13,000 petitions with more than two million signatures were sent in against the Bill in its original shape, and a further 6,000 against the amended version (Hodder, *Shaftesbury*, p. 245; Manning, *Dissenting Deputies*, p. 343). Ashley, who knew a great deal about the industrial areas and Dissent generally, told Graham that the instructions of the Wesleyan Methodists to their ministers and congregations 'have been more arbitrary than at any preceding period; they have *commanded* petitions'. As far as the Church was concerned, on the other hand, 'the Clergy have not petitioned partly because so many are hostile, and partly because the remainder knew not how to commence action. Had the Bishops given any hint, we should have received many petitions. The operatives in Lancashire and the W. Riding will send up several. They have however been much tampered with by various parties' (Ashley to Graham, 26 Apr. 1843, Graham MS.).

[2] Graham, with that clarity in detecting large issues which was in such contrast to his uncertainty over tactical details, had seen this as early as the spring of 1843. 'The failure [of the scheme]', he told Gladstone on 25 Mar., 'will mark the point beyond which an advance is impossible'; though he continued to the end to regard his measure as one of comprehension and concord (Graham MS).

[3] Parker, *Graham*, i. 345. Ashley was of the opinion that the Bill, even if passed, would have been rendered inoperative as much by the lukewarmness of the Church as by the opposition of the Dissenters. He told Peel later that 'you might have carried your Bill through the House by unwilling voters and small majorities, but you could not have carried it into practical operation. Your difficulties would have been less from the fierceness and determination of the Dissenters and Wesleyans than from the utter coldness and apathy of the Church, both lay and ecclesiastical. Not a hundred men would have been found to introduce and support the system. We must ascribe much—very much—of this resistance to the fears of the people caused and stimulated by the perilous pranks of Dr. Pusey and his disciples. A vast

The lesson of the crisis was clear. Defence of the Church was one thing; enlargement of the Church another and quite different one. For all its revival since 1832, the Church of England, as a State establishment, could no longer in practice call upon the State either for wider pastoral privileges or even for peculiar financial assistance. This in itself marked a fundamental change in Church–State relationships which no amount of Anglican activity or confidence could undo. In 1818 Parliament had granted £1,000,000 to the Church of England for building new churches; in 1824 another half-million.[1] Twenty years later such an event was impossible. The contrast was the index of the new position in the State of the regenerated Anglican Church and it affected a wider field than education. The programme of church-building started in 1818, though impressive in its scope and speed,[2] was scarcely keeping pace with the rise in population; and the problem of 'the evangelisation of the manufacturing districts'[3] was still a primary task in the eyes of those who thought in social rather than theological terms. The legal obstacles to the building of new churches and creating new parishes, which had handicapped the State Church in meeting the growth and shifts of population in the early Industrial Revolution, had been largely met by the creation of the Church Building Commission of 1818–56; and the work of extending the parochial system went hand-in-hand with the multiplication of National Society schools. Nevertheless, it was not enough to build a church and create a parish; endowments of livings and provision for upkeep of fabric were equally necessary. When

body of Churchmen actuated by these alarms rejoiced in the opposition. The clergy are not to be blamed for their backwardness. The Church has never made so great concessions: *they went to the very verge of what a man of principle could vote for*' (Add. MS. 40483, f. 114, partly printed Parker, *Peel*, ii. 561).

[1] The second grant was only made possible by the unexpected payment by the Austrian Government of a war-time debt.

[2] A total of over £3 million was spent between 1818 and 1856 (half from public funds and half from voluntary sources) under the auspices of the Church Building Commission. Over 600 Commissioners' churches were built and in addition many more assisted or enlarged. In the country generally it has been estimated that a grand total of £8 million was expended on new buildings and enlargement of old. Church building doubled in each decade between 1811 and 1851 and by the end of the period probably a quarter of the total population was provided for, the most notable improvement being in the industrial areas (see Port, *Six Hundred New Churches*, pp. 125–7.

[3] The phrase was used by the Archdeacon of Chichester in 1844 (Brose, *Church and Parliament*, p. 198).

Peel came into office in 1841 there was considerable pressure on him to embark on a policy of church extension. Inglis was active for Oxford University; Goulburn, his Chancellor of the Exchequer, was being primed by his Cambridge constituents.[1] Indeed, Peel and Graham themselves were as good churchmen deeply concerned about the problem; and there was much correspondence and consultation with the Primate and the Bishop of London on the matter in the winter of 1842–3.

But Peel, if not his High Church supporters, could see from the start the limitations of action. 'I dread', he wrote to Graham in December 1842, 'for the sake of the Church and its best interests, stirring up that storm which large demands on the public purse would inevitably excite.' His own view was that every means of combining voluntary subscriptions with the Church's own revenues should be exhausted before calling for State aid. Even then, he did not think that the Government could do more than give interest-free loans. 'Can we', he added sceptically, 'go so far?' The unrealistic logic of the High Churchmen—a State Church, *ergo* State support—merely irritated his practical sense. 'You and I know that the Church and religion would suffer, and peace and charity would be sacrificed, were we in practice to push these arguments to their just logical conclusions.'[2] What he did do, less conspicuously and more effectively than Graham's disastrous Factory Education plan of the same year, was to pass a Bill[3] in 1843 which authorized the Ecclesiastical Commissioners to create new parochial districts, where the population exceeded 2,000, and

---

[1] Goulburn had told Peel in Jan. 1842 that though the state of public finance made it impossible to do all that was required, the Government should certainly do something by way of a grant of money; and he suggested that an additional way of raising revenue would be for the Crown to sell some of its advowsons (Add. MS. 40443, f. 100). Cf. also Peel's letter to Henry Hobhouse, 21 Jan. 1843. 'The question of Church extension is occupying as much of my thoughts and attention as I can . . . devote to it. . . . Sir Robert Inglis thinks the whole difficulty would be readily solved by the proposal of a large parliamentary grant, two or three millions. I totally differ from him.' What Peel feared was not only that such a proposal would meet with general opposition from Dissenters, Scotland and Ireland, but that the opposition would take the form of a demand for an inquiry into the property of the Church. 'If you are to consider Church Extension at all, the enquiry into Church property will infallibly come' (Parker, *Peel*, ii. 563–5).

[2] Parker, *Peel*, ii. 550–1; see also Add. MSS. 40443, ff. 100–2; 40444, ff. 1–3; 40448, ff. 1, 116.

[3] *An act to provide better provision for the spiritual care of populous parishes* (6 & 7 *Vic. cap. XXXVII*).

to provide stipends for the ministers. The Commissioners were empowered to take an advance of £600,000 from the Queen Anne's Bounty Board, on the security of the existing fund from surplus Church revenues created by the Commission. This was to be used for new permanent endowments and to augment small livings, in supplementation of voluntary subscriptions from local sources. In private Peel set a personal example by donating £4,000 to the Ecclesiastical Commission for furthering the objects of the Bill in London, Lancashire, Staffordshire, and Warwickshire.

The fate of Graham's education scheme was soon to provide complete justification for the refusal of the Prime Minister to propose a State policy of church extension. In 1845 Goulburn, chastened by experience, thought that even a proposal to increase the educational grant to the societies would defeat its own object by drawing attention to the practical exclusion from its benefits of Roman Catholics, Wesleyan Methodists, and Congregationalists.[1] How well founded were his apprehensions was seen scarcely a year later; but by this time the Conservatives were out and it was Russell's Whig Ministry which had the courage to essay that new trial of executive fortitude. Like Anglican opposition in the 1830's, Dissenting opposition in the 1840's was a major conditioning factor of ecclesiastical and educational policy. There was in fact, in the complex, divided, and emotional society of early Victorian England a kind of self-acting principle of equilibrium which prevented any party or interest from gaining too much power. Just as the initial wave of Dissenting and Radical success contributed to the regrouping of Anglican strength, so in turn the greater intellectual and moral energies of the Church witnessed after 1834 produced their own hostile reactions. If Anglicanism was previously disliked as an Establishment, it was beginning by the accession of Victoria to be feared as a Church.

[1] Add. MS. 40445, f. 20.

IV

CHURCH AND DISSENT:
THE COMPROMISE

THE shift in emphasis from questions of power to questions of doctrine which marked ecclesiastical conflicts in the opening years of the Victorian era was not entirely to the advantage of the Anglican Church. Historically it had always occupied a position to the Right in a fundamentally Protestant nation, but in the days of its greatest unpopularity in the earlier part of the century the Evangelical revival had strengthened its ties with Dissent. In the subsequent period of recovery, however, the doctrinal revival which accompanied its resurgence emphasized the differences with Dissent.

Many elements went to the renaissance of Anglicanism after 1828, but that which inevitably attracted most publicity and evoked most controversy was the restatement of its apostolic character and spiritual authority by the Oxford Tractarians. For the Church at the centre of a great political debate this was an equivocal advantage. The Oxford movement was essentially a clerical movement which only gradually spread its influence downwards among the mass of parochial laity; and it acquired an early notoriety in the public eye because of the presumed and indeed overt similarity of its doctrines with those of the Roman Church. This was particularly important because anti-Roman Catholic feeling in England steadily increased in the twenty years after the grant of emancipation in 1829. In the 1820's the Roman Catholics, as one of the repressed and inferior sects, gained at least the official support of Dissent. Even though the unregenerate sentiments of the rank and file of Dissenters and Evangelicals were never so academically ranged on the side of religious toleration for all as those of their leaders, yet from 1825 onwards the Dissenting Deputies, for example, impartially supported Catholic Emancipation. The years 1828–9, however, formed the peak of friendly Dissenting–Catholic relationships.[1] It was followed by a steady disillusionment at the consequences of that epoch-making act of liberal faith. The grant of equality in 1829 did not end either Irish agitation or Catholic pretensions; and an increasing number of Protestants, without distinction of Church, began to feel, as the Master of Trinity College, Cambridge, expressed it in 1845, 'how little liberal concession could allay Roman Catholic hostility'.[2] Anglicans were perturbed by attacks on the Church of Ireland which could never be bought off as long as Protestant Ascendancy in Ireland remained; the Dissenters by the emergence of a policy of State assistance to Roman Catholics in Ireland which in their eyes amounted almost to the creation of another Establishment.

The dilemma for both Whig and Conservative Ministries, however, was that to improve the religious and educational state of Ireland meant inevitably giving money to the Roman Catholic Church. The idea of State stipends for the Irish Roman clergy had a history as long as Emancipation and it continued after 1829. In 1833 Russell could record privately his opinion that State assistance should be given to all three Churches

[1] Cf. Manning, *Dissenting Deputies*, pp. 203–5. In this instance the Deputies, always more intellectual and wordly-wise than their co-religionists in the country, were in danger of losing contact with the real feelings of popular Dissent. The additional weight of the Methodist and Evangelical movements, which in many respects strengthened early nineteenth-century Dissent, probably added to its Protestant, anti-Papal animus (cf. U. Henriques, *Religious Toleration in England 1787–1833* (1961), pp. 146–7).

[2] Add. MS. 40445, f. 6 (Goulburn to Peel, 6 Jan. 1845). Talking to Haydon the painter in Feb. 1834, the Liberal Duke of Sussex gave vent to a characteristic expression of disillusionment on the part of a plain and unsophisticated man. 'As far (as) the Catholick question for Ireland went, I go,' said the Duke, 'but no further. When I find after they & O'Connell said, "We only want this", that directly they got this, they talked of repeal, I begin to hesitate,' said the Duke. 'So with the Dissenters. The Test & Corporation acts were unjust; it was right to repeal them, but when the Dissenters begin only to make this repeal a ground for encroachment, then I stop also' (*Diary of Benjamin Robert Haydon*, ed. W. B. Pope (1963), iv. 170). For a more ornate version of the same sentiments by a quondam Liberal Whig, cf. Graham's lament in 1839. 'It is quite clear that the Roman Catholics have basely cheated all those Protestants who trusted them, when the grant of equal civil rights was conceded, and they are pleased even to mock us with insults, and to laugh at our credulity, when we gave credit to their Oaths and written Declarations, and believed that they would rest satisfied with Civil Equality, while the Ascendancy of the Protestant Church in Ireland is maintained' (Graham MS. To Serjt. Jackson of Dublin, 23 Jan. 1839).

across the water—the Church of Ireland, the Presbyterians, and the Roman Catholics;[1] and the hope of solving part at least of the complicated problem of Ireland by subsidizing its Catholic clergy haunted the inner councils of Russellite Whigs and Peelite Conservatives alike. Even with the lesson of the Maynooth controversy before him, Russell still hoped after 1847 to carry such a policy into effect, and it was the opposition of the Roman hierarchy in Ireland rather than that of his Cabinet colleagues in London which killed the plan at birth.[2] Outside those political arcana, however, the writing on the wall was clearly visible whenever the fate of the Church of Ireland was discussed. 'The "colossal injustice of the Irish Church" not only cannot be permanently upheld in all its magnitude', observed the *Eclectic Review* in July 1834, 'but the claims of the Romish Church to a legal provision, on the principle upon which alone State Establishments can be defended, are so strong, that we do not see how they can be ultimately evaded, but by placing the Episcopalian Protestants on the same footing with those of other denominations, and leaving each form of Christianity to the free working of the voluntary principle'.[3] In other words,

---

[1] Walpole, *Russell*, i. 205 n. (memorandum of 18 Oct. 1833).

[2] Russell hoped after the general election of 1847 to round off the Whig record of political and constitutional achievement in Ireland by making specific provision for the Roman clergy. For obvious reasons he was disinclined to burn his fingers again with an appropriation clause; but Irish famine and Irish disorder offered tangible motives for a further effort to ease Anglo-Irish relationships. In Mar. 1848 he proposed to his Cabinet the payment of Irish Catholic clergy as a remedial and pacifying measure; and there was much correspondence on the subject in the autumn. The basis of the scheme was: previous agreement with the Pope; a comprehensive arrangement to cover all three Churches in Ireland; and raising the necessary funds from Irish taxation. Clarendon, the Lord-Lieutenant, was strongly in favour; Grey (3rd Earl) doubtful at imposing fresh financial burdens on Ireland; Lansdowne and Palmerston agreeable in principle. In Oct. Russell formally proposed to the Cabinet to proceed by Act of Parliament for the payment of the Irish Catholic priesthood. His colleagues consented though without enthusiasm; but consultations with the Irish Roman hierarchy revealed once more that nationalist and confessional reluctance to accept payment from the British Protestant State which had been a continuous strand in Irish religious politics since Grattan's Bill of 1813. In Dec. Russell announced to his colleagues the abandonment of the scheme—'to the great comfort of some of us', recorded the irreverent Hobhouse in his diary. The relief of the Cabinet was understandable. A proposition to tax Ireland on one hand, and endow the Roman Church on the other, seemed nicely calculated to unite both islands against the Government (Broughton Diary, Add. MS. 43753, pp. 46–48, 62; Russell, *Later Corr.*, ed. G. P. Gooch (1925), i. 219–31; Walpole, *Russell*, ii. 60–75).

[3] Vol. 12, p. 59.

no Establishment at all for Ireland, if the alternative was to have two.[1]

When the nettle was finally, and cautiously, grasped by Peel in 1845 with an increased Maynooth grant, the opposition came from two main quarters and with different points of emphasis: from Anglicans who feared the danger to their own Church; and from Dissenters who disliked both Rome and the principle of State endowment for religion. Back from a Christmas vacation tour in Low-Church Cambridge, Goulburn reported to Peel in January 1845 that 'there is a greater feeling of hostility to the Roman Catholics than has for some time past prevailed. May-nooth was more than once adverted to and its extension depre-cated as putting arms into the hands of the enemy.'[2] When the crisis arrived, Ashley the Evangelical and Bright the Quaker were united in their view that the Maynooth scheme admitted the principle of State endowment for the Roman Church in Ireland.[3] Once again the clash was between Parliament and

---

[1] The fear that the Irish Roman Catholic Church would, if once recognized, become by degrees first an endowed and then an established Church, was present even at the time of the great controversy over the Irish Union in the late eighteenth century; though the fear was always expressed by Anglicans who saw that two established Churches could hardly co-exist in one country (Cf. Henriques, *Religious Toleration in England*, pp. 140–1). The formal opposition of Dissenters in the 1830's and 1840's was to the principle of establishment in itself, more particularly to the extension of the principle; though underneath their opposition was a lively antagonism to Roman Catholicism in practice.

[2] Goulburn cited particularly the opinions of the Master of Trinity, the great William Whewell, 'who has always been of very liberal opinions in such matters. . . . He certainly stated to me how much his fears and those of others had been excited by the idea of the extension of Maynooth to which your speech of last session gave encouragement and expressed an earnest hope that you would not attempt to carry your views into effect without taking real securities. He added that the results of the Relief Bill had made people feel how little liberal concession could allay R. Catholic hostility and that he felt satisfied that any attempt to repeat such an experiment in the case of Maynooth would cause universal excitement in the Protestant mind. I think his view is correct. It is impossible not to see that there is among the better class of the Clergy a growing dread of Roman Catholic doctrine, a fear of its extension and an unwillingness to extend by an enlarged education of the Priesthood, its authority and influence. This is not an unnatural consequence of the division which has lately grown up in the Church but it will, I fear, throw great difficulties in the way of the measure which you may contemplate for the improved education of the Romish Priesthood and if such a measure should lead as it probably may to the secession of any important member of the Government, I should not be surprised if the flame of real religious apprehension of the conse-quences of the measure was to burn as fiercely as ever' (Add. MS. 40445, ff. 5–6).

[3] 'This endowment and elevation lead necessarily to the endowment and eleva-tion of the whole priesthood of Ireland—you must, having raised them to a certain

public opinion. 'The House, as I foresaw,' wrote Ashley in his diary, 'would readily pass it, but the country is becoming furious. The Free Church of Scotland, the "religious public" of England, Wesleyans, Dissenters, all alike are protesting and petitioning, probably with little chance of success, but with fixed resolution, so far as in them lies, to cashier their representatives at another election.'[1] To fail in securing disestablishment of the Anglican Church in the 1830's only to see the germ of an established Roman Church in Ireland in the 1840's, was peculiarly bitter to the Dissenters. Yet this increased hostility to Rome which characterized the early Victorian years had a direct and damaging effect on the Church of England. In the eyes of many the Church was tainted by the Anglo-Romanism of the Tractarians and to that extent less representative and less influential as a national Church; less united; less fit to be entrusted with national tasks. There was a double irony here. First that the Tractarians were of all the elements in the Church most disposed to criticize its involvement with the State and to renounce the benefits of the Establishment. Second, that the Tractarian Movement, if pushed back to its origin in the 1828-9 period with Bishop Lloyd as Regius Professor at Oxford,[2] began as an anti-Roman, though not anti-Catholic (in the theological sense), reaction to the Emancipation Act. But irony has no place in popular movements.

What is clear is that Tractarianism inflamed the fears of Dissenters and strengthened their hostility to the Establishment. The *Eclectic Review*, for example, declared as early as January 1836 that 'the Church of England is a halfway house between Popery and Protestantism', and renewed the attack the following month in an article offensively entitled 'The Popery of Protestantism'. Three years later it was warning its readers that 'the Church of England is the last hope of Rome' and that the

level, keep them there, and this can be effected by adequate endowment only. Thence the establishment by law of the Roman Catholic Church, and the concurrent existence of two Established Churches!'—Ashley, 8 Apr. 1845 (Hodder, *Shaftesbury*, p. 327). For Bright's attitude, given sharper emphasis by his disbelief in the virtue of any establishment for religion, see G. B. Smith, *Life of John Bright* (1881), i. 117-20.

[1] Hodder, op. cit., p. 326.

[2] Especially his lectures on the Prayer Book (cf. Stoughton, *Religion in England*, i. 164, ii. 34-35; R. W. Church, *The Oxford Movement* (1891), pp. 41, 187).

only safeguard of the Protestant faith in Britain was to be found 'not in the forms of the Protestant Church, but in the strength of Evangelical Protestantism'.[1] Miall in 1839, when he tendered his resignation from the pastorate at Leicester to take up religious journalism, gave as one of his foremost reasons the fact that 'the Clergy of the Establishment, both evangelical and otherwise, are reviving the arrogant pretensions of the papal priesthood, and are very generally setting forth the doctrines of Popery under the garb of Protestantism'.[2] In 1842 the *Chartist Circular*,[3] no lover of any Church but quite pleased to take up this additional argumentative cudgel, approvingly quoted the description in *The Nonconformist* of the Church of England as 'a church just ready to make common cause with Rome, whilst preparing to practise increased extortion upon a Protestant people'. Over Graham's educational proposals in 1843, the Dissenting Press could proclaim that 'instead of being instructed in the Holy Scriptures, the rising generation will be drilled in Puseyite obeisances',[4] and the same fears played a large part in producing the alliance of the Wesleyan Methodists with orthodox Dissent which was the death-blow to Graham's hopes. 'It is right that you should have the real history of the vigorous opposition to the factory bill', Ashley told him in April. 'The Wesleyan Methodists, hitherto friendly to the Church, as they showed in 1839, are actuated by a deep and conscientious fear of Popery in the Church of England.'[5] Graham had to sacrifice his education scheme in 1843; Peel, by exerting his authority

[1] Vol. 15, pp. 29, 97; N.S., vol. 5, p. 33. The first two references were when Conder was still editor. [2] *Life of Miall*, p. 31.
[3] 12 Feb. 1842. [4] Smith, *Life of Kay-Shuttleworth*, p. 146.
[5] Graham MS., 26 Apr. 1843. Even before this date Graham had realized the situation. 'It is quite clear', he wrote to Peel on 13 Apr., 'that the Pusey tendencies of the Established Church have operated powerfully on the Wesleyans, and are converting them rapidly into enemies.' The formal protest he had received from them 'is more hostile than I anticipated, and marks distinctly a wide estrangement from the Church. In some of the principles announced, this declaration goes the whole length of the bitterest dissent, and the sole reservation opposed to perfect equality of sects is against the Roman Catholics alone'. (Parker, *Peel*, ii. 560). Peel came to the same conclusion. 'Puseyism has alienated the Wesleyans, and redoubled the hostile activity against the Church, of other Dissenters, and made many sober and attached friends of the Church lukewarm in its defence' (*Croker Papers*, iii. 10). So also did Russell: 'With the encroaching spirit of the Oxford Catholics, as they call themselves, I cannot expect that a Bill to place education in the hands of the Church will be acquiesced in' (To Kay, 2 May 1843, *Life of Kay-Shuttleworth*, p. 151).

to the utmost, splitting his party and relying on Opposition support, got Maynooth through. But the ground-swell of angry Protestant feeling remained, to ensure that the next general election in 1847—repeal of the Corn Laws notwithstanding—was fought on the religious rather than the economic records of the Peel and Russell Ministries in so far as it was fought on any general issue at all. It left a strong though unorganized and unaffiliated Protestantism as a prize of immediate advantage, though ultimate liability, for any political party bold enough to angle for it.

That it was not exploited to any great extent was because neither Peel, Russell, Stanley, nor Bentinck were qualified by past performance or existing circumstance to beat the Protestant drum. Of the four, it was left to the impulsive John Russell to deliver one more resounding blow on that ancient instrument of British politics with his famous Durham Letter of 1850 on Papal Aggression and the ill-fated Ecclesiastical Titles Bill of the following year. The significance of Russell's action in 1850, however, was that it was aimed not so much at the Court of Rome as at the native crypto-Romanists of the Tractarian movement still lurking in the bosom of the Establishment. In this Russell was merely giving a lead to a large and confusedly articulate feeling of resentment among wide elements of British society both inside and outside the Church.[1] Nor was he without support from some of his colleagues. G. C. Lewis, for example, thought it important to administer a check to the Tractarians, and argued that 'in its ultimate origin this movement has been a reaction against Puseyism. It is an insurrection of the middle classes against *mummery* which they do not understand and with which they have no sympathy. The man in the omnibus has nothing in common with Tractarianism and ecclesiology.'[2] Nevertheless, for the Liberal party, which stood

---

[1] So good a churchman as Sir James Graham, for example, was seriously concerned in 1849 about the choice of an Oxford college for his second son. He inquired from Peel whether Oriel was 'clear of Newmanism' and observed wryly that 'the fit selection of an Oxford college for a future clergyman is now no easy matter' (Add. MS. 40452, ff. 410, 412).

[2] Lewis (then Financial Secretary to the Treasury) to Graham, 27 Jan. 1851 (Graham MS.). In an earlier letter (10 Jan. 1851), he had told Graham that the Papal Aggression crisis was of no real importance in itself. 'What however is of real importance in this movement is that the Puseyites should be brought to their bearings, that the Pope and those who pull the strings of the Pope, should be made

traditionally for religious toleration, the Ecclesiastical Titles Bill was something of an anomaly. It was an anomaly that was particularly striking among the Protestant Dissenters. Their own historical tradition pointed to the side of individual liberty for all Churches; their instinctive anti-Popery, reinforced over the previous two decades by fear of a semi-establishment of the Roman Church in Ireland and fear of Roman influence in the Church of England, carried them over to the side of Russell. Caught in the prevailing intellectual confusion, the Dissenting Deputies both protested against Papal aggression and condemned State endowment of any religious organization. It was left to a losing minority on their Board to proclaim the true nonconformist principle in a defeated resolution of regret at legislative interference even with the 'Romish Church'.[1]

If this could happen among the Dissenting intelligentsia, there was little hope of any greater clarity among their followers. Cobden, Bright, and Miall might deplore Russell's Bill, but Cobden himself had to admit in terms that explained as vividly as they reprobated, that 'the majority of dissenting politicians have violated the rights of conscience by supporting the Ecclesiastical Titles bill'.[2] It was easy enough for Stanley the same year to talk of the Whigs of thirty or forty years earlier being brought into 'an unnatural combination' with the Papists 'in the general cause of "Civil and Religious Liberty" '. In fact it was the back-bench Protectionists who came nearest to forming a Protestant party in politics. Major Beresford, their Chief Whip, and the man mainly instrumental in forcing Bentinck from the leadership at the end of the year, announced at the time of the 1847 election that 'the only real cry in the country is the proper and just old No Popery cry. . . . I say just, because it is no longer the same cry which refused the Catholics equal rights, it is a cry against their attempt at domination.'[3] But a party headed by Stanley, the former Liberal Whig; Bentinck,

to understand that England is thoroughly Protestant and unchanged in its faith, that the Oxford movement which was Romanizing so many of the more weak-minded or more ambitious of the Clergy, should be checked. This will now be done effectually. The Puseyites must now go to the right or to the left. They must either declare themselves spiritual subjects of the Pope, or relapse into the old High Church principles such as were recognised even when I was at Oxford' (Lewis had been at Oxford 1824–8).   [1] Manning, *Dissenting Deputies*, pp. 206–9.

[2] J. Morley, *Life of Richard Cobden* (1920), p. 560.

[3] *Croker Papers*, iii. 116, 236.

the ex-Canningite and a 'Catholic' in the sense in which politicians were labelled in the 1820's; and Disraeli, the sceptical Jew baptized a Christian, could find little encouragement among its leaders for such a simple electoral platform. Anti-Catholicism was, and remained for many more generations, a strong element in English life; but it was not a politically manageable element. It was a fact in, rather than an issue of, politics; but it was a fact that worked against the growth of Anglican power in the 1840's.

II

By the late 1840's the formal battleground between Church and Dissent had broken up into a medley of cross-alignments and secondary issues. The inability of either side to impose its will on the other was the underlying reason for the disintegration of the conflict. In turn they could not impose their will on the Government, even if the Government (after the experience of the Whigs in 1839 and the Conservatives in 1843) were understandably shy of any attempt to override them. Neither pure voluntaryism for all, nor the full claims of the Establishment, nor undenominational secularism was capable of gaining an outright victory. A wide gap continued to exist between the utilitarian, undogmatic attitude of the leading politicians on the one side, and on the other the intransigent religious convictions of the multiple society which they had to govern. It was a gap which could only be filled by a series of partial and illogical compromises.

As far as English Dissenters were concerned, their hostility to the Establishment in the late 1840's was as inveterate as ever and their confidence in the Whig Government even more tenuous. The pacific Dissenting Deputies in London had been moved by Graham's educational scheme in 1843 to enter the unquiet field of parliamentary politics and were able to close ten weeks of incessant and victorious activity with 'esteem for each other and gratitude to Divine Providence'.[1] But the experience increased both their efforts for voluntary education and their distaste for any kind of State intervention even at the

---

[1] Manning, *Dissenting Deputies*, p. 344.

hands of their former allies. How sensitive their susceptibilities were on this point was shown in the educational controversy of 1846–7. In August and December 1846 two minutes of the Educational Committee of the Privy Council announced changes in the method of awarding school grants, the main objects of which were to encourage the training of pupil-teachers and to secure a higher status for the profession by means of rewards for efficiency and pensions on retirement. The scheme required no fresh legislation, only an increased parliamentary grant; but it did involve an extension of governmental inspection and the principle of professional examinations for intending teachers. It was the most that could be done to improve the quality of teachers and the conditions of the profession without disturbing the essential sectarian and voluntary basis of English education; and despite some misgivings by the High Church party, the National Society welcomed the scheme. The mass of Evangelical Dissent, however, at once declared its opposition. Coming after Graham's 1843 proposals and the increased Maynooth grant of 1845, the Whig plan of 1846 seemed to be of a piece with all the rest of previous governmental activity in the educational field.

Dissenters hardly knew what to fear more: the overt secularism of Russell's proposals, or the danger that Anglicans would so monopolize the additional facilities provided as to throw out a new wing of the Establishment.[1] Either was obnoxious. Edward Baines, in his paper the *Leeds Mercury* and his *Letters to the Right Honourable John Russell on State Education*, in the autumn of 1846 had already been condemning Dean Hook's proposals for a final assumption by the State of the responsibility for secular education;[2] and as soon as Russell's scheme

[1] Cf. *The Nonconformist*, 10 Feb. 1847. 'Twenty years will not elapse, after the adoption of their new scheme, before the educational training of the masses will, by a silent process, slide as effectually under government control as if they had enacted a law to forbid all instruction which they had not themselves previously and formally licensed.' The conclusions were obvious. 'From this measure we may learn the folly of looking to government for any educational plan which does not violate our most cherished convictions' (*Eclectic Review*, N.S. vol. 21 (Mar. 1847), pp. 357, 370).

[2] The main author of the Privy Council's minute was Kay-Shuttleworth, who also supplied most of the ammunition for Hook's demonstration of the inadequacy of Church and voluntary schools for the education of the mass of the nation, in his pamphlet *On the Means of rendering more Efficient the Education of the People*. Hook's main point was that lack of money, of trained teachers and of compulsory powers,

was made public the *Mercury* went in to the attack. 'He is now', it declared of the Prime Minister on 20 February 1847, '. . . doing the most deadly injury to the Dissenters, and pandering to the unjust and arrogant pretensions of the Church. He may rely upon it that the Dissenters will not support an administration which does them such cruel wrong.' But the storm was not confined to north-country Radical Dissenters alone. The *Nonconformist*, the *Patriot*, and the *Eclectic Magazine*, the three chief organs of Dissent, all joined the agitation. In April 1847 there was a special national educational conference of Dissenters in London, attended by nearly five hundred delegates, which not only condemned the Whig measure and passed a resolution against all Government patronage of popular education but recommended Liberal electors to adopt means of securing the return of 'such candidates as not merely profess to hold sacred the claims of religious liberty, but also clearly understand what those claims imply'. Not content with this, in view of the approaching general election, it constituted a Dissenters Electoral Committee to encourage and organize parliamentary opposition. In its *Address to the Nonconformist Electors of Great Britain* the Committee stated that there was so little difference between the two great national parties that 'no damage, therefore, can be done to any great national interests by your refusal to take part in contests which allow you no opportunity of bearing witness against the ecclesiastical policy recently pursued by parliament'. In commenting on this address, the *Eclectic Review* observed bitterly that 'should our measures result in the unseating of any Whig candidates, it will be no just cause for regret. We have done with parties.'[1] In London, the Dissenting Deputies, when noting in 1846 Russell's proclaimed purpose of extending public education while maintaining religious liberty, had already observed sceptically that 'whether the

made voluntary efforts merely the 'lighting a lantern which only makes us sensible of the surrounding darkness'. On the other hand, as he had told Archdeacon Wilberforce in 1843, 'I really do not see how the Church can fairly ask the State to give it money for the purpose of giving a Church education when the money is to be supplied by Dissenters and infidels, and all classes of the people, who according to the principles of the Constitution, have a right to control the expenditure' (C. J. Stranks, *Life of Dean Hook* (1954), pp. 74–79).

[1] *Eclectic Review*, N.S., vol. 21 (May 1847), article on 'National Education—What will the Dissenters do Next?', pp. 635 seq.; vol. 22 (July 1847), article on 'The General Election—Position and Duty of Dissenters', pp. 103 seq.

legislature can interfere at all with public education without at the same time interfering with religious liberty has been doubted'. A conference with the Prime Minister failed to remove their doubts that any State system would be biased in favour of Anglicanism; and the following year they aligned themselves with the general body of Dissenters by publicly affirming that State intervention in education was 'uncalled for, inexpedient, necessarily unjust in its operation, and dangerous to public liberty'.

It was a clear proof of the hardening of Dissenting temper over the preceding half-dozen years. In 1839, less than a decade earlier, a resolution in the Board of Deputies that the education of the lower classes was not 'a legitimate function of the government' had failed to find a seconder.[1] The rapid slide into voluntaryism could hardly be better illustrated. But voluntaryism in this sense meant a rupture with the Whigs,[2] and in the 1847 general election the Dissenting Deputies in London and the Home Counties, like the Anti-State Church Association in the provinces, actively worked in favour of voluntaryist candidates and against the orthodox Ministerial men. Not surprisingly, some of the Dissenting and Radical candidates who now came forward expressed some even more far-reaching opinions. W. J. Fox, the Corn Law agitator and ex-Unitarian minister returned for Oldham, made disestablishment one of the planks of his electoral platform.[3] Bright, elected at Manchester, described the recent creation of the new bishopric there as a 'calamity', declared that 'hierarchies, state-manufactured clergies, are in themselves evils', and ventured the prophecy that the time would come when they would be as extinct as prehistoric monsters.[4] Even Chartism, that repository of lost Radical causes, caught the prevailing mood, and Ernest Jones, for

[1] Manning, *Dissenting Deputies*, pp. 339–49.

[2] As early as 21 Mar. 1847 Charles Wood warned Russell that 'in most of the large towns the very best friends we have had are the persons now leading the anti-government education movement; amongst them are also to be found the Quakers and peace societies' (Russell, *Later Corr.* i. 244). And in Apr., when attacking the Government's education scheme, Bright said that like every step taken by government since 1839 (the date is significant), it had a tendency to give increased and enormous power to the clergy of the Established Church (Smith, *Bright*, i. 287).

[3] Along with tax revision, universal education, Poor Law revision, and Irish land reform (R. Garnett, *Life of W. J. Fox*, p. 289).

[4] Smith, *Bright*, i. 241.

example, running in alliance with Miall at Halifax, put forward as one of his electoral objectives 'the separation of Church and State'.[1] When the elections were over, the embattled forces of Dissent claimed twenty-six of their number returned to the Commons, and some sixty M.P.s pledged against the principle of the extension of State-endowed religion.[2]

But this limited success had been gained at the cost of disrupting conventional alignments in a way which made the 1847 general election one of the most confused of the century. The Dissenters, as one of their organs said afterwards, 'have ceased to act as a section of the Whig party'. From their sectarian standpoint Conservatives and Whigs were now branded as one aristocratic party—'so far as we are concerned, they are one'.[3] Macaulay was thrown out at Edinburgh by a combination of Radicals, Tories, Dissenters, Voluntaryists, Free Churchmen, and spirit-drinkers.[4] In London the Dissenting Deputies helped to return Baron Rothschild, an ineligible Jew; and Russell's position at the head of the poll was ascribed to the support of the Conservatives. There was a Whig–Conservative alliance in the West Riding,[5] where, as Charles Wood wrote, 'but for the extreme and really incredible violence of the non-conformists we should have been triumphant. They are wrong-headed beyond measure, and with very strong feeling about Maynooth and R.C. endowments, they formed a very strong opposition and nothing but the support of the Conservatives carried us through at Leeds and Halifax.'[6] An even more curious whirligig of time and temper was seen at Bath. In 1832 the young and Radical Roebuck's successful electioneering programme there

---

[1] J. Saville, *Ernest Jones* (1952), p. 96.

[2] Cowherd, *English Dissent*, pp. 162–3.

[3] *Eclectic Review*, N.S. vol. 22, pp. 363–5, article on 'The Electoral Policy of Dissenters—What are its Results?'

[4] G. O. Trevelyan, *Macaulay* (1876), ii. 185–7.

[5] Marshall only got in at Leeds with Conservative votes; and Conservatives also helped Wood to win at Halifax along with the Tory Edwards. See also *Life of Miall*, pp. 126–8.

[6] Russell MS., 1 Aug. 1847 P.R.O. 20/22/6. Hobhouse was told by Bright in Apr. that the Dissenters all over the kingdom were up in arms against the Government, and admitted in his diary that 'from my communications with Nottingham and other places, it is certain there is great excitement amongst all classes of Dissenters except the Catholics and Unitarians'. But, he comforted himself, 'the Church is for our schemes, and the Bishops give us open support, all but the very High Church'. (Broughton, *Recollections*, vi. 188.)

had included disestablishment of the Church of England and the secularization of its property; but as an Anglican and a prominent educationist he found his Dissenting supporters at Bath in 1847 in an uproar. When he refused, as he said, though no supporter of the Establishment, 'at once, and without further ado, to propose the utter subversion of this Church as by law established', and reaffirmed his belief in the duty of the State to educate the people, his fate was sealed. Left at the foot of the polls,[1] he angrily told the crowd at the hustings that 'I shall go a member of the Church of England—mind you, Dissenters, a member of the Church of England, remembering well that the Dissenters are not worthy of freedom'.[2] But the anger was not all on one side. In July the *Eclectic Review* published a scarifying attack on Russell, not only comparing him unfavourably with Peel but (unkindest cut of all) with Lord Melbourne, whom it described as 'more liberal than Lord John Russell . . . much less of a Whig, much less of an oligarch'.[3]

The fractional gains of Dissent in 1847 were in fact a political disaster, for they were achieved by splitting both the Whig–Dissenting and the Dissenting–Radical alliances; and to no practical purpose. Disestablishment was an academic gesture, not a real issue; on the old and vexed question of Church rates the Dissenters could get no support from Russell;[4] and on the matter of education they alienated many intellectual reformers. In the winter of 1846–7 for example, the *Westminster Review*, the organ of the Philosophic Radicals, strongly criticized the stand taken by many Dissenters in opposing the extension of State education; and declared that a 'voluntary system' of

---

[1] The successful candidates were Lord Ashley, a Conservative, and Lord Duncan, a Whig.

[2] Leader, *Life of Roebuck*, pp. 44, 183–7.

[3] n.s. vol. 22, article on 'The late and the present Administrations' (July 1847), p. 17.

[4] In the debate in Mar. 1849 on Trelawney's motion to abolish Church rates, Russell spoke against it and was cheered by the Protectionists. When Cobden observed that while gaining new friends, Russell was losing old, the Prime Minister turned to Hobhouse and said that he had never used any other language on the subject (Broughton Diary, Add. MS. 43753, 13 Mar. 1849, p. 126). This was true of Russell personally, but not of the previous Liberal Administrations of which Russell had been a member and from whose actions Russell could hardly dissociate himself. Nevertheless, it was clear that the Whigs had given up their earlier policy and, despite intermittent agitation in the 1850's and 1860's, Church rates were not finally abolished until 1868.

education was in any national sense a mere phantom. It rubbed theological salt into this wound by observing further that the Dissenting agitation against Church rates was a 'capital mistake' and arguing that the Church of England should be regarded as a national church open to all.[1] Roebuck thought that momentary sectarian animosities rather than considered principle dictated the attitude of the voluntaryists; and three years later, at a meeting of the National Public Schools Association at Manchester, Cobden made an appeal to the 'large and most influential portion' of Dissenters to forget the passions raised by Graham's Bill of 1843 and return to their support for a general plan of national education.[2] They were not alone in raising their voices against the departure of English Dissent from a wider view of its tradition and duties. Dale of Birmingham, the great Congregationalist minister who succeeded James at Carr's Lane, could later record[3] that 'the protest in 1846–7 against all State interference with popular education was really a temporary departure from the policy which Congregational Dissenters originally professed'. But for many years they were lonely voices. Despite Cobden's public educational activities, in private he despaired of the cause of national education. It could only come through a middle-class movement and such a movement could never succeed without Dissenting support. At the end of 1848 he told Baines of the *Leeds Mercury* that 'education is the main cause of the split amongst the middle-class Liberals'.[4] Meanwhile the Whig ministry, undeflected by the storm at the 1847 elections, had gone resolutely ahead with its plans, increasing the educational grant of 1847 to £100,000 and conciliating the Wesleyans[5] with pledges as to Roman Catholic schools. Nor were all Dissenters voluntaryists. The Wesleyan Methodists, through their own education committee, came under the recognition of the Edu-

[1] Vol. 46 (Oct. 1846–Jan. 1847), pp. 182 seq.; 195–6; 636 seq. The *Westminster Review* itself, however, had experienced a change of heart on the subject of Church rates. In 1837 it had said, with reference to the Whig plan of that year, that 'the measure seems to us almost perfect' (vol. 27, p. 127, Apr. 1837).

[2] 31 Oct. 1850, printed in *Reminiscences of Richard Cobden*, by Mrs. Salis Schwabe (1895), p. 134.

[3] In a letter of 2 Jan. 1868 (*Life of Dale*, p. 271).

[4] Morley, *Cobden*, pp. 485–6, 495.

[5] Largely through the instrumentality of Lord Ashley (Hodder, *Shaftesbury*, p. 381).

cational Committee of the Privy Council in 1847; and even a section of the Congregationalists consented to bow the knee to Mammon, though they successfully resisted the right of inspectors to report on their religious teaching.[1] But Free Trade in education had taken too firm a hold on the Baptists and the majority of the Congregationalists to be soothed away by more and more easily obtainable State assistance.

In consequence the Anglicans continued to receive the lion's share of the Government grant. The figures for the allocation of State funds for new school buildings between 1839 and 1850 tell their own tale. Of a total of half a million, 80 per cent. went to the Church of England; 10 per cent. to the British and Foreign Society; 7 per cent. to workhouse schools; and 1½ per cent. to the fourth largest category, the Wesleyans.[2] The clear fact was that despite all the heat and conflict, the country had settled down to an untidy, inadequate, but workable compromise of voluntary schools, largely run by organized but different churches, and partially supported by the taxpayer. It was to remain so for another generation of Victorian life.

The paradox of the late 1830's and 1840's was that the more Dissenters clarified their attitude on Church–State relationships, the more they lost their ability to carry their doctrines into practice, except in the limited sphere under their immediate control. The coolness and division that had opened up between Whigs, Radicals, and Dissenters on education and the role of the Anglican Church made the continued talk of disestablishment an exercise in rhetoric rather than politics; though this was not finally to be demonstrated until the age of Gladstone and Joseph Chamberlain. Disestablishment indeed had been a millstone round the neck of Dissenting political activity. They had never been completely united on the issue, and in the 1830's, when their influence was greatest and the reforming movement still in spate, their real objectives were different: lay appropriation, tithes, Church rates, and the stigmata of Dissent represented by the Anglican quasi-monopoly of baptisms, marriages, and funerals. Yet once the controversy on these secondary topics started, it was impossible to exclude the

---

[1] Smith, *Life of Kay-Shuttleworth*, pp. 189–90.
[2] Cowherd, *English Dissent*, quoting census figures for financial grants 1839–50, p. 161.

theoretical question of the continued existence of the State
Church. Enough was said by the more extreme Dissenters to
alarm; not enough was done to wound. Anglicans accused Dissenters of harbouring the ulterior design of disestablishment;
Dissenters retorted that they had been forced into hostility
to the Establishment by the rejection of their more moderate
requests. The hardening of the dogmatic belief in the necessity
for disestablishment was an emotional reaction to their political
defeats on other issues; it was a gratifying concept rather than
a practical possibility. The Whigs were at no time prepared to
lead a central attack on the Church of England, and without
Whig parliamentary leadership organized Dissent could do very
little. They were formidable in agitation; they were effective in
obstruction. Given a suitable issue, they could make a Ministerial policy, even when backed by a House of Commons
majority, unpopular, difficult, and sometimes impracticable.
What they could not do was to formulate and impose a policy
of their own. They lacked the unity, the positive organization,
and still more the human material for parliamentary strength.
The Dissenters were never a homogeneous element in society;
they never formed a political party; and it was impossible for
them to do so. They could not provide enough eligible parliamentary candidates from their own ranks, and if they repudiated Whig–Liberal leadership, they were politically paralysed.
It is not surprising that this was so; all their historical conditioning conspired to make them political amateurs. Though
1828 had been a formal act of political emancipation for English
Dissenters, the matrix of a century and a half of second-class
citizenship had left an imprint on their minds and habits of life
which could not in a single generation be easily erased.

A revealing article in one of the greatest Nonconformist
periodicals of the time, when contrasting the political weakness
of Dissenters with the social and religious dangers surrounding
them, bore unconscious witness to this inherited handicap.

They are not in themselves a separate political party, or capable
of becoming such. They are, in the counties, a religious minority.
Their wealth, though very great in the aggregate, is chiefly mercantile or invested in the great branches of manufacturing industry.
Their education does not fit or dispose their more opulent or leading
men to devote themselves to the thorny and precarious persuit of

politics. Their resources, their energies, their enterprise, their public spirit, have been expended upon other objects, have been directed into other channels—those of an enlarged philanthropy or religious benevolence. And the very liberality of their political principles, together with a repugnance to intolerance, has led them to give their support and confidence, without hesitation, to representatives having no connexion and little sympathy with them as a religious body.

In the face of 'Romanism . . . Anglo-Catholicism . . . a hideous mass of unreclaimed popular ignorance and infidelity', it called for unity and action. 'Not to be a politician in these days . . . is to be a traitor to those principles which are identified with the advancement of Christ's kingdom.'[1] But the plea itself was an open confession of the defensive position to which many Dissenters felt they had been reduced in the opening years of Victoria's reign.

III

There was lastly the state of the Anglican Church, stronger in 1852 than anyone could have foreseen twenty years before. A survey of those two crowded decades could hardly fail to note that the organizational recovery of the Church dated from Peel's Ecclesiastical Commission of 1835; and that the turning point was the defeat of Russell's educational scheme in 1839. As the Bishop of Gloucester said in his Visitation Charge of 1847,[2] 'this must be regarded as the great crisis of the education question'. It was fundamental because it raised the question whether education should become secular or remain a province of religion. Yet the limits of the Anglican revival were reached only four years later with the abandonment of Graham's Factory Education Bill. This was the second great crisis; because it raised the question whether national education was to be a monopoly of the Established Church or shared with others.

---

[1] *Eclectic Review*, N.S., vol. 5 (Jan. 1839), article on 'Proceedings and Position of the Dissenters'. A later historian of Nonconformity, himself a strong disestablishmentarian, has gone so far as to write that: 'on the surface, nothing is more puzzling . . . than the comparative apathy with which the question of disestablishment was regarded by Nonconformists as a whole through a period when in other respects the struggle for Nonconformist rights was so keen'. His own answer to the puzzle was that Nonconformists conceived the struggle as one for their own rights rather than for their own principles (Clark, *History of English Nonconformity*, ii. 409). But this is only part of the answer.

[2] Quoted by W. Johnston, *England As It Is* (1851), i. 312.

Nevertheless, the Establishment had survived the hostility of the 1820's and 1830's; the danger of reform at the hands of its enemies; the demand for the appropriation for secular purposes of part of its revenues; the threat of disestablishment which seemed real enough at the time. Once given leadership and confidence; once relieved from the consciousness of long-entrenched defects and abuses, the strength of the national Church returned like a tidal stream. Even if appropriation of Church revenues had passed the Commons, it would never have got through a House of Lords which secured even for the vulnerable Irish Church protection for its property against the appropriating hands of Whigs, Radicals, and O'Connellites.

Yet even in this record of recovery and reconstruction there were flaws. Given the numbers, wealth, and tradition of the Church, its close ties with the upper classes, its connexion with the Crown and the legislature, it would have required a major social and constitutional revolution for it to have been disestablished or disendowed in the 1830's. Nevertheless, if it had maintained and rehabilitated itself as a Church, it had perceptibly failed to strengthen itself as an Establishment. It had been unable to make good its title to superintend national State education; it had, in a wider field, been unable to maintain its old relationship with the State. What was abundantly clear in the 1840's was that the Church could never again lay claim to the loyalty of the legislature through the acid test of specific financial contributions. At the most it was the favoured daughter in the distribution of money that was in theory available to all its sister Churches. The reform of the Church was primarily an internal reform, even though it had been facilitated—or rather made possible—by parliamentary machinery; and while it received the greater part of the State educational grant, this was in fact a subvention to match and assist its own voluntary efforts. In a real sense indeed the Church of England had become more and not less like a voluntary sect. As a Church it was infinitely stronger in 1852 than in 1832; stronger in zeal, devotion, education, efficiency, and confidence. As a State Church its weakness and limitations had been exposed by events between 1838 and 1843 as never before.

The problem was not merely the external issue of the survival of the Church but the internal issue of the nature of the Church.

The heart-searching among Dissenters over their proper relation to the State was matched by the parallel debate within the Establishment. From 1832 onward there was growing divergence among High Churchmen between those who wished to unite all shades of opinion within the Church in common defence against liberal legislative encroachments, and those who wished to emphasize the inner authority of the Church as a spiritual body and were disposed if necessary to dispense with the State connexion since the State was no longer Anglican. The opposition of the extreme High Churchmen was not merely to Radicals and Whigs but to all forms of secularism, including Peelite Conservatism. Indeed, the latter, because it came in the guise of friendship, expedience, and political alliance, was more feared than the outright attacks of professed enemies. From the start there was considerable animus, for example, against Peel's Ecclesiastical Commission as a secular-dominated body which would soon achieve supreme authority in the Church. Bishop Phillpotts of Exeter, in his widely publicized Visitation Charge of 1836, declared that 'a machinery of the most formidable and portentous nature has been created, threatening us with a series of changes in our ecclesiastical constitution so often as the convenience of any government, which may be dependent on the will or caprices of a faction hostile to the Church, shall dictate such changes'.[1] The Oxford Tractarian party, more logical and doctrinaire, carried this criticism to the point of questioning altogether the value of the Establishment. 'Every day's experience proves', said the Tractarian *British Critic* in 1837, 'that the real dangers of the Church are not so properly caused by those who are opposed to its establishment, as from the very fact of the establishment itself on its present terms', and it went on to

---

[1] Quoted in the *British Critic* (vol. 21 (1837), p. 230), which had similar or even stronger views. Cf. an article in Apr. 1838 (vol. 23, p. 526): 'In a short time, if things go on thus, each ecclesiastical measure will be absorbed into the Commission; we shall live under the supremacy of the Commission; it will be our legislative, executive, the ultimate appeal of our bishops; it will absorb our Episcopate; the prime minister will be our Protestant Pope.' On this particular issue, the enlargement of the Commission in 1840 did much to allay fears of High Churchmen. The *British Critic* itself admitted that 'in all this we see indications of strength. We seem also to see a body whose passive resistance will be enough to save the Church from further innovation' (vol. 29, p. 150). For the attitude of Bishop Phillpotts see also G. C. B. Davies, *Henry Phillpotts, Bishop of Exeter* (1954), pp. 154–7.

anticipate the time when 'as the broken reeds of establishments on which the Church of England has so long and so unhappily rested, and which have pierced and crippled her hands, are withdrawn . . . in proportion as human enactments either desert her or intrude, her independence may be seen, and her spiritual nature acknowledged—she will be thrown back from acts of parliament on . . . her sacred fundamental charter.'[1] In many respects, indeed, the internal significance of the Tractarians was not that they instituted a Catholic doctrine in the Church —that had always been present, and was held before and after 1832 by churchmen who were not Tractarian—but that they applied that doctrine to the government of the Church[2] and formed an 'anti-Establishment' party within the Establishment. If there was any historical analogy here it was with the Non-Jurors of the eighteenth century; and it is worth remembering that the Revolution of 1688 was denounced in the *British Critic* as 'a foul and horrible sin'.[3]

---

[1] Vol. 22, pp. 218–19.

[2] Cf. G. C. Lewis in 1851: 'There was always a Romanizing party in our Church, at one time more, at another time less, but as far as I know it romanized only in *doctrine* and not in *church government*' (to Graham, 10 Jan. 1851, Graham MS.).

[3] In a highly favourable review of Pusey's 5 Nov. sermon at Oxford in 1837. The date was of course the anniversary of both the Gunpowder Plot and the landing of the Prince of Orange in 1688; and Pusey, consistently applying the High Church doctrine of obedience to lawful authority, argued in his sermon that the rebellion against James II had been as bad in principle as the action of Guy Fawkes. The uncompromising nature of his logic, if not of his language, attracted some attention. 'I suppose', wrote James Mozley, 'it is the first time of the Revolution being formally preached against since Sacheverel' (H. P. Liddon, *Life of E. B. Pusey* (1893), ii. 25–30; *British Critic*, vol. 23 (Jan. 1838), p. 147). Mathieson, *English Church Reform*, p. 144, connects the extremism of this review article with Newman's assumption of the editorship of the *British Critic* the same year. But though Newman had been connected with the *Critic* since Mar. 1836, he only took on the editorship in July 1838 (*Letters & Corr. of J. H. Newman*, ed. A. Mozley (1891), ii. 177, 251). The Tractarians, however, were not the only ones to whom the religious conflicts of the Reform era recalled the passions of the seventeenth century. It is a sidelight on the mood of the time that in Dec. 1843 Peel flatly refused to sanction the removal of the statue of James II to a new position in front of the Admiralty. 'Considering what is going on in Ireland, the feverish state of the public mind as to Puseyism and Catholicism, the ferment just roused by the arrival of the Duc de Bordeaux,' he wrote to the First Lord, the Earl of Haddington, 'the time is not very happily selected for stirring the statue of James, and with it, possibly, other things than the statue. . . . I own to you that I think it would cause the greatest surprize to place James the 2nd. as the *Figure-Head* of the Admiralty in the Reign of Queen Victoria' (Add. MS. 40457, f. 56). The Duc de Bordeaux, later known as the Duc de Chambord, was the French Bourbon claimant (as Henri V) to the throne of France. His visit to England in the winter of 1843–4 was suspected by the

The storm which eventually broke over the doctrinal views of the Tractarians between 1840 and 1845, and the migration of some of their leading figures to the Church of Rome, did something to diminish Tractarian influence; but the general High Church uneasiness, of which they had been the extreme spokesmen, remained to trouble Church–State relationships in the latter part of the decade. The resultant confusion of principle and purpose was evident for example in the friction between the Education Committee of the Privy Council and the National Society over the degree of control to be exercised in the constitution of new church schools, which dragged on between 1846 and 1850. The prime object of the Education Committee was to ensure efficient management of schools by insisting on due representation of the subscribers, the official sponsoring society, and the Committee itself; and its management clauses (based on the National Society's own forms) were in fact accepted by the Society in 1846. But there was considerable laxity in small schools run by parochial clergymen and the attempt by the Committee to enforce a uniform system of management raised strong opposition from a powerful section of the High Church party who continued up to 1852 to battle for the rights of the parish priest. At a meeting of the National Society in June 1849, held in protest at what was described as the attempt by the Privy Council to secularize education, it was bitterly alleged that the Privy Council treated the sects as though they were the Church and the Church as though it were a sect. Archdeacon Wilberforce evoked cheers when he asserted that 'the Legislature of England was neither a Church nor a Christian legislature, and therefore if they were to have a system of national education under Government, it must of necessity be irreligious. The government must be pleasing all parties, and this they could do only by withdrawing all true religion and all strict dogmatic theology. . . . This was no question between clergy and laity; it was not as laymen that they were to be feared, but as a Government representing all parties', and therefore by definition no one religion and perhaps no religion at all.[1]

Court and the Government as being a political demonstration designed to embarrass relations with France.

[1] *The Times*, 7 June 1849, report of meeting of the National Society in London on 6 June; Johnston, *England As It Is*, i. 318–19.

The confusion was seen again, in a different form, in the Papal Aggression crisis of 1850–1. On any analysis, it was a curious reversal of tradition that the Whig Russell should bring forward a Bill overtly framed to protect the royal supremacy and the monopoly of the Anglican hierarchical system from Roman competition; and the attempt embarrassed and divided rather than united good churchmen. Once the first moral indignation of county meetings and diocesan clerical assemblies was over, there was a perceptible slackening of wholehearted enthusiasm for the Ecclesiastical Titles Bill; and if few opposed, not many supported without reservations. Behind the firm front of the twenty-six bishops who gave it their votes in the Upper House was perhaps a larger admixture of doubt. Even in Cambridge opinion was divided. 'The feeling there', Goulburn reported 'was generally speaking very moderate. Everyone was sensible of the difficulty of Lord John's position and anxiously expecting his measure and with one or two exceptions, all were most desirous not to aggravate the difference between the High and Low Church parties, though among the elder portion of the University the inclination is decidedly to the latter.'[1] At High Church Oxford, Lord Portman could say in November that he found several Heads of Houses and many dons delighted at the Durham Letter;[2] but some High Churchmen, whether Tractarian or merely sympathetic to the ideals of Tractarianism, were equally clearly on the side of religious liberty. They had not yet accustomed themselves to regard Lord John Russell and the Whigs as champions of the Church; and recent secular action in Church affairs—the appointment of Dr. Hampden in 1847 to the see of Hereford (denounced by half the Episcopal Bench)[3] and the upholding of Gorham's presentation by the Judicial Committee of the Privy Council against both his Bishop and the Dean of Arches Court in 1850 —had done nothing to strengthen their confidence in the value of existing Church–State relationships.[4] Gladstone, though he

[1] Graham MS., Goulburn to Graham, 1 Jan. 1851.

[2] Russell, *Later Corr.* ii. 52.

[3] 'The greatest mistake the government have made since they have come into office is the appointment of Hampden', wrote G. C. Lewis to a colleague in Dec. 1847. 'They have utterly thrown away all the Church popularity obtained by the Bishop bill of the last session which greatly offended the Dissenters' (Clarendon MS., 22 Dec. 1847).

[4] Hampden, as Regius Professor of Divinity at Oxford, had virtually had his

disapproved of the Gorham decision, was plunged into despair at the 'dismal' state of the Church and confided to Acland that he would consider his political life at an end if he raised his voice in favour of separation from the state.[1]

When the Ecclesiastical Titles Bill controversy entered Parliament in 1851, it was noticeable that nearly all the leading Peelites—Gladstone, Sidney Herbert, Graham, Newcastle, Aberdeen, Cardwell, St. Germans, together with young men like Roundell Palmer and Frederick Peel, in the incongruous company of Hume, Roebuck, Cobden, and Bright, were ranged in the Opposition minority. Gladstone spoke in words that might have been used by a Whig of the 1820's when he condemned 'all attempts to meet the spiritual dangers of our church by temporal legislation of a penal character'.[2] In private, however, what weighed with the Peelites was that the same parliamentary machinery could be used against the Church of England as was used against the Church of Rome. 'I believe', wrote Acland to his father, 'Johnny is getting up the steam to alter the Prayer Book, and legalize a new form of loose Protestantism open to all except honest high Churchmen, whom (as a Whig should) he hates.'[3] Goulburn, though in the end he voted for the Bill, had similar misgivings. 'I fear in common with you', he wrote to Graham in January 1851, 'legislation as to the Liturgy and attacks on Episcopacy which will call on all sincere members of the Church for great exertions to resist, for they will have to fight the motley crew of Papists, dissenters, and Infidels.'[4]

The deeper question was whether the Church should be thinking in terms of Establishment or of spirituals, rather than indulging in confused and emotional anti-Popery prejudices; and the agitation of 1850–1, evanescent and unimportant as it was for its proclaimed purpose, revealed in fact the dilemma which lay behind the successful defence of the Church in the 1830's and which had steadily widened since 1828: the dilemma

views condemned as heretical by his own university eleven years earlier; Gorham was refused presentation to a living by Bishop Phillpotts of Exeter on grounds of unsound doctrine on baptismal regeneration.

[1] *Life of Acland*, pp. 163–4; Morley, *Gladstone*, i. 283.
[2] Ibid., p. 305.
[3] *Life of Acland*, p. 165.
[4] Graham MS., Goulburn to Graham, 1 Jan. 1851.

of a State Church that could no longer depend on the State for its defence and an Anglican Establishment that was subject to a Parliament no longer Anglican. It was a paradox felt acutely by the Tractarians and logically solved by some of them by transference to Rome. It was equally cogently felt by men like Gladstone, whose mind was impervious to logic except of his own peculiar manufacture. He had touched on it when, for instance, over the Unitarian Chapels Bill in 1844, he declared that it heightened his churchmanship but depressed his Church-and-Statesmanship. As he said in a letter to Manning in 1846, when the end to be attained was for the Church to help herself, and when it was recognized that active help from Parliament could no longer be given, 'the function of serving the church in the state . . . dies of itself'.[1] The internal disagreements in the Church over doctrine and government; the divisions between High, Low, and Broad Church; the limited value of the Establishment; and the dangers still feared from parliamentary supremacy: all these elements meant that the Church, though it had maintained itself in the Age of Reform, had become in the process a different kind of Church. It was not surprising that the Archbishop of Canterbury, in answering a plea for the restoration of Convocation in July 1851, replied sadly but firmly, 'I think that the assembling of Convocation with active powers would tend to increase discord in the Church'.[2]

Yet in the last analysis, perhaps, these were the fears of the professional clerics and committed churchmen; and Gladstone's dilemma that of a high-flown and idealist minority. For the sober practical men, who had to deal with the Church as it was, in the society which existed after 1832, the main aim after all had been secured. To borrow the prosaic specification laid down by Peel as early as 1828[3] of the essentials of the Establishment: the Anglican monarchy created by the Act of Settlement;

[1] Morley, *Gladstone*, i. 238–9.

[2] *Hansard*, vol. 118, 525. For a typical Low Church Anglican view of the divisions in the Church, cf. Graham's remark in 1844. 'The Protestants, weary of abusing the Papists, are disposed to turn semi-Papists themselves; and neglecting the "weightier matters", they fight about Albs and Copes and Surplices and Credence Tables, with all the Bitterness of Unbelievers in the Gospel of Peace; and the Church, which has overcome her Enemies from without, is now in imminent danger from the Feuds within her Pale' (to Croker, 11 Dec. 1844, Graham MS).

[3] Peel, *Memoirs*, i. 80. This point is made by Olive Brose in *Church and Parliament*, pp. 16, 208.

the participation of bishops in the House of Lords; the inalienable claim of the Church to its ecclesiastical property—all these criteria were still in existence. It was an untidy and anomalous situation, when viewed against all the other developments in English social and religious life; and to some churchmen these bare essentials were bare indeed. To maintain them might appear in 1852 a limited end; but it was an end that had seemed difficult enough in 1832 and ultimate success could not then have been taken for granted. Yet the success had been achieved in the most testing period that the Church had passed through since the seventeenth century; and it had been achieved mainly by prosaic and moderate men. Moreover, for all its untidiness and illogic, the result had possibly answered the needs and wishes of the majority of the nation as well as those of the ordinary church clergy themselves, as they would not have been answered by the logic of either its extreme champions or extreme enemies. Historical processes are never tidy and rarely doctrinaire. For those churchmen who were concerned more with what could humanly be done as distinct from what ideally was desirable, the state of the Church and its role in early-Victorian society was neither dismal nor ineffective.

The most eminent of all these practical men, Bishop Blomfield himself, in the last Visitation Charge (1854) of his long episcopal career, found it a matter for congratulation that the different classes of English society were evincing more goodwill and mutual kindliness than he had ever known before; and he ascribed a portion of the credit for that increasing social harmony to the clergy of the Establishment—to their pastoral work, their educational efforts, and their interest in social problems and improvements.[1] What at least was undeniable was that

---

[1] *Memoir of Bishop Blomfield*, ii. 164–5. As against the activity of Dissenters in the Anti-Corn Law movement, there had been a notable Anglican element—especially among the Yorkshire and Lancashire clergy—in the Oastler and Ashley factory reform movement—Bull of Brierley, Boddington of Horton, Fawcett and Hook at Leeds, Heap, Scoresby, and Burnett at Bradford, supported at longer range by the Archbishops of Canterbury and York, among the bishops by Ryder of Coventry, Longley of Ripon, Phillpotts of Exeter, and by Archdeacon Wilberforce. When the Ten Hours Bill was finally carried in 1847 there was a strong episcopal attendance in the House of Lords for the debate on the second reading; the Bishop of Oxford delivered a powerful speech in favour of the Bill; and nearly every bishop voted in support. 'This will do very much', recorded Ashley gratefully, 'to win the hearts of the manufacturing people to Bishops and Lords' (Hodder, *Shaftesbury*, pp. 368–9).

there was still a real function for the Establishment; and that it was carrying it out with greater efficiency than when Blomfield first took his seat on the Bishops' Bench in the age of Liverpool and Canning. Even doctrinally, perhaps, between the Anglo-Catholicism of the Tractarians and the new German-inspired higher criticism of the rational theologians, there was still an innate stabilizing force that kept the Church on an even keel. 'Depend upon it,' wrote Sidney Herbert consolingly to Graham in December 1850, when all England was in an uproar over papal aggression, 'Tractarianism has had its day. . . . The Germanizing process will, I think, now be tried at the other end, and that, in my opinion, will fail too. There is a fund of good sense in England, and a strong prejudice in some, and attachment in others, to the Bible and Prayer Book.'[1] In both politics and theology, despite the upheavals of the Reform era, the traditional *via media Anglicana* had not yet exhausted its purpose.

[1] Lord Stanmore, *Memoir of Sidney Herbert* (1906), i. 135.

V

PARTY IN POLITICS:
THE CONSERVATIVES

'No period of our history from the Revolution of 1688', observed a political writer in 1836, 'was so remarkably distinguished by the absence of party spirit as the reign of George IV.'[1] It was a sentiment for which there was ample contemporary corroboration.[2] No doubt Liberal and Radical impatience with the aristocratic faction fights contributed to the belief that the names of Whig and Tory were the vanishing emblems of an outmoded era; but there was much in the actual circumstances of the time to justify that belief. Party was the basis neither of Government nor of any Opposition likely by itself to become a Government. The traditional party names were in use and indicated certain differences of tradition, temperament, and attitude; but though the Whig Opposition cheerfully accepted a party label, there was no great inclination on the part of leading Ministers to style themselves Tory.[3]

[1] Sir John Walsh, *Chapters of Contemporary History* (1836), p. 69.

[2] For example: *Edinburgh Review*, 1818 (vol. 30, p. 182), 'Even the more thinking classes of the community, unconnected with government, are apt to see something factious in a systematic opposition'; Francis Place in 1821 (*Life*, by G. Wallas, p. 185) spoke of the Whig party as 'distrusted if not despised . . . even its name will probably in a few years be lost. Or if it remain, it will be received as the name of Tories out of place, and will be simply applied to any opposition not composed of Radical reformers'; the Duke of Clarence in 1828 (*Croker Papers*, i. 401), 'The names Whigs and Tories meant something a hundred years ago but are mere nonsense nowadays'; Francis Jeffrey in 1830 at a public meeting at Edinburgh, quoted by W. Hone, *Annals of the Revolution in France* (1830), p. 226, 'The time . . . was not far distant, indeed it was almost present, when the names of Fox and Pitt, and the designations of Whig and Tory, as party distinctions, would fall into utter disuse; and when, in all the practical points of good government, all parties would be united. Party animosity was every day going down'; *The Extraordinary Black Book* (1832), p. 229, 'Upon the whole, both Whiggism and Toryism may be considered defunct superstitions'.

[3] Only one occasion seems to be recorded when Peel used this description of himself, and that was ironical—in his well-known speech after resigning from the Government when Canning became Prime Minister in 1827: 'I may be a Tory, I may be an illiberal, but etc.' (N. Gash, *Mr. Secretary Peel* (1961), p. 437).

Liverpool's Cabinet was primarily, and in direct succession through Perceval and Portland, a continuation of Pittite central administration. In its early years it was a war-time Government of order and national survival, and later simply 'the Government', attracting the young men of talent and ambition and addressing itself to national tasks. That it had an unreconstructed Tory-reactionary element among its supporters, and often faced Whig and Radical opposition, did not prevent it from becoming an Administration of change and reform.

As the Austrian Ambassador acutely if jealously observed as early as 1820, 'it is not the real Radicalism which presents to the Government its greatest difficulties but rather the disguised Liberalism. . . . This peril . . . the Government encounters not only in the ranks of its enemies but also of its friends . . . if ever there was a Liberalism of good faith, it is found in this country.'[1] On Catholic Emancipation, foreign policy, fiscal policy, administrative reform, it was increasingly difficult to distinguish liberal elements in the Cabinet from those in opposition; and the lines of division in the House of Commons had to be redrawn on almost every issue. If the Whigs were the safety-valve of the oligarchical constitution, the Administration (at least from 1822 to 1830) was not obviously in need of such a device; it supplied its own brand of liberal and reforming legislation. Moreover Liverpool, Canning, and Wellington were not so much heads of parties as heads of executives, facing the legislature rather than based upon it, and working unpopular measures through Parliament by varied appeals to different interests and elements. On the most difficult problem of all, Catholic Emancipation, there was a frank abandonment of executive guidance until 1829. Hence Canning was able to take over with a partial reconstruction of the Cabinet and a partial amalgamation with the Whigs; and the proclaimed intention of Peel and Wellington in 1828 was to reconstruct the old Liverpool 'party'. Wellington's Ministry fell, perhaps needlessly, certainly wantonly, in 1830; but the Duke's essentially coalition Government of 1828 was merely replaced by Grey's coalition Government of 1830.

Grey's courageous decision to bring forward an extreme and

[1] Esterhazy to Metternich, quoted by C. Webster, *Foreign Policy of Castlereagh 1815–22* (1925), pp. 22–23.

controversial Reform measure in 1831 was a landmark in English political history and is sometimes taken as the starting point of a new party system. In a broad chronological sense there is meaning in this, but the exact meaning requires some definition. The crisis was not a party crisis. Party is not in any case the most illuminating method of analysing pre-1830 politics; but the crisis involved among other things the swamping of the House of Commons as an institution by a great weight of public opinion. This opinion affected the traditional political classes and to some extent the traditional modes of influence and control, once Grey had produced his Bill and the cards were on the table. It was not to be expected that politicians would stand idly by when policy, office, and seats were in question. Yet there was much more to the crisis of 1831–2 than a change of attitude by any segment of the ruling classes. It was also a national crisis which affected the temper and composition of the House of Commons as it had not been affected for a long time. In particular the dissolution of 1831 was an appeal by the executive over the heads of the legislature to the electorate and to an even wider and more influential if more shapeless 'public opinion' which could work on and through the electorate and those who had means of influencing the electoral system.

In 1829 over Catholic Emancipation Peel had declared that he would look not to public opinion but to the legislature; Parliament alone would be his arbiter.[1] That was not the line taken by Grey: hence Peel's anger and despair in April 1831. Parliament in 1829 passed Catholic Emancipation when it must always remain doubtful whether the country would have done so; in 1831 the country carried the Reform Bill against a Parliament which had rejected it. Grey in a sense broke the rules of the parliamentary game and by breaking them ensured that the Cabinet would have its way. But the result was if anything an even greater weakening of party and executive influence.[2]

---

[1] *Mr. Secretary Peel*, p. 571.

[2] To Peel in 1833 it seemed as though in retrospect the 1820's had been a period of much more closely marked party differences, at least as far as Parliament was concerned. 'The great change that had recently taken place in the constitution of the House', he told the Commons at the start of the first session of the reformed Parliament, 'justified and required from public men a different course of action. Formerly there were two great parties in the state, each confident in the justice

If the Government seemed in control of the House of Commons in 1831–2, it was because of the Reform issue, and only on the Reform issue. Althorp's first Budget of 1831 was mangled out of recognition, and at the height of the controversy over the third Reform Bill in 1832 the Government was brought within 24 votes of defeat on the Russian loan issue. It was probably only fear of a Government resignation which produced even that narrow majority. Lord Grey's tart comment that members cared only for Reform and not for the Administration[1] had more than a little justification. The general election of 1832, the first under the new system, produced a House of Commons no more amenable to party or executive influence than that of 1831. It was only manageable because of two factors: the widespread desire for further changes, for which the Reform Act seemed the foundation-charter and the Whigs the honorary trustees; and a sense of responsibility among the leading men in opposition who had more in common with the Government than the wild men on the back benches.[2]

The year 1832 was the point of origin for a new party system in the sense of a redefinition of party.[3] It was not an immedi-

of its own views, each prepared to undertake the government upon the principles which it espoused. . . . He doubted whether the old system of party tactics were applicable to the present state of things.' The significance of this comment, however, relates more to the state of the legislature in 1833 than in the previous decade (*Speeches*, ii. 612, 7 Feb. 1833).

[1] Le Marchant, *Althorp*, p. 392; Aspinall, *Three Early Nineteenth Century Diaries*, p. 197.

[2] Cf. Peel, in his speech on the Address in Feb. 1835, in which he referred to 'the assumption that the House of Commons, since the passing of the Reform Bill, has been divided into two parties—the advocates and the opponents of the reforming government. A reference to facts will show that such has not been the case; but, on the contrary, that I, an anti-reformer, so far as the constitution of the House of Commons is concerned, have been the supporter of the government, and that it is the reformers themselves who have opposed them'. He listed the occasions on which he had supported the Ministers since 1833: O'Connell's amendment to the Address; Disturbances (Ireland) Bill; Attwood's motion on general distress; Harvey's motion on publication of division lists; Grote's motion on the ballot; Rippon's motion for exclusion of bishops from the Upper House; repeal of the malt tax; Corn Laws; pecuniary relief to Irish clergy; Tennyson's motion for repeal of the Septennial Act; Harvey's motion on the pension list; Ingilby's motion for reduction of the malt tax; Buckingham's on impressment; Hume's on corn laws; Althorp's proposal for Church rates; O'Connell's motion for repeal of the Union (*Speeches*, iii. 12, 24 Feb. 1835).

[3] Cf. Ellenborough's letter to Hardinge (30 Aug. 1830) even before the collapse of the Wellington Ministry, in which he argued against the admittance of men who would destroy its unity. 'The question of Reform could not be made an open

ately complete or universally satisfactory redefinition; it would have been odd had it been. There were several secessions and regroupings to mark the political uneasiness of the first twenty years of the reformed era: the Stanleyite defection from the Whigs in 1834; the splitting of the Conservative party in 1846; the Aberdeen coalition in 1852; besides many unnoticed shifts and modifications by obscurer politicians during these years. Yet substantially the foundations for the Victorian two-party system were laid by the divisions of politicians into Reformers and Conservatives over the Bill of 1831. Nevertheless, the reconstruction of parties came about not so much over the Reform Bill itself as over the significance of Reform in terms of subsequent policy. It dates less from 1831–2 than from 1834–5, following two confused sessions in which party was at a discount in parliamentary politics. The reason for this is not hard to find. The initial effect of the Reform Act was to weaken party divisions because in a real sense that was what Reform was meant to do; and the characteristic Radical rejoicing in 1830–2 over the approaching demise of Whigs and Tories as political parties arose mainly from their wish to see them supplanted by some other form of political government. A regenerated electorate would return good men to the legislature, and a good legislature would instruct the executive on good measures. It was a naïve outlook but a popular one; and even the Whigs had to pay lip-service to it for a time. The pamphlet on *The Reform Ministry and the Reformed Parliament*, published as a symposium by the Whigs at the end of the 1833 session[1] in defence of their administrative record, referred to the change which had taken place in the constitution since the days when 'the House of Commons consisted of partisans, when every speech and vote was part of a system', and went on to declare that 'to get rid of this wretched

question. It was best for the country that parties should be decidedly separated. It might then choose which it preferred, and men would be obliged to take a side' (Ellenborough, *Political Diary* (1881), ii. 348).

[1] It was edited by D. Le Marchant with contributions from Stanley, Graham, Althorp, Palmerston, Drummond (Althorp's Private Secretary), Bellenden Ker (a barrister), Jeffrey, Kennedy, and Lefevre; the fifth edition was corrected by Brougham. The pamphlet, which appeared soon after the prorogation at the end of August, had considerable success, running through four editions in a fortnight. By 1834 it had reached a tenth edition and was translated into French and German. The quotations are from the 10th edn., p. 107 (see Le Marchant, *Althorp*, p. 476 n. and Aspinall, *Three Diaries*, pp. 369–70).

system was the great object of the Reform Bill, and it *has* been got rid of. A majority of the Members of the House of Commons are partisans not of the Ministry or of the Opposition, but of good government.'

Even on the Tory side of the House, there was a section of disgruntled country gentry who had detected in the Government's more liberal financial and fiscal policy during the 1820's, and above all in Catholic Emancipation, the sinister hand of executive and Treasury tyranny, and who wanted therefore a reformed ˏand independent legislature. Admittedly their thoughts ran on a legislature controlled by themselves and reform in a somewhat different manner than envisaged by Place, Hume, or Macaulay.[1] Even so, this element had not been without its successes in 1831. They had protested against the reduction in the representation of England and Wales and helped in securing an enlargement of the county representation as well as the enfranchisement of the tenant farmers. If the independent county members were not necessarily more independent after 1832, at least there were more of them to be independent; and the agitation against the Malt Tax demonstrated the existence of a sympathetic 'country party' grouping among the agriculturist back-benchers on both sides of the House.

In so far as unregenerate politicians began after the Reform Act to reconstruct a party system more formidable than any that had preceded it, it signified not merely a reaction to the inevitable confusions and weaknesses of 1830–4, but in a deeper sense a defeat for that species of old-fashioned political idealism which believed that, in an honest and representative legislative assembly, government could be conducted on a basis of public opinion.[2] The victory for the party system was, however,

---

[1] See, for example, the pamphlet on the *Alarming State of the Nation* by a Country Gentleman (1830) which, after rehearsing all the sins of the Administration since the passage of the Currency Act in 1819, called for a reform of the House of Commons, not on the Radical or Utilitarian model, but in such a way as to place the power of returning members exclusively in the hands of 'the *middle classes of society*; a *decided preponderance* being assigned to the interests of *agriculture* in the National Councils, over the interests of *manufactures and commerce*' (p. 65) by the simple expedient of creating twice as many county members as town, with a high property qualification for voters.

[2] Besides the more modern radical reformers, the old-fashioned squirearchy had an equally strong if less vociferous tradition of the personal independence of an M.P. Sir Thomas Acland, for example, in his parting address to his constituents

neither easy nor complete. The dilemma for the Whigs was how to transform a party of opinion into a party of administration. The dilemma for the Conservatives was how to attract public opinion without compromising their autonomy as potential Ministers of the Crown. Between 1832 and 1841 the Conservatives were a party of government adapting themselves to opposition; the Whigs a party of opposition adapting themselves to government. Both processes involved a strengthening of party discipline and organization, and inevitably therefore a good deal of uneasiness and friction. Ministers and followers alike chafed under a new relationship, unsweetened by the arts of eighteenth-century management, and soured by the necessities of nineteenth-century politics. There were protests against both the tyranny of leaders and the tyranny of party. Parliamentary majorities rose and fell like barometer readings indicating the degrees of popularity of individual measures. On one or two well-known occasions the House of Commons was forced to rescind its own votes: by Althorp in 1833 over the reduction of the malt duty, by Peel in 1844, in even less palatable fashion, over the factory Bill and the sugar duties. The problem of indiscipline was most apparent when a party was in power; but there were difficulties at all times. Leaders of a party in office had to take national responsibilities as Ministers which were not always appreciated by their rank and file. The leaders of a party in opposition lacked the ultimate sanction of resignation or dissolution which fenced in the discipline of the Government side of the House. Quite apart from the self-styled independent members, a stubborn tradition of personal political independence lingered on among politicians at all levels. Ministers and followers alike were apt to claim the right of individual judgement and to follow their conscience, their interest, or their responsibilities. Moreover, the argument cut both ways. A tightly disciplined and monolithic party would

in W. Somerset in 1847 (he resigned rather than face a contest with two Protectionists) said that 'it does not accord either with my principles or my professions to give adherence to the extreme views of any party or blindly to follow any political leader. The great ends of all government are paramount to the immediate objects of party combination however important, and public men who steadily pursue these ends with a single eye to the good of the country will sooner or later be justified by its good sense and right feeling' (*Life of Acland*, pp. 104–5). Cobden and Bright could have subscribed to every word of this.

have been regarded as an intolerable servitude by both leaders and led; and claims by the rank and file for a measure of latitude also justified a similar latitude by leaders whether in or out of office. For both, the ramshackle electoral structure left by the Reform Act, despite the novel forms of central and constituency party organization improvised since 1830, made possible a considerable freedom of behaviour.

Yet it would be a mistake to lay the emphasis on the laxity and indiscipline of party life, and to conclude sceptically that this period did not see in any real sense the emergence of a modern party system: that is to say, a body of politicians with coherent organization and a rudimentary philosophy of action, who provided the legislative foundations either for a Ministry or for an Opposition aiming at its replacement. Indeed, the late thirties and forties are remarkable for some highly modern statements by professional politicians on the function of party. H. L. Bulwer could write in 1836 of 'times like the present, when two parties, professing two perfectly distinct creeds, are struggling for power'.[1] Graham observed to Peel in 1839 that 'the constant legitimate object of an Opposition is the overthrow of an Administration which they consider bad, and hope to replace by a better';[2] and even the detached and mild Aberdeen, in explaining Peel's anomalous position in Parliament to the Queen in 1847, expressed the view that 'the only permanent bond of Party, according to my notions, was the possession of office, or the pursuit of it', and since neither was the case with Peel, even though some individuals regulated their conduct by his example, this 'would not constitute what is meant by a Party, as there could be no permanent union, or concert, or any personal objects in view'.[3] In 1851, a year not conspicuous for tight party divisions, the intellectual Whig G. C. Lewis confessed that 'my attachment to party is the result more of reason than of feeling. I believe it to be the only means of government

[1] In his pamphlet, *The Lords, the Government and the Country*, p. 87.

[2] Parker, *Peel*, ii. 421. Cf. his remark to Stanley the same year: 'The possession of power in our popular form of government is the sole object of political warfare' (Parker, *Graham*, i. 289).

[3] Add. MS. 40455, f. 442 (Aberdeen to Peel, 18 Sept. 1847, giving an account of his conversation with Victoria). Peel himself had written to Goulburn the previous year that 'competition for power and the determination to take every legitimate advantage of your opponents in possession of it, are the indispensable cement of a compact and growing party' (Goulburn MS. 20 Dec. 1846).

in our political system and it is impossible for a party to continue if everybody insists on his opinion to its full extent'.[1]

This was not idle theorizing. Politicians talked in this way because they had grown accustomed to the use and necessity of party affiliations. In 1837, for example, Raikes noted that eloquence in the House of Commons had little influence on divisions. 'Party influence is so defined that there are few, if any, floating voters who are sufficiently independent or unprejudiced to be gained by any sudden convictions; so decidedly are the minds of all made up on the subject, before the discussion takes place.'[2] The party calculations of strength indicate the truth of this observation. Russell told the Queen that the result of the 1837 election was Ministerialists 340: Opposition 313: doubtful 5. Greville's analysis of the House in February 1839 was Government 267, Radicals 66, doubtful 5, Conservatives 315, with 4 vacancies.[3] The figures supplied to Peel by his Whips at the start of the 1840 session were: Ministerialists 316, Opposition 317, doubtful 8, Radicals 8, and 8 vacancies.[4] The striking feature of all these calculations is the small number of doubtful, that is to say, genuinely non-party or independent members. One mark of the increasing hold of party allegiance was that it was becoming more difficult for a prominent politician to cross the House. Stanley and his group of dissentient Whigs refused to join a Conservative Ministry in 1834;[5] and though they consulted with Peel over parliamentary tactics as early as 1836,

[1] Graham MS. (to Graham, 27 Jan. 1851).

[2] *Journal of T. Raikes* (1858), iii. 207.

[3] *Greville*, 10 Feb. 1839; Walpole, *Russell*, i. 295 n.

[4] Apsley House MS. (Peel to Wellington, 5 Jan. 1840). The doubtful were Sir G. Heathcote, G. J. Heathcote, J. Bennett, W. F. Chetwynd, H. D. Goring, R. Ingham, Sir R. Howard, C. B. Wall. All of these except the last are listed by Dod as Liberal at this date. But the two Heathcotes and Howard were absent from the no-confidence division of June 1841 and Bennett voted against the Government, while Ingham voted against his party on the sugar resolution in May. G. J. Heathcote was elected as a Liberal in 1841, as a Protectionist in 1847 and 1852; Bennett as a Conservative in 1841 and a Protectionist in 1847. Wall, on the other hand was listed by Dod as a Conservative in 1837, and as a Liberal-Conservative in 1847 and 1852; but he voted with the Ministers in 1841 both on sugar and no confidence. See also Appendixes A and B.

[5] 'The sudden conversion of long political opposition into the most intimate alliance—no general coincidence of principle, except upon one point, being proved to exist between us—would shock public opinion, would be ruinous to my own character, and injurious to the Government which you seek to form.' (Stanley to Peel, 11 Dec. 1834, Parker, *Peel*, ii. 258.)

it was not until the following year that Graham accepted an invitation to Drayton or Stanley attended a party meeting at Peel's house in London; not until the very end of 1840, 'after some years of mutual probation', as Stanley expressed it to Graham,[1] that the two men decided to join the Carlton Club. Similarly, one of the main causes of the bitterness of the Conservative split in 1846 was the fact that a real party and not merely a heterogeneous collection of groups was being disrupted; and one of the reasons why the Peelites floated in a political limbo for six years after the break-up over the Corn Laws was the inherent psychological difficulty of uniting with their former opponents, however much they agreed on policy. As one of their lesser members, Lord St. Germans, wrote to Russell in 1847, when refusing the presidency of the Poor Law Commission, 'I will moreover acknowledge that I am reluctant to separate myself even in appearance from those with whom I was officially connected and to whom I am bound by the ties of personal friendship as well as those of political alliance.'[2] These close party ties and equally bitter party animosities, when persisting over years of parliamentary life, produced deep divisions between politicians which it was not easy to overcome.[3] 'The great fault of the present time', Melbourne ruefully remarked in 1835, 'is that men hate each other so damnably.'[4]

But the hatreds, suspicion, and habitual depreciation of each

[1] Stanley told Graham that 'if his accession to the Carleton would reconcile or prevent differences, the Time is in his opinion come, when our junction is a matter of course; for after some years of mutual probation, it is more natural than otherwise that we should be members than we should not' (Add. MS. 40416, f. 185, Graham to Bonham, 27 Dec. 1840).

[2] Russell MS., 2 Oct. 1847, P.R.O. 30/22/6).

[3] 'The contact of party produces a warmth of feeling towards those who sit around us, while the eye is a cold and jealous scrutiniser of those that are opposite us' (*Croker Papers*, ii. 352, Croker to Brougham, 1839).

[4] Torrens, *Melbourne*, p. 349. There was a neat illustration of the psychological effect of past party differences in 1852 when Gladstone observed to Aberdeen that in 1835 the Whigs had run Peel to ground over the appropriation clause, worked it as long as it suited them, and then cast it to the winds. Russell retorted to Aberdeen that he might as well say that in 1841 the Conservatives had held the Government up to odium for not giving sufficient protection to agriculture, worked the Corn Law as long as it suited them, and then turned round and cast it to the winds. He added also that there was no chance of agreement with men who entertained such notions of the Whigs. (Russell MS., Russell to Aberdeen, 13 Aug. 1852, P.R.O. 30/22/10.)

other's character and motives which affected even the best men on both sides, arose because politics was not a mere game of ins and outs but about serious issues. The mechanism of party warfare elaborated in the 1830's rested on real differences of ideas, interests, and social composition. The refined mathematical analysis to which the division lists of the 1841–7 House of Commons have been subjected by an American scholar[1] has tended to confirm what a common-sense empirical judgement might suggest: first, that behind the broad scale of differences on various issues from Chartism to the import of foreign cattle there was an interconnexion in men's minds on many important topics and not a mere random voting according to personal taste, economic interest, or constituency pressure; and secondly that the two great political parties fitted into this general pattern. They fitted into it in the sense not that all voting was on strict party lines, but that the two main parties did in fact occupy broadly different, if overlapping, territories in the political field; that is to say, they stood for something different in politics, even though there were cleavages of opinion on specific issues within each party and no rigid party discipline in voting. What has helped to obscure this central feature is that Parliament also dealt with matters, notably social legislation, on which there were no clear party distinctions. *Laisser-faire* versus State intervention was not a dividing line between Liberal and Conservative, however much individuals might differ on the application of these principles. The stereotype of Conservatives as the party of the landed interest and Protection, as against the Liberal party of industrialism and Free Trade, is capable of such limited application as to be more misleading than illuminating; and over social welfare, and the 'Condition of England' problem, party affiliations are almost undetectable. When the plight of the poor and defenceless came under the attention of the legislature, the general attitude of the politicians was pragmatic and undoctrinaire, and their solutions, therefore, piecemeal and experimental improvisations. But social legislation was not the primary issue of contemporary politics, and it is only retrospective interest that makes it so. 'The central issue

[1] Professor W. O. Aydelotte of Iowa State University, on whose paper 'Voting Patterns in the British House of Commons in the 1840's' this paragraph is primarily based. See Appendix C.

of politics', observes Professor Aydelotte, 'was not the welfare of the poor but the divergent interests of the rich.'

II

Of the two great parties on the morrow of the Reform Act the Conservatives had politically the more formidable, although ideologically perhaps the simpler task; certainly the more clear-cut and intelligible. They stood in the first place for strong executive government as the rock on which all else must stand —'that restraint', as Peel expressed it to Croker as early as 1831, 'which is indispensable to the existence not of this or that, but of all Government'. Opposition for its own sake therefore was not only in certain circumstances dangerous, but a fundamental inconsistency; and the excesses of the Opposition Tory Press in 1833 evoked the private comment of Lord Melville that 'those Doctrines and anti-governmental principles (I use the word advisedly as opposed to anti-administration) are much more at variance with our sound principles than with those of our Whig ministers'.[1] This feature of Conservatism was the burden of Peel's first major speech to the reformed House of Commons;[2] it was referred to in the Tamworth Manifesto; and again in Peel's important party speech at Merchant Taylors Hall in 1838. It was an appeal which was profoundly effective not only in the legislature in the confused years after 1832, but in the country at large in the years of Chartist discontent.[3] In a society

[1] See my article on 'Peel and the Party System' in *Trans. R. Hist. Soc.* 5 Ser., vol. 1, pp. 52–54, for a discussion of this aspect of Peelite Conservatism.

[2] 'It was his duty to support the Crown in relation to the measures for Ireland, and the support he gave was dictated by principles perfectly independent and disinterested. He had no other views than to preserve law, order, property and morality. . . . He saw principles in operation, the prevalence of which he dreaded as fatal to the well-being of society; and whenever the king's government should evince a disposition to resist those principles, they should have his support' (*Speeches*, ii. 612, 7 Feb. 1833).

[3] Arbuthnot in Apr. 1839 quoted his son as saying that the great manufacturers in Manchester and other large towns were complaining of Chartism—'the general cry is for a strong Government and those who were loudest for Reform are now dreadfully alarmed' (Add. MS. 40341, f. 72). For the cool attitude of the *Manchester Guardian* towards further Corn Law agitation after Peel's reform of 1842 and its argument that agitation would only damage trade and industry, see Read, *Press and People*, pp. 148–50. Haydon the painter was probably not alone in his reflection (despite his liberal view in politics) during the crisis of Dec.

where popular agitation ran high and the machinery of public order was fragile, it had a potent influence. Indeed, order and authority was the great taproot of Conservatism which preceded the growth of the visible parliamentary party. In the disturbances of the Reform crisis men were talking about the conservative party in the State when it is clear that they did not mean a political parliamentary party. Professor Wilson's reference, for example, at the constitutional meeting at Edinburgh in November 1831, to 'the great Conservative party' which rallied round George III at the time of the French Revolution indicated something of the historical soil in which this organic conservatism was rooted.[1]

But authority was not only for its own sake; it was also to preserve the traditional forms of constitution—the Church, the monarchy, and the House of Lords. It was this and not any particular fiscal or administrative programme which was the essence of the great Conservative Party which came into power in 1841 and split—not over strategy but over tactics—in 1846. It was a constitutional and religious, not a social and economic party. 'The Conservative Party', wrote *Blackwood's Magazine*, the outstanding organ of independent Toryism, in 1837,[2] 'are more firmly united on every great constitutional principle, on every true party question, than any similar body of men have ever been before. They are resolved to oppose any invasion of the privileges or property of the Protestant Establishment throughout the three kingdoms; they are resolved to maintain the independence of the House of Lords, and to resist further alteration in the constitution of the House of Commons; they are resolved to preserve the full prerogative of the Crown and

1845. 'What a curious thing it is, I never feel comfortable with Sir Robert & the Duke out!' (*Diary of B. R. Haydon*, ed. Pope, v. 501.)

[1] *Report of the Speeches at the Constitutional Meeting in the George St. Assembly Rooms, Edinburgh, on Monday, 28 November, 1831* (Edinburgh 1831). The anonymous introduction to the pamphlet declared outright that 'the conservative portion of the state unites in its ranks men of all parties and of all political opinions'.

[2] In an article on 'The Elections', Sept. 1837 (vol. 42, p. 304). For early examples of the use of the term 'Conservative', see Halévy, *History of the English People 1830–41* (1927), p. 68 n. It was, however, not Croker who used the expression 'Conservative Party' in the *Quarterly Review* of Jan. 1830, but probably either Fullerton or Miller, the regular writers of political articles in the *Review* at this time. Croker did not begin to write again for the *Quarterly*, after the lapse of five years, till July 1831 (M. F. Brightfield, *J. W. Croker* (1940), p. 403).

the integrity of the Empire.' The views of the two Conservative
party leaders coincided exactly with this general statement. 'It
is very desirable that the public should understand clearly what
the difference of opinion between the two parties is', wrote
Wellington succinctly to Peel in 1837, 'that you are determined to uphold the Protestant religion, the Church of England
in Ireland as well as in England; that you are determined to
maintain the independence of a House of Lords.'[1] A year later,
in his Merchant Taylors Hall speech, Peel gave the fullest
public definition of Conservatism in his career to a crowded
and enthusiastic party audience of 315 Conservative M.P.s.[2]
'If you ask me what I mean by Conservative principles, I shall,
as we have been so often taunted with the use of vague generali-
ties, in conclusion briefly state the meaning I attach to them.'
He listed them in order: the maintenance of the prerogative of
the Crown and the just constitutional powers of King, Lords,
and Commons; that along with perfect equality of civil rights
'there shall always be in this country an established religion,
fostered and encouraged by the State; and that that established
religion shall maintain the doctrines of the Protestant reformed
faith'; and that the alienation of Church property from spiritual
uses would be resisted. Finally, 'by Conservative principles we
mean the maintenance of our settled institutions in Church and
State and also the preservation and defence of that combination
of laws, of institutions, of usages, of habits and of manners which
has contributed to mould and form the character of Englishmen'. All the succeeding speakers, including Stanley and
Graham, followed the same line. Stanley in fact defined the
essence of Conservatism as the 'preservation of the British Constitution in Church and State'. Corn Laws and Protection to
Agriculture had no place on this level of party principle; and
indeed, except for a passing observation by Peel that the Conservatives had come to the rescue of the Government in opposing their repeal, the Corn Laws were not even mentioned. This
silence was not felt as an omission. Francis Egerton, in proposing
the health of the chairman, the great agricultural champion
Lord Chandos himself, observed that 'there was not any topic

---

[1] Add. MS. 40310, f. 168, quoted Parker, *Peel*, ii. 342 (23 Mar. 1837).
[2] *Authentic Report of the Conservative Festival at Merchant Tailor's Hall*, London
(12 May 1838), published by the Conservative Journal Office, London.

connected with the policy of the country that had not been touched upon'.[1] Time and disruption did not alter this fundamental concept. 'In the main it is undoubted that the Whig Governments fell, and the Conservative party was formed,' wrote Stanley to Croker in 1847, 'upon questions affecting the maintenance of the Established Church, and the integrity of the institutions of the country, the House of Lords included.'[2] Any discussion of the 'betrayal' of the party in 1846 must start from this fact.

The social elements to which this religious and constitutional conservatism could look for support scarcely need rehearsing: wealth and property, the Church, most landowners, many of the great manufacturing and financial classes, the professions, the universities, the respectable and the genteel—'the best portion', as Graham in his usual florid style once described them, 'of the entire Community which claims to itself a great preponderance of property, of learning, of decent manners, and of pure religion; and which, by the rejection of all former ties and party distinction, selects these very Elements, as the vital Principle, the distinguishing Mark, the avowed Bond of their Present Union'.[3] Conservatism was wider than the landed interest, and in the process of gathering strength during the 1830's tapped almost unsuspected sources of social recruitment.

---

[1] For a more literary contemporary definition of Conservatism, see Walsh, *Chapters of Contemporary History*, pp. 77–88. 'A Conservative is a man attached upon principle, to the English Constitution, to the Established Church, to our mixed institutions.' If Whigs of the old school could be similarly described, 'there is another characteristic—a Conservative is one who, having this loyalty to the Constitution, believes it is threatened with subversion by the encroachments of democracy, and is prepared to defend it against that danger. The Conservative party, therefore, includes all those shades and degrees of political opinion, from the disciple of moderate Whig principles to the most devoted champion of ancient usages, who agree in these two points—attachment to King, Lords, Commons, Church and State, and a belief that there is a pressing danger of these institutions being overborne by the weight of the Democracy.' Finally, 'the Conservative Party is not identical with the Tory party' because it did not oppose all innovation in principle nor entertain an 'illiberal and contracted view of politics'.

[2] *Croker Papers*, iii. 113.

[3] Add. MS. 40318, f. 106 (to Peel, 15 Nov. 1837). For a similar but more succinct analysis, cf. Wellington: 'The great landed, commercial, and manufacturing and funded proprietors of the country; the Church almost to a man, the Universities, the great majority of the learned professions in the three kingdoms, and of the Professors of Arts and Sciences, of the Corporations of the Empire etc.' (*Croker Papers*, ii. 217).

After his resignation in 1835, for example, Peel received an address of confidence from some 1,100 solicitors resident in the metropolis. He told Croker that he did not know there were so many, still less that they were nearly unanimous in Conservative principles.[1] When this strength was translated into electoral terms, two other aspects were noticeable. The Conservative party was in the first place the party of England. As Campbell the Scots lawyer put it in 1841, 'the English nation is determinedly Tory: not only the Peerage, the Church and the land are Tory, but commercial and professional men think it more genteel and fashionable to take the Tory side and to such an immense body of property and influence there is no counterbalance'.[2] By the year of Victoria's accession the Conservative Opposition, as their party managers were proud to boast, were already in possession of a distinct majority of the English seats. Bonham calculated that in England and Wales the distribution was Conservative 264, Ministerial 232. Hardinge reported a Conservative majority of 30 in the English seats; in Scotland a Ministerial majority of 10; for Great Britain as a whole, therefore, a Conservative majority of 20, which the Irish representation turned into a minority of 20–25.[3] It was a significant religious as well as regional party grouping.

Secondly, it was broadly speaking the party of the counties and the smaller boroughs, as opposed to the industrial areas and the large towns.[4] Any generalization about the politics of the towns between the first and second Reform Acts needs caution. The results of parliamentary contests in the boroughs

[1] *Croker Papers*, ii. p. 273. The previous autumn, on an unheralded visit to Blackburn to look at his estate there, Peel found himself unexpectedly the object of much popular interest and applause, of a degree and from quarters which surprised him. 'The professional men', he told Goulburn, 'and chief shopkeepers were Conservatives' (Parker, *Peel*, ii. 250).

[2] He went on to say that 'the Dissenters are completely cowed, and though merchants and manufacturers privately disapprove of the Corn Laws, they quietly submit' (*Life*, ii. 161–2, 13 Nov. 1841).

[3] Graham MS., Peel to Graham, 11 Aug.; Hardinge to Graham, 13 Aug. 1837. The final figures in Peel's possession at the end of August indicated a Conservative gain of 24 in England and Wales (almost entirely in the counties); no change in Scotland; a loss of 9 in Ireland. The final position was therefore: Ministerial 341, Conservatives 317, leaving the Government a majority of 23 together with the Speaker (Add. MS. 43061, f. 205, Peel to Aberdeen, 20 Aug. 1837).

[4] An analysis of the largest and smallest boroughs in terms of electorate bears out this generalization. Taking the categories supplied in 1834 (*Parl. Papers* ix. 590 seq.) on the basis of the first registration after the Reform Act, and the party

were notoriously difficult to forecast and every general election produced its crop of unexpected failures and successes. Yet even with all the cross-currents at work, a certain pattern is visible. According to a list drawn up for Peel after the general election of 1841, which represented the high-water mark of Conservative strength during this period, the party had gained only 9 and lost 11 in towns with a population over 30,000; gained 6 and lost 3 in towns with a population over 20,000; gained 11 and lost 5 in the towns over 10,000: a net gain of only 7 seats, or a turnover of 14 votes in a division.[1] The distinction between the towns is not of course clear-cut. In some of the larger towns it is possible to discern a tendency for more wealthy and settled urban communities like the City of London,[2] Westminster, Liverpool, Leeds, Hull, and Bristol, to return a Conservative candidate, even if accompanied by Liberals. The more suburban London constituencies, on the other hand—Marylebone, Tower Hamlets, Lambeth, Finsbury, and Greenwich—along with middle- and lower-class industrial centres like Birmingham, Manchester, Sheffield, Bury, Oldham, Rochdale, Salford, South Shields and Wolverhampton, were virtually impervious to Conservative efforts even in 1841. Unless the party had not

affiliations indicated by Dod, *Electoral Facts, 1832–53*, the results for the general election of 1841 are as follows:

Size of electorate	No. of boroughs in each category	M.P.s returned	
		Liberal	Conservative
Under 200	5	2	4
Under 300	26	16	21
Totals for small boroughs	31	18	25
Over 1,000	32	34	29
Over 2,000	28	43	15
Totals for large boroughs	60	77	44

The actual lists of these boroughs are given in my *Politics in the Age of Peel* (1953), pp. 75–76. I have omitted East Retford, Aylesbury, Shoreham, and Cricklade, which were pre-1832 corrupt boroughs enlarged to form semi-rural areas.

[1] Add MS. 40485, ff. 322–4 (Bonham to Peel, 29 July 1841).

[2] The Conservative success in winning two of the four City seats, after an unbroken run of defeats at every general election since the Reform Act, was a feature of the 1841 results. Rous's victory at Westminster, another Liberal stronghold, was almost as significant.

only made but consolidated its inroads on the borough constituencies, however, the Conservative revival would have worn
a different look; and much of Peel's political effort was in
fact directed towards the Liberal-Conservative elements in
the towns. Without the 44 Conservative M.P.s returned for the
larger boroughs (with electorates of over 1,000), there would
have been no Peelite victory in 1841. Urban Conservatism was
necessary to give landed Toryism its parliamentary majority.

In terms of the specific party victory of 1841, however, the
outstanding feature was not the hard-won and limited gains
in the large boroughs, but the sweeping successes in the county
constituencies. Here there was a gain of 34 and a loss of only
5 seats; and of the lost 5, the only English constituency was
Rutland, which was hardly a county in the political sense. It
was this net gain of 29 county seats, a turnover of nearly 60
in a division, which provided the bulk of Peel's working majority
in the 1841 Parliament. It was decisive not only for the fate
of the Whigs, but for the future of the Conservative party,
that the triumph of 1841 was achieved not by massive gains in
the urban constituencies but by a continued reduction of the
remaining Whig strongholds in the English counties. In 1831
the reformers won all but 6 of the 82 county seats; in 1841,
of the 159 English and Welsh county seats, all but 23 were held
by the Conservatives. This striking success was not merely the
result of the 1841 Whig budgetary proposals. The Whigs had
been losing ground in the counties ever since 1832 and their
losses in the English counties in 1835 were heavier than in 1837
and 1841. Even before Russell announced his fixed duty scheme
for corn in 1841, his party was resigned to a continuation of their
decline in the counties.[1] It would be a distortion, therefore, to
regard the Conservative party as merely an alliance between an
intellectual Peelite minority on one hand and a Tory agricultural interest on the other, held together by the brittle bond
of agricultural protection. The Conservative revival after the
Reform Act started earliest and continued more effectively
in the counties because the gentry and the clergy provided
the natural social basis for the constitutional defences which the
Conservative party was designed to erect. It was only during the
later stages that the question of the Corn Laws came in as an

[1] See Appendix A,

important reinforcement to this existing electoral situation. Yet if the English counties were the natural home of Conservative feeling, it meant that the economic interests of the counties naturally took a place among the major national interests of their representatives. At the heart of this English and Anglican party was the land.

It was not solely, perhaps not primarily, an economic interest. Landed property had for centuries been the basis of the political and administrative structure of the State, and was surrounded by a nexus of traditional powers, privileges, patronage, and duties.[1] It was this which gave it a unique position among other species of property; though this in turn needed the buttress of the laws of inheritance and primogeniture to ensure the necessary permanence of estates and fixity of family tenure. Not land, but land in the possession of families, was the essence of 'the landed interest'. As yet it was relatively uncorroded by the attractions of other forms of wealth more fluid and less onerous because less responsible—even though as a purely economic asset land was not the most profitable investment. As late as 1885 Gladstone could write that,'I . . . regard it as a very high duty to labour for the conservation of estates, and the permanence of the families in possession of them, as a principal source of our social strength, and as a large part of true conservatism.'[2] Yet though the land was a unique form of property, it was still property and could not escape the economic interest. Here, it could be said, were the feet of clay of the Conservative party; but clay is a necessary ingredient in any durable party substance. Passion and interest count as much in politics as patriotism and intellect, because they are equally constant and equally powerful human factors. 'I am aware to what extent our Conservative party is a party pledged to the

[1] These considerations apply of course to the landed interest irrespective of party. It was a Whig, the descendant of a city merchant, who wrote to his son when entering Oxford in 1843: 'Your position is fixed—that of an English country gentleman; and it will be your business in life to do your duty in that state of life to which it has pleased God to call you. . . . Have the English country gentlemen, then, any business? To my mind no one more. All men are not fitted for the performance of all these duties, but it is in the discharge of some that men of property in this country do their duty to their God, benefit their country, and contribute to their own happiness. . . . I shall be as satisfied if you are a *worthy* country squire as if you were a leading Whig speaker' (B. Mallett, *Earl of Northbrook* (1908), p. 26, Sir Francis Baring to his son, Thomas George, later Earl of Northbrook).

[2] Morley, *Gladstone*, i. 258.

support of the land', wrote Lord Ashburton in 1841,[1] 'and that, that principle abandoned, the party is dissolved.' It was, in the conditions of the post-Reform era, a double-sided principle: positive as far as agricultural protection was concerned; negative as far as it represented a latent hostility to the other great interests in the country.

There was an element of what a Dissenting theologian might have called a 'particular' aristocratic and landed interest in the Conservative party, even if it did not involve all or the best of its members. C. P. Villiers, an aristocratic Radical, expressed the view to his brother in 1836 that

what keeps the aristocracy here in a constant fret is that, while they have been trained to the expectation of political power, independent of any qualification of merit or fitness for its exercise, the circumstances of the country have so entirely changed with the progress of civilisation, a constitution on such a system has become impossible, and they feel that they are already in this respect less fortunate than their ancestors.[2]

This was perhaps bitter and exaggerated; but it was not without some home truth. Graham told Greville in 1846, for example, that Stanley disliked the manufacturing interest and its progress in Lancashire and all round Knowsley, because it diminished his territorial power. Greville himself, in his obituary notice of Peel's career, wrote of the jealousy and fear with which the Conservative party regarded the middle classes—'those formidable masses, occupying the vast space between aristocracy and democracy'.[3] The naked class language of the Anti-Corn Law League did nothing to dispel this latent antagonism. Indeed, the numerous Agricultural Protection Societies which sprang up in the 1840's in direct answer to the attacks of the Leaguers further widened the gap between classes and interests, and provided a formidable and angry substratum of agricultural feeling to stiffen the ranks of their representatives in Parliament in 1846.

Yet even with class hostility set aside, it was natural for Tories like Croker to argue that it was 'the existence of a landed gentry, which has made England what she has been and is',

[1] Memorandum on the Corn Laws, Parker, *Peel*, ii. 507.
[2] Maxwell, *Clarendon*, i. 124–5 (to George Villiers, later 4th Earl of Clarendon).
[3] *Greville*, 2 Feb. 1846, 6 July 1850.

and fatally easy to proceed from there to the unproven corollary that Protection was necessary for the existence of that class, and that its abandonment would mean 'the overthrow of the existing social and political system of our country'.[1] Peel's disagreement was not with Croker's thesis but with his conclusion.

> I believe it to be of the utmost importance [he said when it was too late for his words to be any more than an expression of faith] that a territorial aristocracy should be maintained. I believe that in no country is it of more importance than in this, with its ancient constitution, ancient habits, and mixed form of government. I trust that a territorial aristocracy, with all its just influence and authority, will long be maintained. I believe such an aristocracy to be essential to the purposes of good government. The question only is—what, in a certain state of public opinion, and in a certain position of society, is the most effectual way of maintaining the legitimate influence and authority of a territorial aristocracy?[2]

This was the crux of the matter.

For the sake of the landed interest itself Conservatism as a national party could not take its stand on landed Toryism alone, whether that implied land as the only important national interest or Toryism in the sense impatiently defined by Goulburn in 1834 as 'deaf to all improvement which comprises change, however much on other grounds to be desired'.[3] Peel's work was meaningless if it did not stand for a widening of the party's social foundations and for a policy of action which would strengthen the old institutions of the country by means of controlled reform. The Tamworth Manifesto was a frank appeal to 'that class which is much less interested in the contentions of party, than in the maintenance of order and the cause of good government', and that this appeal necessarily involved a forward policy was clear, for example, to the young intellectuals of the party he was already beginning to gather round him. As Acland, an Oxford Double First and Fellow of All Souls, wrote to Gladstone, another Double First, in the same month, 'the only true conservative principle is destructive of real abuses, never sacrificing a jot of the institutions or laying the blame on them but on the abusers', and Gladstone in reply, in a burst of

---

[1] *Croker Papers*, iii. 13 (to Brougham, Feb. 1843).
[2] *Speeches*, iv. 684 (4 May 1846).
[3] Add. MS. 40333, f. 177 (in a letter to Peel, 8 Dec. 1834).

unusual brevity, spoke of 'the task of rescuing, rectifying and securing the institutions of the country'.[1] As for the land, Peel had already privately described to Croker the contention that 'the landed interest, as the most important, ought to be a favoured class, for the benefit of which the rest of the community may properly be taxed' as an 'invidious and startling argument'.[2] The Reform Bill debates had certainly raised the spectre of the field of coal arrayed against the field of corn, but Peel's approach to the mercantile and industrial interests —as befitted a politician in line of descent from Liverpool, Huskisson, and Pitt—was essentially conciliatory and comprehensive. He refused to accept that a collision between land and industry was either logically inevitable or politically desirable, any more than he could accept industry or the land as ends in themselves, distinct from the wider national community that embraced those and all other interests, including the labouring poor.[3]

III

These, however, were questions for the future. The immediate issue in 1833–4 was whether there could be a Conservative party at all in any proper political sense. The opposition to the Reform Bill in the two previous years had been divided, and if not leaderless, at least with no single leader. The opening of the first reformed Parliament saw little improvement. Though there was a move to elect Peel as leader of the Conservative Opposition, it broke down on the unwillingness of malcontents like Knatchbull and Vyvyan to accept unity under his leader-

[1] *Life of Acland*, pp. 75–76. It was a characteristic intellectual Peelite reaction that Acland, when rejected in 1847 by W. Somerset for supporting repeal of the Corn Laws, took a course of agricultural chemistry at King's College, London, won a prize from the Royal Agricultural Society with an essay on Somerset agriculture, and played a leading part in the revival of the Bath and West Agricultural Show (ibid., pp. 140–3).

[2] *Croker Papers*, ii. 222 (Peel to Croker, 24 Mar. 1834, with reference to the recent debate on the Corn Laws in the House of Commons).

[3] Cf. his speech of 4 May 1846. 'I said long ago, that I thought agricultural prosperity was interwoven with manufacturing prosperity; and depended more on it than on the Corn Laws. . . . I believe that it is for the interest of the agriculturalist that you should lay a permanent foundation of manufacturing prosperity; and as your land is necessarily limited in quantity, as your population is increasing, as your wealth is increasing, that the true interests of land are co-existent with the manufacturing and commercial prosperity. . . . I believe the interests, direct and indirect, of the manufacturing and agricultural classes to be the same' (*Speeches*, iv. 685).

ship without stipulations as to men and measures which Peel at least regarded as ludicrous. If he was by far the outstanding politician on the Conservative benches in the first two sessions of the new Parliament, he was not the head of a party. There was no acknowledged head and no real party. Althorp did not think it impossible that Manners Sutton would be Prime Minister if a Conservative Government had been formed in 1833[1] and he was still being tipped in club gossip as a candidate for that post in the autumn of the following year.[2]

It was this which made the importance of 1834. It gave Peel, first, authority as the chosen Minister of the Crown. If anyone made Peel the leader of the Conservative party it was William IV. Secondly, it gave him as head of the Government a platform for his views. He said virtually nothing that was new in the Tamworth Manifesto; but though he had said it before, the difference was that he was now saying it as Prime Minister. What matters in politics is often less what is said than who says it. The more novel and interesting feature was his preoccupation with public opinion and his clear wish to destroy the Wellingtonian image of the party, deriving from November 1830 and unavoidably renewed by Peel's absence in Italy when the Ministry was formed. He was not alone in this. Indeed, he was pressed from several quarters to make some gesture which would reassure the country that a Conservative Ministry in 1834 would not be merely resurrected Wellingtonianism. Hence his public offer of temperate review and reform, his conciliatory approach to Dissenters, his attempt to bring in Stanley and Graham, and the Tamworth document itself—in form an address to his constituents, in reality a manifesto to the country.[3] His appeal was to those who regarded the Reform Act as a proper but conclusive work of organic constitutional change; but it would be a mistake to regard as the primary purpose of the Manifesto his need to announce his acceptance of the Reform Act. He had done that already in 1833.[4] The document was primarily

---

[1] Le Marchant, *Althorp*, p. 474.

[2] Lord Wharncliffe, for instance, heard rumours in his club in Nov. that if the Government resigned, the King would send for the Speaker; and he thought it not unlikely (*Lady Wharncliffe and Her Family*, ii. 207).

[3] The word 'Manifesto' is a contemporary one and was used by Peel himself to describe his address.

[4] For example, in his speech on the Address, 7 Feb. 1833. 'The King's government

an election address, arising not so much from the events of 1832 as from those of November 1834. 'My address to Tamworth', he wrote to Croker in criticism of a draft article for the *Quarterly Review* in January 1835, 'is . . . too much referred to necessities imposed by the Reform Bill. I think the necessities rather arose from the abruptness of the change in the Government, and to say the truth, from the policy of aiding our friends at the election.' What he wanted was 'the adhesion of moderate men, not professing adherence to our politics'.[1]

But for the parliamentary party, too, the Hundred Days of 1834–5 worked a revolution. Office heightened their morale and improved their discipline. Over Chandos's disruptive Malt Tax motion in March 1835, for instance, there was a large party meeting called by Peel and attended by some 200 M.P.s, at which leading agriculturist members declared that they would throw over their pledges and disappoint their constituents rather than risk the existence of the Government.[2] Outside Westminster the glimpse of power and the heartening successes at the elections gave a powerful stimulus to those unorganized forces in the country which had been disturbed by developments in politics in the previous two years. From this point indeed they were increasingly organized for electoral purposes. The main wave of Conservative and Constitutional Associations in the constituencies, far more important electorally than the foundation of the Carlton in 1832, dates from the winter of 1834–5. The achievement of winning a hundred or so seats in the general election was due primarily perhaps to a natural reaction from the temporary Reform excitement which had conditioned the election of 1832; but from 1835 the Conservative party grew steadily as a national movement, organized as

had abstained from all unseemly triumph in the king's speech respecting the measure of reform. He would profit by their example, and would say nothing upon that head; but consider that question as finally and irrevocably disposed of. He was now determined to look forward to the future alone, and, considering the constitution as it existed, to take his stand on main and essential matters.' He also said in the same speech, 'he was for reforming every institution that really required reform; but he was for doing it gradually, dispassionately, and deliberately, in order that reform might be lasting' (*Speeches*, ii. 613).

[1] *Croker Papers*, ii. 256–7.

[2] A hundred of them went off afterwards to form a deputation to ask Chandos not to persist with his motion (Ellenborough Diary, 7 Mar. 1835, P.R.O. 30/12/28/5). See also *Croker Papers*, ii. 267 for an account of the meeting.

no political party had ever been organized before for the purpose of winning parliamentary elections. The peculiarities of
the reformed electoral structure made a landslide impossible,
but the new techniques of party organization provided a direction and a solidity which gave promise of not too remote
victory.

The emergence of a recognizable party Opposition made
possible a recognizable Opposition policy: initially, and until
1840, what Graham called the 'Fabian policy' of a waiting and
elastic defence on behalf of the 'establishment' both lay and
ecclesiastical. After 1834 regular party consultations, especially
of the inner conclave of leaders in both Houses, discussions by
groups of leading debaters, and on occasions general party
meetings, brought greater co-ordination to tactics and a growing sense of unity. It was not done without friction and sometimes angry feelings—between those who would compromise
and those who would resist; those in favour of controlled and
limited change and those against any change at all which
affected their interests; between the majority in the House of
Lords and the minority in the House of Commons. The conflicts themselves indicated the diversification of thought and
temper within the party. The task was not easy, as Peel put it
afterwards,

to conciliate and keep together some of the authors and chief
advocates of the Reform Bill, and some of its most determined and
unforgiving opponents; so to regulate the course of debate that it
should not revive the half-extinguished animosities that the years
1829 and 1830—the Catholic Question and Reform—had kindled;
to conduct an Opposition on Conservative principles—almost a
contradiction in terms; for the recourse to faction, or a temporary
alliance with extreme opinions for the purpose of faction, is not
reconcilable with *Conservative* Opposition.[1]

Yet it was done and whenever the opportunity offered (which
was rare enough in those days of inhibited oligarchical politics),
Peel continued to emphasize to a wider public his conception
of the new Conservatism. It was in this fashion, rather than in
the details of party management, that his capacity for party

---

[1] Parker, *Peel*, ii. 338 (Memorandum of July 1837 on discussions during the
session on the course to be pursued in the House of Lords with reference to the
Irish Municipal Bill).

leadership was shown. His main motive, for example, in accepting the Rectorship of Glasgow University in 1837 (he told
Graham) was the 'state of public affairs and the necessity of
unremitting exertion on this behalf of all who wish to preserve
a National Church, and the Constitution of their country'.[1]
He declined an invitation to talk to the High Tories of Edinburgh, and reserved his main effort not for the university
students—to whom he delivered a rather stereotyped address
on the virtues of a classical education and the opportunities
open to talents and industriousness—but for the great civic
banquet at Glasgow, where for some time there had been an
alliance between the Tories and Right-wing Whigs. There, to
an audience of over 3,000, he made an impressive appeal for
widening the foundations on which the defence of the constitution and of the religious establishments of the kingdom must
rest, and for the construction on that foundation of an active
Conservative Government 'animating industry, encouraging
production, rewarding toil, correcting what is irregular, puri-
fying what is stagnant or corrupt'.[2]

[1] Graham MS., Peel to Graham, 29 Nov. 1836. For another example of Peel's
extra-parliamentary speeches, which by the conventions of the day were necessarily limited in number, see his speech at the opening of the Tamworth Library
in Jan. 1841, which gave great offence to ultra-Tories. It consisted largely of
an advocacy of the need to open up knowledge to all classes of society and to
strengthen the bonds between them; and of a liberal declaration of faith in the
reconcilableness of intellectual inquiry and Christian revelation (*Sir Robert Peel's
Address on the Establishment of a Library and Reading Room at Tamworth on 19 January
1841* (London 1841)). For the garbled version that went the rounds in some
quarters, cf. Lady Palmerston: tho' he (Peel) bids for popularity in all his Speeches,
he disobliges his followers thereby. They do not like . . . a speech he made at Tamworth at some Literary meeting, in which he said all classes were alike and that
education should not be merely confined to the Church of England (very dis-
pleasing to his bigot followers)' (*Letters of Lady Palmerston*, ed. Sir Tresham Lever
(1957), p. 248). B. R. Haydon recorded on 4 Mar.: 'bought Peel's Pamphlet;
heard him abused by his party' (*Diary of B. R. Haydon*, ed. Pope, v. 36).

[2] *Speeches delivered by the Rt. Hon. Sir Robert Peel Bt. on his inauguration into the
office of Lord Rector of the University of Glasgow . . . and at the Public Dinner at Glasgow, etc.* (London, 1837). The visit lasted several days, and besides making his
inaugural speech on 11 Jan. and the civic speech on 13 Jan., Peel received the
freedom of Lanarkshire; entertained deputations from many royal burghs; and
accepted the freedom of Glasgow, originally withheld by the Town Council, but
purchased for him by the contributions of three thousand operatives and presented
to him in a silver box with an address. 'His liberalized tone', reported Graham
afterwards, 'and avowed abandonment of the High Tories may have been felt by
many to deserve encouragement, and were, I am persuaded, the immediate cause
of a Portion of the Enthusiasm' (Graham MS. 15 Jan. 1837, Graham to Stanley).

The crucial point in the Conservative recovery after Peel's first Ministry was passed in 1837. The continued electoral gains in the hard-fought election of that year made the Conservative party a more powerful Opposition than any known before. Croker in 1827 had opined that an Opposition of 250 would stop all public business; ten years later the Opposition numbered over 300; and the fact that the Government remained in office another four years was at least in part an index of the solidification of party discipline after the Reform Act. Office for the Conservatives would have come earlier but for the fiasco of 1839; but ultimate victory could not be denied, and after 1837 the Fabian policy of the leaders severely taxed the patience of followers straining at the leash with power in sight. The by-elections from 1837 to 1841 slowly narrowed the margin of the Ministerial majority,[1] and Graham could write happily in June

[1] According to a paper prepared for Peel by his Whips and used by him in the debate on the motion of no-confidence in May 1841, there were 104 by-elections between 1837 and 1841, excluding changes on petitions arising out of the general election of 1837. In 82 of these there was no change (34 were held by the Conservatives and 48 by Liberals). Of the remaining 22, the Conservatives gained 17 and lost 5; or, excluding Ludlow (lost by the Conservatives in 1839 and regained in 1840), Conservative gains 16, losses 4. The 4 lost seats included Helston, won in 1840 by Bassett, who (as Charles Ross said) was scarcely an opponent and in fact is listed in Dod, *Electoral Facts*, as a Conservative. He absented himself from the no-confidence division in June 1841 and voted with the Conservatives on the sugar resolutions in May. Two other losses were in Sutherland and Rutland, which Ross pronounced as 'nearly close boroughs'; so that the only remaining loss was St. Albans, a notoriously corrupt borough which was disfranchised in 1852. The balance-sheet was as follows:

	Conservative gains	Losses
1838	Bridgnorth	
	Devizes	
	Marylebone	
1839	Ayr co.	Ludlow
	Cambridge borough	
	N. Devon	
	Ipswich	
1840	Carlow co.	Helston
	Lewes	Rutland
	Ludlow	Sutherland
	Radnor co.	
	Totnes	
1841	Canterbury	St. Albans
	Monmouth co.	
	Nottingham	
	Sandwich	
	Walsall	

Totals: gained 17, lost 5, balance 12.   (Add. MS. 40429, f. 287)

1840 of the Conservatives 'floating into harbour on the full and rising tide of public confidence'.[1] In so far as one general factor can be disentangled from the welter of special and local influences in the general election of 1841, it was perhaps this matter of confidence. It was true that the Whig budgetary proposals of 1841 made it inevitable that the issue of the Corn Laws should be raised and Big Loaf parade with Little Loaf on innumerable election flags and hustings placards. Nor could there be any uncertainty about the protectionist feeling in the agricultural counties. 'I was elected', wrote Ashley long afterwards in words that could have been uttered by many county members, 'by an agricultural body, who expected, undoubtedly, that what they called "Protection", should be maintained. I was not tied, by their language or by my own, either to mode or to extent'; but, he added, had the issue of total abolition been raised (which it was not, by either party) it would have been one 'on which the electors would have had a right to ask, and possibly I should have been ready to give, a decided engagement.'[2] Peel himself did nothing to disclaim this. He could not do so because he still believed that the special position of agriculture, particularly in view of the financial burdens resting on it, made some means of Protection expedient and just. But he argued from expediency only; he did not give the issue prominence; and he reserved his freedom of action when in office.

Over the whole Free Trade question in 1841 there was in any case a certain unreality, since if the parties offered a choice, it was not between Free Trade and Protection, but between two systems of Protection, or, it might equally well be said, two modified versions of Free Trade.[3] If there was a national issue before the country it was, for the first time in British parliamentary history, which of two parties and which of two sets of men were to rule the country; and to this the

---

[1] Add. MS. 40318, f. 190.

[2] Hodder, *Shaftesbury*, p. 337 (Ashley's diary, 23 Dec. 1845).

[3] C. P. Villiers even welcomed the change of Government as an indispensable preliminary to securing a Free Trade policy. 'We shall now have a large political party interested in converting the community on the subject.' 27 Aug. 1841 (*Free Trade Speeches of the Rt. Hon. C. P. Villiers* (1883), i. 272). And Lord John Russell reminded the Queen in May 1841 that 'Sir Robert Peel, Lord Stanley and nearly all the eminent leaders of the party, profess their adherence to the principles of Mr. Huskisson' (*Victoria Letters*, i. 278).

Opposition held firm.[1] If it meant anything, the election was a vote of no-confidence in the Whig Ministry, confirming not only the formal parliamentary vote of June 1841, but the steady drift of electoral tendencies ever since 1835. The Whigs were beaten, in a sense, not by one general election but by three; and it is this which deprives the controversies of 1841 of much of their apparent importance. 'The change is very constitutional and legitimate', observed one Whig Minister dispassionately. 'The worst feature is that the House of Commons assumes the choice of Ministers without asserting any principle whatever. The Whigs are cashiered without any condemnation of any one of their measures, and the Tories who succeed are at liberty to follow all the policy of their predecessors.'[2]

In 1841 Peel claimed and won for himself a free hand; but this necessarily had its limitations. It entitled him to decide what he wished; but what decided whether he could carry it out was the available material in Parliament. He held office as the leader of a party: the brute votes in the lobby which had put him into power. That party was not a *tabula rasa*. It had opinions and interests, and a conception of its own character and significance. The Conservative members were neither mutes nor janissaries. Like all parties, moreover, it had a range of opinions from Right to Left; and what was important was not merely the range of opinion but the relative strength behind

[1] Cf. the letter from Graham to Peel, 6 Aug. 1841, on the need to discuss men not measures, when moving the amendment to the Address in the new Parliament, and to refuse to be inveigled into arguments over the Whig Budget (Add MS. 40318, f. 291). It may be noted that when that unpolitical, mildly Liberal, middle-class Londoner B. R. Haydon turned his thoughts to politics at the time of the general election of 1841, he thought in terms of national and not local issues. He had a vote for Marylebone and cast a plumper for Napier on 1 July; but his first reaction was to reflect whether the Whigs deserved to be ousted by the Conservatives as the Government of the country. 'If there be a dissolution, what shall I do? The Whigs have not done *all* I wish, but they have done a great deal. Will Peel do as much? I fear not. When he feels himself strong, will he not East Retford *again*? . . . Nobody considers what difficulties they [i.e. the Whigs] have had to contest with. Nobody does justice to the hideous struggle to do Reform and in reforming not to destroy. For rendering "Reform available in strengthening & not crushing the principle reformed", they have incurred the hatred of the Radicals; for reforming at all, they are detested by the Tories; for not going to the extreme of Revolution they are sneered at by the people!' (*Diary of B. R. Haydon*, ed. Pope, v. 52–53, 24 May 1841). For the East Retford reference, see *Mr. Secretary Peel*, pp. 469 seq.

[2] Campbell, *Life*, ii. 160.

each section. Whatever the proportions of Conservative strength in the country, in the parliamentary party the intellectual liberal Peelite wing was in a minority. In 1837 a generally accepted newspaper analysis[1] was Conservative 80, Tory 139, Ultra-Tory 100: that is to say, Peelite Conservatives numbered only between a quarter and a third of the parliamentary party. This corresponds reasonably accurately with the actual voting in the 1846 crisis when approximately a third of the party voted with Peel over the Corn Laws. The proportions were ominous, for the moment of victory in 1841 was also the moment when the fundamental unity of the party appeared to lose its *raison d'être*. What had provided that unity was the defence of the Church, of the monarchical constitution, and of the House of Lords; but these were no longer in danger. The mere fact that Peel was in power was proof of that. In many ways the party had accomplished its main work in the 1830's without being more than a few months in office. By accepting some reforms, modifying others, and blocking the rest—doing in fact (as Peel claimed in his Merchant Taylors speech) the work of government—it had shaped events very much to its own pattern. Whig legislation, on the basis of actual achievement, was very little different from Conservative policy. This was a major triumph for Conservatism; but what did it leave to be done? It was the fate of the great Conservative party of 1841, as of many other political parties, that the problems it had to face when it came to power, were not the problems it had been created to solve. From 1834 to 1841 it had been trained in defensive measures, even if it had been an elastic defence rather than stubborn resistance at advanced and untenable points. It now had to turn to positive policy for which it had not been educated and its very success in the previous decade made it more vulnerable to the new stresses after 1841.

It was here perhaps that Peel's administrative mind showed his limitations as a party leader. The challenge of the 1840's he welcomed. It was the great opportunity of his career and he used it to the full. It was different for many of his followers for whom winning the victory had been an end in itself. After 1841 the problems to which the Government had to turn were trade and finance, unemployment and poverty, Irish agitation and

[1] *Ann. Register*, 1837 p. [17 n.

Irish famine. What had Conservatism, as defined in the Merchant Taylors Hall, to do with these? Superficially very little; in Peel's mind a great deal. What happened was that the flexible reforming Peelite Conservatism of the 1830's moved with office to a fresh plane of detailed constructive policy and in the process began to lose contact with the less flexible and less imaginative members of the party and their constituents. Yet though the problems of Conservatism in office were different from those of Conservatism in opposition, the central principles remained. Peel's Budgets, the income-tax, the Bank Charter, concessions in Ireland, the studied understatement of Church policy, even the repeal of the Corn Laws, were all parts of an intellectual sophisticated Conservatism of the only kind which Conservative leaders in office could take as their guide. A Conservative Government had after all to govern. At the start of the Ministry Gladstone wrote to the Prime Minister:

I regard you as holding the conviction that it is ... possible to adjust the ancient and noble institutions of this country to the wants and necessities of this unquiet time ... as having the rarest discernment of the manner in which such adjustment is to be effected; as having resolution to adhere to principle which you believe to be such, and the perhaps still greater courage to divest of the cover and shelter of the name of principle such matters as you do not hold entitled to it, and as is rightfully subject to the ordinary and more flexible rules of politics.[1]

The essence of the internal conflict of the Conservative party in 1841–6 was precisely over what was principle and what was subject to the 'flexible rules of politics'. Peel could claim with justice that he never embarked on any policy that was not at bottom a conservative one.[2] To encourage trade and industry, to dampen class and sectarian conflict, to remove the sting from Irish discontent, to kill Chartism by prosperity and the League by timely concession, were in his view the surest means of preserving aristocratic leadership and the traditional structure

[1] Add. MS. 40469, f. 19 (17 Oct. 1841).
[2] For example, in discussing the relationship between his duty to party, the country, and the Crown at the start of the 1846 session, he declared outright that the power conferred on him had been used for public advantage and 'I cannot charge myself with any conduct at variance with the true and comprehensive policy of a conservative minister' (*Speeches*, iv. 581, 22 Jan. 1846).

of power.[1] It took the administrators and intellectuals to see this,[2] though for a long time party loyalty and his own prestige carried his followers with him. But when the breaking-point came, the dead weight of the party which was also the indispensable weight of Peel's majority, in default of any obvious challenge to Church and Constitution and with what seemed a very real threat to their material interests, followed their instincts and prejudices, their political honour and consistency, and the angry pressures of their constituents.

Yet it is easy to overestimate the degree of cleavage in the party and the lack of management by its leader. No party in office is without difficulty, for difficulties come with office. To the normal vicissitudes of politics in the 1840's was added the relative novelty of close party organization and discipline. The striking fact perhaps was not the disruption of 1846 but the generally good discipline beforehand. Clearly there was much discontent, and Peel—essentially an authoritarian—pushed party discipline and executive dominance to the limit. But in the end the discipline of the party only effectively broke down on two issues.[3] One was significantly religious, the Maynooth

[1] It would be easy to multiply examples of Peel's settled view of this concept of Conservatism, but two may suffice: one public, the other private. The first from his speech at the opening of the stormy session of 1846: 'I have thought it consistent with true Conservative policy, to promote so much of happiness and contentment among the people that the voice of disaffection should be no longer heard, and that thoughts of the dissolution of our institutions should be forgotten in the midst of physical enjoyment. These were my attempts, and I thought them not inconsistent with true and enlarged conservative policy' (*Speeches*, iv. 581, 22 Jan. 1846). The second, Peel's long letter to Arbuthnot in Oct. 1842, defending himself against the grumbling of the ultra-Tories over the measures of the preceding session, especially the Budget and the revision of the Corn Laws: 'The true cause of alarm to Ultras and to all other agriculturalists is not the reduction of prices from a good season, or even from the Tariff, but it is from the increase of the Poor Rate, from outbreaks from distress and above all from the inability to buy agricultural produce on account of poverty and distress. . . . The true friend to the astounded and complaining ultra is the man who would avert the consequences which would inevitably follow, if some of them could have their own way' (Apsley House MS., 30 Oct. 1842, printed with some verbal changes in Parker, *Peel*, ii. 532).

[2] Cf. Lord Lincoln's conversation with Gladstone, 6 Dec. 1845, in which he expressed the opinion that the Conservatives were in a false position over the maintenance of Protection and that the real problem was how to get rid of the Corn Laws. 'He conceived it especially desirable to disengage the Corn Laws if possible from the general interests of the aristocracy which were now most seriously compromised by it' (Gladstone's Memoranda, Add. MS. 44777, f. 233).

[3] The defeat of the Government over the factory clauses in 1844 was not quite a case in point. The voting on the crucial issue was low: 179–170 on Ashley's

grant—a premeditated policy; the other, the repeal of the
Corn Laws, which in a sense was an unpremeditated emergency
measure. The real fissure came in the spring of 1845 over
Maynooth, which of all Peel's actions came nearest to an
apparent repudiation of the basic Conservative principles enun-
ciated in the 1830's—and when half his party voted against
him.[1] Graham, the Home Secretary, was given to melancholy,

amendment and 186–183 on the 12 hours clause. When the Bill was re-introduced
and the Government made it a vote of confidence, they secured a majority of 297–
159. Similarly, over the sugar duties defeat on 14 June 1844, there had been a
somewhat inconclusive party meeting beforehand and it was not clear that the
issue was regarded as of fundamental importance. When the Cabinet decided to
make it an issue of confidence, a second party meeting of some 200 M.P.s at the
Carlton Club (with some 5 or 6 dissentients, including Disraeli and Ferrand) agreed
to give the Government general support; and despite a hard and rather injudicious
speech by Peel, he secured a majority of 22 when the matter was again put to the
House on the 17th (Add. MS. 40438, f. 302; *Greville*, 21 June 1844). Lord Sandon,
in an interesting letter to Peel, argued that the actual issue was 'of no great
Ministerial importance. . . . On no principle of finance is Government defeated;
on a detail it is. Now, in this point of view, a Government with a majority, on questions of principle, of about a hundred, has no right to consider such a defeat a
fatal affront. There has no doubt been from time to time an expression of dissatisfaction among some of the supporters of Government. But is it not inevitable when
questions of protection to particular interests are concerned? . . . You are not
deserted by your friends in Parliament. . . . Try their attachment by any real test,
and you will see, as you have seen, how they will answer to it. But you cannot
expect that upon all points, whether of individual interest, or class interest, the
whole of your supporters should sacrifice everything to this general but honest
allegiance.' Peel replied dryly: 'Declarations of general confidence will not, I fear,
compensate for that loss of authority and efficiency which is sustained by a Government not enabled to carry into effect the practical measures of legislation which it
feels it to be its duty to submit to Parliament—at least not enabled to carry them
without the dissent and disapprobation in many cases of a large and respectable
portion of the party with which that Government is connected.' In this instance it is
Peel arguing for a tighter party system and his supporter for a looser one (Parker,
Peel, iii. 150–2).

[1] The voting figures on Maynooth supplied to Russell by the Liberal Whips
were:

Second Reading	For	Against	Majority
Liberals	165	31	146
Conservatives	159	147	Conservative majority *for* of 12.
Totals	324	178	
Third Reading			
Liberals	169	35	133
Conservatives	148	149	Conservative majority *against* of 1.
Totals	317	184	

(Russell MS. P.R.O. 30/22/4, Tufnell to Russell, n.d.; cf. Walpole, *Russell*, i.
416 n.)   [*Footnote continued overleaf.*]

but it is difficult to contest the force of his conclusion when he wrote that 'the bill will pass but our party is destroyed. The result may probably resemble the consequences which ensued on the carrying of the Relief Act.' And again, 'a large Body of our supporters is mortally offended, and in their anger are ready to do anything either to defeat the bill or to revenge themselves upon us'.[1] When the next unexpected and intolerable strain came less than twelve months later, the party split irretrievably; and of the 147 Conservatives who voted against Peel on the Maynooth Bill, only 19 voted for him on the repeal of the Corn Laws.[2]

In the end Peel's Government was defeated not over corn but the subsidiary issue of the Irish Coercion Bill, on which in effect he invited defeat. He did so because he was not prepared to conduct an executive not in proper control of the legislature; and because he did not think that a premature general election would yield a firm and cohesive, that is to say, a party majority. He accepted a party system as the only basis for effective government,[3] though he still held that the party was wrong in splitting

Hodder, *Shaftesbury*, p. 328 gives a variant for the second reading:

Liberals	165	31	
Conservatives	158	145	
Totals	323	176	with 64 Conservatives absent.

The official figures in *Hansard* (vol. 79, 1042) give totals on the second reading of 323 and 176 also, but Tufnell's figures are confirmed by Professor Aydelotte.

[1] Graham MS. (Graham to Lord Heytesbury, the Lord-Lieutenant of Ireland, 12 and 18 Apr. 1845). To Hardinge, Governor-General in India, he wrote in similar terms. 'We have lost the slight hold which we ever possessed over the hearts and kind feelings of our followers. Never was a measure more wise or more necessary . . . but in a party sense it has been fatal and the old High Tories will not see that they can only govern on Peel principles in a Reformed Parliament, and if they reject the only man who has the wisdom and capacity to lead them thro' the difficulties of the Age in which we live, they must be content to see power transferred to their political opponents; and in the present generation at least there is no prospect of a Conservative opposition conducted on High Tory principles returning to power' (ibid., 23 Apr. 1845).

[2] Of the 159 Conservatives who voted *for* the Maynooth Bill on the second reading, 82 voted for repeal of the Corn Laws in the division on the third reading in 1846; 59 voted against repeal; and 18 did not vote. Of the 147 Conservatives who voted *against* the Maynooth Bill, only 19 voted for the repeal of the Corn Laws (third reading); 111 voted against repeal; and 17 did not vote. The figures for the voting on the Corn Laws include the tellers and 20 pairs. (I am indebted to Professor W. O. Aydelotte for these figures.)

[3] 'A Government', he wrote in a memorandum for his colleagues when about

and he was right.[1] The significant aspect of his conduct was therefore not so much the decision to repeal the Corn Laws as the decision to repeal even if it meant splitting the party. Whatever the grounds for repeal, it could be argued that the preservation of the party was an even greater Conservative interest. Goulburn, a friend and colleague, put the case in forcible terms.

> In my opinion the party of which you are the head is the only barrier which remains against the revolutionary effects of the Reform Bill. So long as that party remains unbroken, whether in or out of power, it has the means of doing much good, or of preventing much evil. But if it be broken in pieces by a destruction of confidence in its leaders (and I cannot but think that an abandonment of the Corn Law would produce that result), I see nothing before us but the exasperation of class animosities, a struggle for pre-eminence, and the ultimate triumph of unrestrained democracy.[2]

It was an argument to which there was no easy reply; for what was at issue here was the perennial political dilemma: between means and ends, between the particular and the general, between immediate dangers and contingent evils. All that can be said is that events did not bear Goulburn out; and that the repeal of the Corn Laws contributed to falsify his own gloomy predictions.

Perhaps the real answer to Goulburn was that the question he put was not the fundamental question. Implicit in the crisis was a larger issue to which in fact Peel was directing his attention. However hard and brusque his tactics had been, the disruption of the party was a profound if painful and immediately disastrous political education. Conservatism as a party could not remain in being unless it offered the prospect of an alternative Government; and if it was to be a Government, it must

---

to quit office in June 1846, 'ought to have a natural support. A Conservative Government should be supported by a Conservative party' (Parker, *Peel*, iii. 364).

[1] He wrote to the King of the Belgians in Jan. 1846: 'I have done everything in my power . . . to harmonise the action of conflicting authorities in the State, and to maintain order and contentment among very powerful and enlightened classes of society, by convincing them that their comfort and happiness is one of the main objects of civil government. This policy may be obstructed; it may temporarily fail; but I have a deep conviction that it is the true Conservative policy, and that another policy, though sanctioned for a time by powerful majorities, would ultimately tend to discord and confusion' (Parker, *Peel*, iii. 478).

[2] Add. MS. 40445, f. 276 (Goulburn to Peel, 30 Nov. 1845), printed Peel, *Memoirs*, ii. 201–4.

paradoxically be ready for adaptation and change. It was not only the last, but the greatest lesson he had to give his followers. Though the land was a great interest, it was no longer enough as a bond of union, still less as a basis of party, even if the Protectionist case for the retention of the Corn Law had been valid.[1] The Protectionists were not a political party in the sense of one able to provide and sustain a Government in the circumstances of the mid-nineteenth century. 'I hope', observed Peel, after Bentinck's deposition from the Protectionist leadership, 'to see Inglis in his proper place as the leader of a real old Tory and Church of England, Protectionist, Protestant party; and Lord Stanley acting in concert with him.'[2] He was not being ironic; but there was a certain disadvantage, which he refrained from mentioning, in that logical and homogeneous party grouping—namely, that it would never obtain power. For Disraeli, at least, that was a perceptible drawback. The fact was that English society was already too diversified to allow either a Tory-Protectionist or for that matter a purely aristocratic Whig party to remain long in power. The lesson of the whole period since 1830 was that a national political party must itself be a diversified party, representing and somehow harmonizing diversified interests. The intelligent politicians on both sides realized this; the rank and file, still less the electorate, was not fully aware of the lesson. The weakness of the Protectionists was not merely that after 1846 they represented the Conservative party with most of the brains knocked out, but that until they could shake off the monolithic character implied by their title, they could scarcely hope to become a national party or form a viable Government. The peculiarities of the limited electoral system, however, made the task of recovery and recon-

[1] Cf. the blunt remark of the Duke of Wellington in his argument with Croker in Jan. 1846: 'The existing Corn Law is not the *only* interest of this great nation, and whatever confidence I may feel in my own judgement, I do not think an administration could be formed in the House of Commons capable of conducting the affairs of the State, consisting of persons only who are of the opinion that the existing Corn Law is preferable to any other' (*Croker Papers*, iii. 52).

[2] Graham MS., Peel to Graham, 1 Jan. 1848; extracts in Parker, *Graham*, ii. 62 under date 2 Jan. In the earlier part of the letter Peel had referred to political gossip about Disraeli's unpopular speech on the Jewish Disabilities Bill, and Bentinck's announcement of the disruption of his party, and to the general ignorance among the politicians he then had staying with him at Drayton of the real state of the Protectionist party and the relations between Lord Stanley and their nominal leaders.

struction a slow one. A wider franchise and a more equitable system of representation would have accelerated the process by demonstrating their national weakness. As it was, the bias of the system still gave great powers of endurance to the country party, as the elections of 1852 clearly showed. But it was not enough; and Disraeli's successive flirtations with Peelites, Radicals, and Whigs represented a vain hunt for short-term solutions within the parliamentary framework for a problem which was essentially a long-term and national one.

The weakness of the Peelites, on the other hand, was that after 1846, though they could have served with efficiency and distinction in any Liberal or Conservative Ministry formed on a wide basis, they were severed by personal and traditional factors from the only two major parties which could offer the substance of a parliamentary majority. A looser and more limited system of politics, of the kind subsisting up to 1830, would have served their turn better. Yet though the party system had been cracked by the events of 1846, it did not disintegrate. From 1846 to 1852 office could only be obtained by the Peelites as individuals entering a party Ministry. It was a price which recent history and their own sense of importance made it difficult for them to pay. Once the favourable circumstances of December 1852 enabled them to join a coalition under a Peelite Prime Minister and virtually on their own terms, the essential fusibility of the Peelites was evident. The Aberdeen Ministry was divided, but not on Whig–Peelite lines, and despite its humiliating end, the way was cleared for the future. Yet the ultimate ability of the leading Peelites to fuse with the Whigs was not a mark of the lack of difference between parties. It derived from the circumstance that they belonged to that section of the Conservative party which overlapped in the centre with the moderate Liberals. That such an overlap existed was already a sign of the maturity of the British party system. With the decline of Radicalism inside the party headed by John Russell, no ideological factor—other than the temporary and uncharacteristic Papal Aggression crisis of 1851 —separated Left-wing Conservatives from Right-wing Liberals. 'I feel certain', wrote Aberdeen to Princess Lieven in March 1852, 'that a Government of progress in these times is indispensable. None can be too liberal for me, provided it does not abandon its conservative character.'[1] It was to be left to Palmerston and Gladstone between them to implement that balanced formula. 'In one sense', observed *The Times* in 1852, 'we are all Peelites.'[2]

[1] Lady Frances Balfour, *Life of Aberdeen* (1923), ii. 166.
[2] 21 July 1852.

VI

PARTY IN POLITICS:
THE LIBERALS

'I ALWAYS thought', wrote Lord John Russell in 1839, 'that the Whig party, as a party, would be destroyed by the Reform Bill.'[1] That, with retrospective wisdom, was perhaps ultimately true. It could equally well be argued, however, that the Reform Bill gave the Whigs a new lease of life. In the 1820's they had come near to extinction as a party,[2] and only Canning's death, and the failure of Wellington to form a second coalition, enabled Grey to reunite them as the preponderant element in a new Government and to endow them in the Reform Bill with a store of political credit on which they lived for another generation. But parliamentary reform was for many Whigs an eleventh-hour conversion; and whether the overriding motive was a genuine conviction that the political state of the country required such a drastic remedy or a party calculation that the Whigs could only retain office if they reformed Parliament,[3] the passage of the Act in 1832 raised—not immediately

[1] Russell, *Early Corr.* ii. 264 (to Melbourne, 9 Sept. 1839).

[2] As late as the 1830 session, for instance, the Whigs in the House of Commons were leaderless and divided, with 'an absence of all system and concert'. Apart from occasional meetings in Althorp's rooms in the Albany there was very little general consultation on the course to be followed in the House. This was the reason why after a month of the session had gone by, Althorp was formally elected head of the House of Commons group in March. But it is important to note the limited nature of the 'election', as described by Althorp to Lord Grey. 'A certain number of members of the House of Commons, much the largest part of whom were members of the old Opposition, have agreed to act together for the purpose of enforcing retrenchment and a reduction of taxes upon the Ministers, but without intending thereby to act in hostility to them, with a view to their removal from office; and they have decided to put me forward as their organ. The number at present amounts just to 40. The principle of our junction is that it is to extend only to measures of retrenchment and reduction of taxes. On all other points we are to continue as much disunited as ever' (Le Marchant, *Althorp*, pp. 243, 245, 267). It is hard to see in this a party, a party leader, or a party policy.

[3] Roebuck in 1851, inquiring from Graham the reason why the Whigs brought forward so extensive a Reform Bill, suggested that it was for the second motive; only popular enthusiasm could retain the Whigs in office and the Bill was brought forward therefore 'not as a mixture of legislation and reform, but as a party

but in the long run inevitably—the dividing question: was the Reform Bill to be a terminus or a point of departure. So long as Grey remained in office, his Ministry retained its fundamentally conservative character, and the legislation of 1833-4 contained little that could not have been brought forward by Peel, or for that matter by Canning or Liverpool.[1] The only exception was the notorious clause 147 in the Irish Church Temporalities Bill, embodying the principle of appropriation, on which the Cabinet was divided and which was later abandoned.

Nevertheless, even in these early years, there was an atmosphere of discomfort. Wider issues had been raised, and the area of public controversy enlarged to a point where some Whigs already felt insecure. The question of the Irish Church touched the raw nerve of these anxieties and produced the first split between the Old Whigs and the post-1832 species.[2] Stanley, in

proceeding' (Graham MS., 2 Jan. 1851). Grey in 1820 had privately uttered opinions which lent some colour to this (Trevelyan, *Lord Grey*, Appendix A). But much had changed between 1820 and November 1830, and it would be unduly cynical to disbelieve the serious arguments of the Whig Cabinet for the necessity of reform. Cf. Lord Melbourne's remark in 1835 that if reform had not been absolutely necessary in 1831, 'it was the foolishest thing ever done' (Russell, *Early Corr.* ii. 153). Lord Milton, son and heir to Earl Fitzwilliam, wrote in 1829, 'I am not a Reformer because I am or have been in opposition (for I was in Parliament, and therefore in opposition, as a very young person, many years before I was converted), but because the experience I have had of the House of Commons this Session as much as any other, has convinced me of its necessity to the ultimate preservation of the Constitution' (to Sir James Scarlett, 29 (?) May 1829, P. C. Scarlett, *Memoir of Lord Abinger* (1877), p. 143).

[1] Cf. Grey himself: 'We have endeavoured to bring forward those measures of reform . . . strictly, I repeat, upon Conservative principles, wishing to cover the weak parts of the Government, and strengthen it against the attacks of its enemies' (speech on second reading of the Irish Church Bill in the House of Lords, quoted in the *Reform Ministry and the Reformed Parliament*, p. 105 n.).

[2] It could be and was argued by Liberal Whigs that the Church of Ireland was in a totally different position to that of the Church of England and that to identify them was to ruin both. As Ellice observed in 1833, 'you may secure the whole concern in England by throwing the Irish lumber overboard. Take care that you do not swamp both by tying them together.' But to Conservative Whigs like Graham the question of the Church of Ireland seemed integral to the Union (and so was not only a religious but a political question) and the attacks on it by Dissenters and Radicals merely one aspect of the general movement against the Church and State connexion. Cf. Graham to Howick in Mar. 1835: 'I, on the contrary, adhering to Whig principles, regard with peculiar jealousy a dominant Catholic Church . . . the Union cannot be maintained, if the Protestant connection be severed . . . especially when in England also a powerful party has arisen eager for the downfall of the Church' (Parker, *Graham*, i. 182, 196-8, 240-1).

his Merchant Taylors Hall speech of 1838, drew a cutting comparison between the Whigs of 1688 and those of 1835: the first combining for the preservation of the Constitution and 'in order to give strength and stability to all, for the maintenance of that bulwark of our civil and religious liberties, a national and Protestant Church. But those who call themselves the Whigs of the present day seem . . . to have combined for the purpose of these institutions being made one and each the objects of uniform and separate attack.'[1] He was not the only one to compare (with greater or lesser degrees of historical accuracy) the past and present versions of Whiggery. Edmund Lechmere Charlton, M.P. for Ludlow, in the debate on the Address in 1835, spoke of himself as having 'imbibed my principles of Whiggism from the early part of the last century, when the principles of Whiggism were laid down, and which consisted, if I remember right, of freedom of election, loyalty to the House of Brunswick, toleration to Dissenters, and the fullest security to the Protestant Church'.[2] On those historical grounds he protested against anything calculated to harm the monarchy or the Church of England, and declared he would vote with the Peelite supporters. When to the attack on the Church was added the threat to the House of Lords and the contingent danger of the ballot, shorter Parliaments, and a wider suffrage, the discomfiture of the Old Whigs was complete. The justification for the radical nature of the Reform measure in 1832 had been that only so would it be effectual, permanent, and final. 'You and I', wrote Graham to Stanley in 1837, 'have always contended for the "finality" of the Reform Bill in a certain sense . . . there are fourteen Gentlemen in England, who were the cabinet of Lord Grey . . . they *alone* in honour and in duty are bound to resist the ulterior changes, against which they tendered their own sweeping Measure as a preventive security.'[3]

---

[1] *Authentic Report of the Conservative Festival at Merchant Tailors Hall*, pp. 25–26.

[2] *Hansard*, vol. 26, 280 (25 Feb. 1835).

[3] Graham MS., 24 Nov. 1837. Cf. Graham's remark to Granville Somerset a year earlier. 'I obtained the representation of my native county . . . as a member of the Old Whig party, pledged to Parliamentary Reform, but the avowed friend of the Protestant Church Establishment, and the enemy of Ballot, short Parliaments, and all the nostrums by which the regal and aristocratic power is assailed. It is needless to advert to my secession from the Whigs. They retain the name, but, as I contend, have changed their principles. I retain my principles and am indifferent to the name' (Parker, *Graham*, i. 249). Or the similar sentiments of a former

The resignation of Lord Grey and the secession of the Stanley-ites in 1834 left the Administration more flexible. Their new head, Lord Melbourne, if less of a statesman than Grey, was more of a political animal. But it also left the question of what the Whigs stood for and how they would react to post-1832 conditions. The defection of 1834 had not excised all old-fashioned Whigs from the ranks of the Ministerialists. There were plenty of what Campbell called the 'Conservative Whigs' who 'were on the Liberal side chiefly from family connection, not from personal inclination'.[1] Family relationship among aristocratic Whigs was undoubtedly an important feature. It tended to make them exclusive, with the toughness and tribal sense which exclusiveness breeds. It also led, within the oligarchy, to a species of patrician equalitarianism which hindered the evolution of strong leadership. Yet it is easy to make too much of this. The aristocracy naturally intermarried, and the consanguinity of the Whig ruling clan was more obvious mainly because there were fewer of them.[2] But there were other factors in promoting homogeneity: ideas, for example, and historical tradition. For a quarter of a century before 1830 the Foxite Whigs had been almost permanently in opposition, and almost —one might add—disqualified from office. The explanation lay in the events of the late eighteenth century, and as an excluded minority the Whigs remembered these events more clearly, certainly more bitterly, than those politicians born to the Pittite purple. In Grey, Lansdowne, and Holland, as well as back-benchers like Fysshe Palmer of Berkshire, they had living survivors of the age of Pitt and Fox; and in Russell the anti-Pittite, anti-Tory tradition was still remarkably alive.[3] In 1838,

colleague of Liverpool and Canning—Lord Ripon (*alias* Robinson, *alias* Goderich), who seceded from the Whig ministry with Stanley and Graham in 1834. 'I consider that the having any question as to the Representation in Parlt. to be an *open question*, would be an unequivocal abandonment of Lord Grey's system, and a renunciation of all the arguments upon which *converted Reformers* (of whom I was one) justified their course upon that question, and a realization of the worst fears, and the strongest arguments of the opponents of that measure' (Graham MS., to Graham, 26 Dec. 1836).

[1] Hardcastle, *Campbell*, ii. 117 n.

[2] Cf. Gladstone's remark (quoted D. Southgate, *Passing of the Whigs*, p. 201): 'Whig selections were . . . made . . . from a narrower circle and with a more close and marked preference for the claims of consanguinity.' The one naturally followed from the other.

[3] Thirty-five years after Fox's death, Russell could refer in a major contribution

for example, he recited to Melbourne a litany of Pittite sins: the Corn Law, £500 millions of debt, bad currency, bad Poor Laws, a bad law for Canada, swamping the House of Lords, and 'every other difficulty we have or shall have'. But, he added ironically, a country that survived being governed by Pitt must last for ever.[1] The conventional Radical concept of fifty years of Tory misrule which preceded the Age of Reform, found an echo among many of their aristocratic allies.[2]

But not all Whigs could attain to Russell's historic plane of family tradition and it is doubtful whether the Prime Minister to whom he addressed his tirade could share his emotions. No seventeenth-century Lamb, as far as is known, had shed his blood for Whig principles either in the field or on the scaffold; and it was perhaps as easy to forget that Melbourne had been a Canningite as to remember at convenient moments that Palmerston was not really a Whig. Yet, besides tradition, there was an idea of Whiggism, however neglected at particular times by historical Whigs, which could attract the sympathetic minds of men who were not originally of Whig or even aristocratic

to a debate on which the fate of the Whig Ministry depended, to 'the great cause of civil and religious freedom which he [Fox] had ever espoused', and referring to contemporary Whigs, declared that 'espousing the principles of Mr. Fox, like him we will not desert the cause in which we have embarked' (*Hansard*, vol. 58, 1210, in the no-confidence debate of 4 June 1841). Even more curiously, when Labouchere in 1850 remonstrated with Russell for making the question of the African squadron (maintained in African waters to repress the slave trade) a question of confidence in the Government, Russell replied that 'he could not abandon the course pursued by *Mr. Fox* and all the great men of the time, who had striven to put down slavery' (*Greville*, 20 Mar. 1850).

[1] Russell, *Early Corr.* ii. 238. It was not only Whigs, of course, who had this historical conception of themselves. The 8th Duke of Argyll, then about seventeen, said of himself in 1840 that 'I simply looked upon that Government as the débris of the party which had been led by Lord Grey, and on Lord Grey as the last survivor of the party led by Charles James Fox, the determined enemy of Mr. Pitt, and who, as I thought, had carried his opposition to flagrantly unpatriotic lengths' (*Memoirs*, ed. Duchess of Argyll (1906), i. 148).

[2] The Ministerial pamphlet *The Reformed Ministry and the Reformed Parliament*, in discussing the Poor Law Amendment Act of 1834, referred sarcastically (p. 82) to 'the mode in which that subject was dealt with, during the forty-five years for which Mr. Pitt and his followers held office'. For a Radical version of the same theme, cf. Bright's address *To the Radical Reformers of the Borough of Rochdale* in 1837. 'By the Tories the government of this country has been conducted for fifty years, at least, previous to 1830 . . . the profligate waste of public money, the shameless system of jobbery and corruption, which has grown up under their rule, has no parallel in the history of any people pretending to the possession of a representative government' (Smith, *Bright*, i. 40).

connexion: the idea of a liberal minority of the aristocracy which stood for civil and religious liberty and could in time of crisis save their order and their country by representing and controlling popular movements. To quote the slightly self-conscious description given by a Victorian Whig of a new family built on trade and finance, Sir Francis Baring, the Whigs were 'a body of men, connected with high rank and property . . . who in bad times keep alive the sacred flame of freedom, and when the people are roused, stand between the constitution and revolution, and go with the people, but not to extremities'.[1] Or, in the less kindly language of Cobden in 1848, the Whigs were 'buffers placed between the people and the privileged classes, to deaden the shock when they are brought into collision'.[2] It was a concept that had its champions among less exalted members of society, like Edward Baines senior, the Leeds newspaper proprietor, who told a Radical in 1835 that he had always thought the Whigs were the mainstay of the country;[3] or Kay, the son of a Yorkshire Nonconformist cotton-manufacturer, who in 1831 urged the commercial interests of Lancashire to put their political trust in liberal Whiggism as 'the enemy of exclusion and monopoly, the friend of non-intervention and peace, the unqualifying advocate of retrenchment, and the stern opponent of profligate patronage'.[4] It was this which gave the Whigs their political strength in the country. Though the party of Grey and Melbourne comprised an important and wealthy section of the peerage, and a respectable following in the squirearchy, it was still, almost by definition, a minority of the aristocracy.[5] Its political significance lay in the leadership it provided for other classes in a mixed society still enmeshed in an oligarchical system of politics. Melbourne himself, though apt in private to look disconsolately at the phalanx of traditional forces arrayed against his party, warned the House of Lords in 1836 that, though the gentry, the clergy, and the universities were

---

[1] Mallett, *Northbrook*, pp. 32–33.

[2] Morley, *Cobden*, p. 487.

[3] N. Gash, *Politics in the Age of Peel*, p. 111.

[4] In a pamphlet published anonymously, *Letter to the People of Lancashire concerning the future Representation of Commercial Interest* (Smith, *Life of Kay-Shuttleworth*, p. 20).

[5] For a full discussion of the economic and electoral basis of the Whigs see Southgate, *Passing of the Whigs*, ch. IV.

behind the majority among the peers, yet, 'these interests are not omnipotent in this country; nor were they omnipotent when other interests, such as those of towns and cities, the interest of commerce and manufactures, the interests of the Dissenters, and the general opinion of the people, were all as nothing compared with what they are now'.[1]

Among wealthy City families for instance there was a notable Whig bias at least up to and into the Reform era; and a number of Whig politicians graduated from the shop and counting house. Hawes,[2] who was as much a Whig as a Radical, was a wealthy soap-manufacturer of Lambeth; 'Bear' Ellice made his fortune in the fur trade before entering politics; Poulett Thomson began his career in the family firm of Thomson, Bonar & Co., specializing in trade with Russia; the great house of Baring was almost solidly Whig until Alexander Baring went over to the Conservatives on the issue of the Reform Bill.[3] It was not without some significance that Lord John Russell as Prime Minister represented the City of London while Peel sat for his family borough of Tamworth. But there were other Whig recruiting areas besides England. Scotland supplied an intellectual strength to Whiggery which in the age of Pitt took young Whig aristocrats up to Edinburgh and Glasgow to sit at the feet of northern professors,[4] made the *Edinburgh Review* a national political organ, and subsequently produced in Horner, Mackintosh, Brougham, Cockburn, Jeffrey, Kennedy, and Campbell a succession of ambitious young barristers to use their tongue and pen on the Whig side in more propitious days. Scotland indeed was remarkable for producing many Whigs but few Radicals. In Ireland also there was a small but important Whig–Liberal element, the significance of which has been obscured by the preoccupation of both English and Irish historians with the more flamboyant figure of O'Connell. In the

---

[1] *Hansard*, vol. 34, 885 (June 27). For the reverse of the picture cf. his lament to Althorp in Apr. 1835. 'We have fearful odds to bear up against, the inclination of the King, the House of Lords, three-fourths at least of the gentlemen of the country, and such a preponderant number of the clergy as may be fairly called the whole of them' (Le Marchant, *Althorp*, p. 538).

[2] Benjamin Hawes, M.P. Lambeth 1832–47, Kinsale 1848–52.

[3] Of the five Barings in the House of Commons in 1831, all but Alexander (later Lord Ashburton) voted for the second reading of the first Reform Bill (22 Mar.).

[4] Including Lord Lansdowne, Palmerston, Melbourne and his brother Frederick Lamb, and Lord John Russell.

existing structure of Irish electoral representation, O'Connell and the Repeal party even at the height of their activity could only secure about a third of the Irish representation. In the 1830's the Irish Liberals were approximately equal in strength to the Irish Nationalists and with the decline in O'Connell's physical and mental powers, and under the seductive influence of six years of governmental patronage, the Whig–Liberals emerged from the general election of 1841 as the largest single group of Irish M.P.s.[1]

Conversely, once the more fundamental features of political life were disclosed by the 1835 election, it was clear that in the English counties, half a dozen years before agricultural protection became an issue between parties, the Whigs were on the retreat. In 1835 they gained not a single English country seat and lost 29.[2] The pattern repeated itself in 1837 and 1841. Their losses in 1837 were estimated at 23.[3] There was another net loss of 22 in 1841;[4] and it was a striking commentary on the weakness of Whig English county representation that more Conservative county M.P.s actually voted for the repeal of the Corn Laws in 1846 than Whig.[5] In the same process their centre of electoral gravity shifted outward. They lost their majority in the English counties in 1835; their majority in the English seats as a whole in 1837; their majority in the United Kingdom in 1841. After 1835 in fact the Whigs were primarily dependent on a combination of urban and non-English constituencies. If the general election of that year did much to amend the shapelessness of the first reformed Parliament, the main result for the Whigs was to reveal the heterogeneous composition of the Liberal majority of the future. Their strength was that they formed the largest and most compact group in the

[1] A. D. Macintyre, 'Daniel O'Connell and the Irish Parliamentary Party' (unpub. D.Phil. thesis, Oxford 1963); J. H. Whyte, 'O'Connell and the repeal party' (*Irish Hist. Studies*, vol. ii).

[2] See Dod, *Electoral Facts* (1853), on which this calculation is based. If Stanley and Graham were counted as Conservatives, the figure would be 31.

[3] *Ann. Register*, 1837, p. 240]. The Whigs also failed in 15 out of 16 contested Conservative-held county constituencies, their solitary success being Graham's defeat in Cumberland.

[4] See the table of gains and losses in *Ann. Register*, 1841, p. 147. The Whigs lost 23 and gained 1 (Rutland).

[5] Fifteen (out of 21) Whig English county members voted for repeal: 18 (out of 122) Conservative county members. (Southgate, op. cit., p. 107.)

party of the Left; their weakness that the social composition of their parliamentary leadership was at odds with their electoral basis and their natural political allies. Fundamentally the Whigs were aristocratic and conservative. Russell could say in 1835 that 'to the Constitution of this country, in all its branches, I stand pledged by feeling, by opinion and by duty';[1] Durham in the 1837 election that 'I wish to rally as large a portion of the British people as possible, around the existing institutions of the country—the Throne—Lords—Commons and The Established Church'.[2] Such language, however, was common form; the test was how they wished to protect those institutions. In Durham's case it did not exclude support for ballot, shorter Parliaments, and household suffrage. In Russell's, it did not exclude a politician's instinct for shaping a course which would build up from the mixture of forces on the Ministerial side a general Liberal party. The name Liberal was in common use by 1834–5,[3] applied both to Government and party; the difficulty was to translate the idea into reality. Macaulay defined its essence in 1834. 'The strongest party beyond all comparison . . .

---

[1] Russell, *Early Corr.* ii. 151, replying to an address from Devonshire (Oct. 1835).

[2] New, *Durham*, pp. 314–15.

[3] Halévy, *Hist. of the English People 1830–41*, p. 183 n., unduly post-dates the general use of the term 'liberal', in place of the older title of 'reformer'. For some examples: Brougham in May 1834 told Lord Grey that if the King brought in Wellington and Peel, 'all the Liberal party' would oppose them (Brougham, *Life and Times*, iii. 370); he told Althorp in July 1834 that his retirement would probably prevent 'a Liberal Government' being formed; C. Wood spoke in Nov. 1834 of 'the Liberal Government which is to go on'; Althorp (now Lord Spencer) talked of the 'Liberal party in the House of Commons' in Jan. 1835; Melbourne in Apr. 1835 of 'the Whig and Liberal party' (Le Marchant, *Althorp*, pp. 510, 523, 532, 538); Parkes in 1836 drew a distinction between the 'clique of office-hunting Whigs' and the general 'Liberal party' to which Durham had attributed his exclusion from office (Reid, *Durham*, ii. 87–88); Russell wrote to the Queen in 1839 that 'the Liberal party has still a clear though small majority in the House of Commons' (*Victoria Letters*, i. 176); Charles Buller spoke of himself in 1841 as 'a member of the Liberal party' and therefore not justified in refusing the offer of a post in the Government (Secretary to the Board of Control) and the chance to identify himself with the principles of which Russell had made himself the representative (Russell, *Later Corr.* i. 38). The *Annual Register*, which in 1835 had given an undifferentiated list of elected candidates in the general election of that year, in 1837 distinguished them by 'the Capital Letters L or C (indicating the general tendency of their politics as Liberal or Conservative)'; and in 1841 gave an abstract of the election returns in modern style, dividing members into Liberals and Conservatives, and analysing the party majorities for the different categories of constituencies with a table of Conservative and Liberal gains and losses.

is what I call the *Centre Gauche*, the party which goes farther than the majority of the present ministry, and yet stops short of the lengths to which Hume and Warburton go. That party is a match for all the other parties in the State together. . . . But it has no head.'[1] To provide a policy and a leadership was the operation facing the Liberal Whigs in 1834; and it was a trifle more complicated than was envisaged by William Russell in his cheerful advice to his brother in 1833 either to set the Radicals at defiance or else 'go full swing down the wind of public opinion, cut and slash and clash and stop when you can'.[2] The business of the Whigs was not to allow themselves to be led by the Radicals but to evolve a brand of Liberalism which would guide Radicalism into manageable paths.

It was a business which they carried out with more success than is commonly allowed. Indeed, a major if unpublicized achievement of the Whig–Liberal majority was the progressive emasculation of both the Radical and O'Connell's parliamentary parties of 1835. What has obscured that achievement is the open and wordy debate after 1834 on what the Radicals should do; the undue prominence given to the relatively small but vocal number of Radical extremists; and the fact that after the 1837 election even small defections from the Ministerial party could be fatal. The argument over the role of the Radicals in politics was in essentials an argument over tactics. On one

[1] Torrens, *Melbourne*, p. 295. Macaulay went on to say that 'Lord Althorp with Stanley's abilities, or Stanley with Lord Althorp's opinions and temper, would be the leader of that party, and consequently the most powerful man in the country'. Failing either, he politely suggested the man to whom he was writing, Spring Rice; a somewhat startling anti-climax. Other people had the same opinion of Althorp. 'The only person', recorded Littleton in his diary in Mar. 1835, 'who could rally the party in the country would be Earl Spencer' (A. Aspinall, *Lord Brougham and the Whig Party* (1927), p. 292). In fact, apart from Althorp's lack of ambition and dislike of office (two unusual defects in a politician), he had many qualifications for becoming a great Liberal leader. Had he been able to develop his ideas on income-tax and the Corn Laws, he would have anticipated much that Peel accomplished in the 1840's; and his popularity, tact, and freedom from social prejudices would have enabled him to win a wider support from the Liberal party in the Commons than was ever secured by Melbourne's philosophic nihilism or Russell's disconcerting blend of timidity, impetuosity, and Whig grandeeism. As it was, Althorp was left as an applauder from the side-lines of parliamentary politics of all Peel's policy, including Maynooth and the Corn Law revision, until his death in Oct. 1845. His increasing admiration and support for Peel was reciprocated. Aberdeen told Gladstone in 1846 that Lord Spencer in his later years was Peel's ideal (Add. MS. 44777, f. 245).

[2] Russell, *Early Corr.* ii. 38.

side it was contended that a Whig Government would be more liberal than a Tory Government; that divisions among reformers would only result, as H. Lytton Bulwer said, in 'two jealous minorities—the Whig minority and the Radical minority';[1] and, finally, that some of the Radical demands were impracticable in existing political conditions.[2] As against the conformists, the dissident Radicals retorted that Whig and Tory politicians were becoming virtually indistinguishable;[3] that only continuous agitation could effect necessary reforms; and that it might even be worth while to precipitate a crisis and let the Tories in for a time in order to produce a Liberal reaction in the country.[4]

More important than the battle of words was the counting of heads. As Melbourne once observed of the Liberal pamphleteers, 'a little quiet voting is worth a ream of writing'.[5] The significant fact here was that the size of the independent Radical group in the House of Commons shrank steadily from 1832 to 1841. In the first reformed Parliament the Radical element, variously estimated as between 100 and 120, was regarded as a separate and hostile party.[6] But by 1837 the 150 Radicals

---

[1] *The Lords, the Government and the Country*, p. 71.

[2] See, for example, the pamphlet, *What ought the Radicals to do?*, by a Radical M.P. (1839).

[3] See *The Politics of 1837*, by An Old Reformer (1837), pp. 13–14, which described the two major parties as 'both weary of warfare, one rejected by the Radicals and the other possibly a little cloyed by possession of them, and both abhorring alike the Ballot and the old Triennial Law'.

[4] Parkes, for instance, thought in 1836 that 'we are now approaching the real consequences of the great events of 1832', and he envisaged a deadlock between the two aristocratic parties, the overturn of the Whigs, the temporary return of the Tories, followed by the advance of 'the whole Liberal party . . . for further organic changes in the representation' (including a remodelling of the peerage, equalization of constituencies, household suffrage, the ballot, and shorter Parliaments)—or, as he put it more realistically, beginning again 'as a virtuous minority'. In Apr. 1837 he still thought that there was no chance of getting a better Ministry until they first got a worse (Reid, *Durham*, ii. 87, 90, 122). The counter-argument to this is seen, for example, in H. Lytton Bulwer's pamphlet mentioned above, where he stated that he was in general a supporter of the Whig Ministry and in a degree attached to them because they were better than any which might be formed in their place and he preferred Radicals to gather round the banner of 'some reform' as against the advocates of 'no reform'.

[5] Quoted in *Diary of B. R. Haydon*, ed. Pope, iv. 328, actually in allusion to one of the Bulwers.

[6] Cf. the Whig pamphlet *Reform Ministry and Reformed Parliament*: 'It is the fortune of the present Government to be encountered by two hostile factions, the Tories and the Radicals' (p. 2); Walsh, *Chapters of Contemporary History*: 'The real

generally accepted as being returned at the 1835 election had changed to 50 Radicals and 100 Liberals.[1] Mrs. Grote indeed said in December 1836 that the Radical party had been thinned down to a mere 20 or so.[2] Even more striking was Bonham's analysis of the House of Commons in 1840, which only allowed 8 independent Radicals separate from the Government party.[3] Clearly all numerical estimates of such loose categories as Radicals and Liberals could only be approximate; but the tendency in these calculations is too clear to be ignored. However fragile and precarious, the apparition of a genuine Liberal party was beginning to take shape. The phenomenon was noted by the *Westminster Review* in 1837. The general election of that year, it pointed out, had reduced the numbers of both the pure Whigs and the extreme Radicals; but the moderate Radicals had increased and they represented the majority of the Reform party among the middle and upper classes. It defined these middle-men as supporters of the Government; constitutionally in favour of King, Lords, and Commons; undecided about the need for a reform of the House of Lords; against universal suffrage; many of them Anglicans though looking to further

effective opposition to Lord Grey's Administration in 1833 and 1834, was that of the Radicals, and not of the Conservatives' (p. 55).

[1] The Conservative party's calculation of the result of the 1835 election was: Conservatives 290; Radicals 150; Whigs and Stanleyites 218, of whom 40–50 were doubtful (Ellenborough Diary, 30 Jan. 1835, P.R.O. 30/12/28/5). Walsh, *Chapters of Contemporary History*, suggested that the Radicals in 1836 numbered 160–70 (p. 60). The *Ann. Reg. 1837*, p. [17 n. gave the following as an analysis appearing in the newspapers just before the opening of the session in Jan. 1837 (i.e. the last session of the Parliament elected in 1835). It remarked that the figures underrated the Ministerial strength, though their approximate accuracy was not disputed.

Radicals, English and Irish	80
Liberals	100
Whigs	152
Total Ministerialist	332
Conservatives	80
Tories	139
Ultra Tories	100
	319

The Speaker and six vacant seats made up the grand total of 658.

[2] *Life of Grote*, p. 109.

[3] Namely, J. Fielden, Leader, Molesworth, J. Jervis, W. Williams, Grote, Hume, and Wakley (Apsley House MS., Peel to Wellington, enclosing memorandum from Bonham, 5 Jan. 1840). See Appendix A.

moderate Church reform. What they wanted was the ballot; shorter Parliaments; improved electoral machinery; abolition or consolidation of the small borough constituencies; abrogation of the Corn Laws; and a radical reform of the Irish Church. 'These are the opinions generally prevailing among the new liberal English members. These men represent the average strength of the Reform spirit.'[1] It was with these men that the future of the Liberal party lay, and with it the future of their aristocratic leaders. As Ellice wrote to Russell in November 1841, since 1832 a stationary policy was out of the question. 'Our Whig party can only do good when leading and moderating the actions of the popular party below and beyond them.'[2]

II

The history of a party whose majority steadily decreased through three general elections is apt to be a study in electoral decline; but the history of the Liberal party in this decade is also a study in parliamentary growth. Three sets of events between 1834 and 1841 mark its development: the Lichfield House compact and the defeat of Peel's Ministry in 1835; the reshuffle of the Cabinet in 1839 and the decision to make Ballot and Corn open questions; and the Free Trade Budget of 1841. Admittedly none bore the stamp of clarity or success. The appropriation clause on which the Whigs drove out Peel in April 1835 they were never able to pass into law. The events of 1839 represented a weak compromise. The Free Trade policy of 1841 went off at half-cock. Nevertheless, they were early milestones on the road towards the Victorian Liberal party. The appropriation clause and the ballot brought up the two basic issues of the Church and the parliamentary constitution on which the two great political parties were clearly divided; and the Budget of 1841 was the first and last Liberal effort until Gladstone's Budget of 1853 to offer a creative financial and administrative leadership that could rival Peel's.

Factually the Lichfield House compact of February 1835 was no more than a demonstration of unity among the three parties of the Left for the limited purpose of bringing down the Conservative Ministry. Politically it established the first solid

---

[1] Vol. 28, pp. 8–9 (Oct. 1837).
[2] Russell MS., P.R.O. 30/22/4 (3 Nov. 1841).

foundation for the construction of a real Liberal party. What gave it this wider significance was the course of events in the preceding twelve months. The internal crisis[1] of the Whig Government in May 1834 had clarified Cabinet policy, especially on the Irish Church, and brought John Russell to the front. Peel's accession to office and the general election of 1835 trimmed down the unwieldy Reform majority and frightened Radical reformers by indicating that an anti-reform Administration was still possible. But if in one obvious respect the Lichfield House meeting gained the English and Irish Radicals for the Whigs, there is also a sense in which it gained the Whigs for Radicalism.[2] For all his initial reservations about an alliance

[1] Primarily brought on by Ward's resolution of 27 May declaring the justice and necessity of depriving the Church of Ireland of part of its temporalities, and the right of the State to regulate the distribution of Church property in such manner as Parliament might determine. A commission of inquiry into Irish Church revenues had been decided on by the Cabinet as an expedient to meet Ward's motion and conciliate Stanley; but it was the general opinion that it would be impossible to carry the previous question against Ward. In the event, a meeting of Government supporters on 3 June (to which day the debate on Ward's motion had been adjourned) was a failure, and Althorp's announcement of the Commission coldly received. Cf. Southgate, *Passing of the Whigs*, pp. 45–50, who emphasizes the opportuneness of Russell's earlier and unheralded declaration in favour of appropriation. Russell certainly helped to get rid of the Crown Prince of the party and so, incidentally, cleared his own path to the leadership of the Commons; but he was probably following his political instincts rather than indulging in a piece of Machiavellian craftsmanship. It is not clear, however, that Stanley would have resigned but for the general weight of feeling in the Cabinet and among the Government's parliamentary following. Russell's speech upsetting the coach was on 6 May; Stanley resigned on 27 May, shortly before and in anticipation of the debate on Ward's motion and the Government's announcement of the Commission of Inquiry, which he thought virtually accepted the principle of appropriation. If any one man was responsible for Stanley's departure, it was Ward rather than Russell; but the real cause of his resignation was the unwillingness or inability of the Cabinet to meet Ward's motion by a direct negative. (Le Marchant, *Althorp*, pp. 487 seq.; Brougham, *Life and Times*, iii. 375; *Greville*, 1 June 1834.) A greater gain to Russell was Lord Spencer's death, opportunely removing Althorp from the Commons. Althorp wrote in Feb. 1835 that 'a great many of the Liberal party are looking to me not only as their leader out of office, but expecting me to take office when it shall be offered me on Liberal principles'. The party memorial to Althorp on his retirement in 1834, signed by 206 M.P.s of all varieties of Liberal opinion, including some not previously in the 1831–2 Parliament and of independent outlook, gave Althorp some title to this position had he cared to exploit it (Le Marchant, *Althorp*, pp. 516–17, 536).

[2] Cf. E. Lytton Bulwer's argument in his pamphlet *Letter to a Late Cabinet Minister*, that the necessity of fighting an election out of office would make the Whigs more ready to act on popular principles. 'If the Whigs return to office, they must be more than Whigs. . . . You are now fighting for things, not men' (pp. 57, 81).

with Radicals, Russell had no doubts at all about the need for a more radical policy; and the alliance solidified a party behind that policy.[1] Even after the election results, Peel still entertained a faint hope that his legislative proposals would detach some of the Opposition. The Lichfield compact killed that prospect at the start. Defeats on the Speakership and the Address at the start of the session, with the trump card of dissolution already played, gave no encouragement to waverers and made Peel's resignation only a matter of time. In effect the alliance of

[1] See A. H. Graham, 'The Lichfield House Compact' (*Irish Hist. Studies*, xii). The Lichfield House meeting was the normal gathering of supporters at the start of session. Circulars requesting the attendance of reformers had been sent, through the agency of Warburton, to O'Connell to pass on to his own followers; and he responded enthusiastically with a letter direct to Russell promising support 'until the Tories are routed'. But though the initiative seems to have been taken by Warburton, not all Radicals were happy at the prospect of a close junction with O'Connell, and it is doubtful whether an effective alliance could have been made except under the general cover of the Whig–Liberal party. Cf. W. Clay (M.P., Tower Hamlets) to Grote, 20 Feb. 1835: 'I could not usefully or consistently belong to a *sub-division* of the Liberals, which numbered O'Connell among its members, however willing I may be to co-operate with him and his immediate friends as part of the *general body*' (*Life of Grote*, p. 99, note). In fact some Radicals also had a private meeting of their own before going on to Lichfield House. Similarly, the joint meeting was a source of disgust to old-fashioned Whigs like Grey and Lansdowne. Both men protested to Russell against any formal alliance with O'Connell. Grey's attitude was to be expected; but even Lansdowne declared against any 'party concert or alliance' and drew a distinction between occasional political 'intercourse' with the leader of a group like O'Connell and 'intimate councils' (Russell, *Early Corr.* ii. 81–82; Walpole, *Russell*, i. 228–34; Mrs. Fawcett, *Life of Molesworth* (1901), p. 73). Russell's own feelings were midway between those of his party Whips and his late leader. Though he approached the Lichfield House meeting with reservations, he had no doubts on the question of policy. He wanted a clear line on the Irish Church question, and the actual issue on which he eventually displaced Peel (the appropriation clause) was one which naturally threw him into alignment with the secular views of the Radicals and to a less extent with the Irish and Catholic views of O'Connell. Even Melbourne, while disarmingly admitting that no one was so much in favour of 'shuffling over differences of opinion and getting over matters as well as one can, as I am', agreed that 'this is really an important moment, and a great start', and that it was right to be explicit over the Irish Church issue. Russell in fact told Melbourne on 11 Feb. 1835 that the kind of cautious mixed Liberal Ministry suggested by Grey would still be divided on the Irish Church and he could therefore take no part in it (Russell, *Early Corr.* ii. 90–91; Walpole, *Russell*, i. 232). In the end, of course, the appropriation clause proved a boomerang. It was adopted as a principle before it was clear that there would in fact be a surplus to dispose of; it was thrown out by the House of Lords in 1835 and 1836; and O'Connell himself began to express the view by the winter of 1836–7 that it should be dropped. Its final abandonment by the Government in 1838 was a severe blow to the prestige both of Russell and the Whig Ministry.

February 1835 not only brought down Peel's Ministry but
formed the basis of the Whig Government's strength for the
remainder of the 1835 Parliament. As Russell later acknowledged, the House of Commons majority was 'pledged to us
from the first day, and stood to its pledge to the last'.[1]

The real difficulties of the Government after 1835 were not
so much with the Radicals as with the King and the House of
Lords. O'Connell showed himself a faithful and accommodating ally; and the argument among the English Radicals was
not whether, but on what terms, they should support the Whigs.
Though left-wing reformers proved wayward at times on particular issues such as Canada, where they thought themselves
to be fighting the same battle as at home against clericalism,
privilege, and oligarchy, they showed no disposition to separate
as a body from the Ministry. The veteran Hume, with over
twenty years' parliamentary experience, played a central role
in bridging the gap between ultras and moderates among the
Radicals; and vociferous extremists like Roebuck, Warburton,
Molesworth, Grote, and Place represented only a small and
quarrelsome minority. The bulk of the Radicals—'Hume and
the Prudents' (as Roebuck called them)—agreed with Parkes
in wanting the Government to go on, not out.[2] It was sympto-
matic, for example, that when on the eve of the 1836 session
Roebuck began a series of pamphlets advising the Radicals to
abstain on the Irish Church question and only support the
Ministers on a promise of radical concessions, the publication
fell flat and was discontinued with a net loss of £150. As he
complained to Place, the only result of his stand was that 'all
you prudent politicians went half mad. There was running to
and fro, and threats and prayers and remonstrances without
end. Even Hume grew frightened'.[3] Moreover, the general
election of 1837 brought no comfort for the extremists; seven
leading Radicals lost their seats[4] and Grote came within six

[1] Walpole, *Russell*, i. 297.

[2] New, *Durham*, p. 305.

[3] Leader, *Roebuck*, pp. 74–77, 81. Hume had good-naturedly tried to raise a
subscription from Liberal M.P.s to support the project but met with many rebuffs
and only collected £70. But he too was critical of Roebuck's refusal to concede a
particle to other men's opinions and there was an open breach between him and
Roebuck at the start of the 1837 session (ibid., pp. 92–95).

[4] Hume (Middlesex), Roebuck (Bath), Ewart (Liverpool), Thompson (Maid-
stone), Hutt (Hull), Gaskell (Wakefield), Trelawney (E. Cornwall).

votes of defeat in the City. Nevertheless, if the Radical wing was not rebellious, it was not content. Melbourne's reconstructed Ministry, with the loss of Althorp, Ellice, and Abercromby,[1] was if anything less Liberal than his first. O'Connell had not been made Irish Attorney-General nor Durham Foreign Secretary nor Brougham Lord Chancellor.[2] At the same time the Government's Reform programme, almost inevitably in the parliamentary conditions after 1835, laboured heavily along in the trough of a reinvigorated Opposition in the Commons and a hostile majority in the Lords. For Radicals it was an added source of resentment to refrain from pressing liberal measures in order to keep in power a Ministry which seemed determined to exclude from office any whose views were more advanced than their own.[3] If the stumbling-block was the peerage, the obvious answer was some further reform which would at any rate strengthen Liberal representation in the Commons. With the increasing realization that the Reform Act had left an electoral structure whose abuses and defects were uncommonly like the pre-1832 system, it was a natural response to call for a second instalment of reform; and the argument, dutifully put forward by the official-minded *Edinburgh Review*,[4] that the

[1] Abercromby had been elected as Speaker in opposition to the Conservative Manners Sutton in 1835. He was chosen in preference to the moderate Whig, Spring Rice, as tactically more likely to receive the general support of the Liberal party (Torrens, *Melbourne*, pp. 331–45).

[2] Hobhouse, taken into the Cabinet, possibly as a sop to the Radical wing of the party, told Melbourne in fact that his Government was not as Liberal as before; to which the Prime Minister characteristically retorted that some people had told him that it was too Jacobinical (Broughton, *Recollections*, v. 34; Torrens, *Melbourne*, p. 355).

[3] As C. P. Villiers wrote to his brother in 1836 with reference to the reconstructed Ministry, 'There is no real disposition in what are called the Radicals to separate from them; but there is a great aversion on the part of the Radicals to be called a set of time-serving, truckling knaves for abstaining from advancing any of those measures of reform for which they were returned, in order to support a ministry who, with less liberality than their Tory predecessors, exclude every man from any share in the government who represents a constituency in advance of their clique in political opinion' (Maxwell, *Clarendon*, i. 107). E. Lytton Bulwer also criticized Whig exclusiveness in this respect. 'The Whigs are doubtless much better masters than the Tories, but the principle of no wages is a danger' (Reid, *Durham*, ii. 118–19). The question of patronage was clearly a sore one. H. Lytton Bulwer went out of his way in his 1836 pamphlet *The Lords, the Government and the Country* to refute the charge of exclusiveness by listing a number of Radicals and Liberals who had been given official employment by the Whigs, but it was not a very impressive or very political list (pp. 88–90).

[4] 'In proportion as Whigs are, and have been true Reformers, they are bound

Whigs, as authors of the Reform Act, had a moral duty to guard its integrity, lost its savour in the face of the Conservative electoral revival.

From this situation came the next hesitant forward step. It was hesitant because the constant dilemma of the Whigs, in Russell's words, was that 'if they attempt little, their friends grow slack; and, if they attempt much, their enemies grow strong'.[1] But under pressure from his energetic lieutenant in the Commons, Melbourne gave way and between 1838 and 1839 reluctantly assented to changes in both men and measures. The general feeling in the party in favour of Cabinet changes was made irresistible in 1838 by affairs in Canada.[2] The re-shuffle was carried out in two stages. First, in February 1839, the incompetent Glenelg (the despair of every Administration in which he served)[3] was succeeded at the Colonial Department by Normanby, and Morpeth came in as Secretary at War. Then, after the Bedchamber incident, there was a further series of changes, the most significant of which were the departure of the Conservative Spring Rice to the House of Lords, the retirement of Howick (the head of the Grey clan) in a huff; and the entry of three Liberal Whigs—Clarendon, Labouchere, and Macaulay —into the Cabinet.[4] The same year saw a shift in principle on the question of electoral reform. The election of a new and unpledged House of Commons in 1837 made it in Russell's view essential 'to carry with us those Whigs who are Whigs in party and Radicals in opinion'.[5] One way was to make the

to watch over the Reform Bill, and to defy the cry of 'woe to those who stop' by which Reform is turned to Revolution' (vol. 64, p. 542, Jan. 1837).

[1] Walpole, *Russell*, i. 297 (Aug. 1837).

[2] Cf. Russell to Melbourne, 18 Oct. 1838: 'The Speaker, Ebrington, and Ellice all say that the opinion of our party is that there must be some change in the *personnel* of the Cabinet' (Walpole, *Russell*, i. 321). Lord Morpeth nearly resigned in protest against Glenelg's handling of colonial affairs, and Russell himself threatened to resign if nothing were done.

[3] This was Charles Grant, whose ineptitude in administration had been demon-strated as long ago as 1819–23 when he was Irish Secretary.

[4] The Cabinet changes would probably have been greater had it not been for the penalty of securing election on appointment (or reappointment). See above p. 4, n. 2.

[5] To Melbourne, 13 Sept. (Walpole, *Russell*, i. 299). On the other hand, there is no evidence that Russell himself had changed his mind on the question of the ballot. In his speech at Stroud at the 1837 election he had declared that if the old names of Whig and Tory were to be dropped, he was ready to take the name of Reformer, but he refused to adopt the popular nostrums of ballot, shorter

ballot[1] an open question, and this he formally proposed to his chief. Melbourne's refusal and Russell's consequent attempt to assert a firm Cabinet policy by his 'finality' speech at the start of the new session, merely diminished his own popularity and the hopes of his Liberal supporters. The consequences were soon seen. On Grote's ballot motion in 1838 (lost by 315 to 198) nearly 200 regular supporters of the Government voted for Grote, against a majority composed of their official leader and some 60 Whigs, reinforced by Peel and 250 Conservatives.[2] It was, in many ways, one of the most important divisions of the decade in party history. Though early the following year the Government rallied their supporters[3] on a vote of confidence in their Irish policy, Leader warned them that on a general vote of confidence in the Government, more than a dozen Radicals would vote against them. In fact, over the Jamaica vote on which the Government resigned in May, ten Radicals

---

Parliaments, household suffrage and an elective House of Lords (ibid., pp. 295–6). In 1838 took place a curious exchange of letters between Graham and Lord Tavistock (Aug.–Sept., renewed in Nov. after the death of Lady John Russell, part printed in Parker, *Graham*, i. 265–72) on the position and policy of the Government, which Graham believed to be a deliberate feeler on Russell's part (Graham MS.). In May 1839 Russell published a pamphlet, *Letter to the Electors of Stroud*, on the principles of the Reform Act as a 'permanent settlement of a great constitutional question', which Greville said would vex the Radicals and satisfy 'all moderate and really conservative men of whatever party' and which certainly pleased Graham (*Greville*, 5 May 1839).

[1] Since the end of 1836 Grote had been waging an intensive campaign for the ballot, even to the extent of having sample ballot boxes manufactured (at 24*s.* each) and distributed to various constituencies at his own expense (*Life of Grote*, p. 109). By 1839 the *Morning Chronicle* was calling on the Government to rally reformers round it by declaring in favour of triennial Parliaments, ballot, and household suffrage (Broughton, *Recollections*, v. 183).

[2] The minority included two official men, Hussey Vivian and R. Steuart, who defied their Whips (probably as a result of constituency pressure). According to Greville (18 Feb. 1838) many more Whigs, either pledged to the ballot or afraid of their constituents, abstained from the division. All the Cabinet members either voted against the motion or absented themselves. Vivian offered to resign but insisted on voting for the motion; and of those who voted with Russell many did so reluctantly and it was thought unlikely that they would do so again.

[3] The actual majority was 22, more than the Government Whips had expected. It was preceded by a curious overture by one of the Whigs (unnamed) to Greville, to get him to urge Peel not to press the Government too hard on the issue. Greville approached Graham, who spoke to Peel about it (*Greville*, 6, 10, 13, 21 Apr. 1839; Walpole, *Russell*, i. 328–9). If Greville's informant was right, Russell at this point was angry and nervous, and half-inclined to throw up office rather than give way to Radical pressure and the criticism of radical-minded colleagues like Duncannon at his 'finality' attitude to reform.

joined the Opposition to transform an expected majority of over twenty into one of only five. When the Government resumed office, it was clear that there would have to be changes in policy as well as in personnel. The Radicals for their part had been alarmed by the narrow escape from a Conservative Administration, and were anxious for a reconciliation on minimum terms.[1] With the Cabinet divided on the ballot and (according to Lord Tavistock) four-fifths of their supporters in its favour, it was now made an open question. When Grote renewed his motion in June 1839, 217 members voted for it, including Poulett Thomson,[2] Campbell,[3] Sir George Grey,[4] and two Russells,[5] while Labouchere and Hobhouse absented themselves.

The concessions of 1839 were something;[6] but they were not very much. They were a half-promise rather than a fulfilment. The device of making the ballot an open question, while a step towards the Radicals, was also a painful confession of weakness. It might satisfy the loyal *Edinburgh Review* to argue, as it did in 1840, that the Administration was weak only because it reflected the variety of opinions within the party; and that with this inevitable return to the normal constitutional channels of weak government, 'Open Questions must come in with them'.[7] It might amuse Lord Tavistock to console Russell with the quip that 'Whiggism, like a spent cannon-ball, is formidable even in its decay'.[8] But in a period of commercial distress and

---

[1] According to Greville, Ward proposed to patch up Government support on the sole condition of the ballot's being made an open question (10 May 1839).

[2] President of the Board of Trade.

[3] Attorney-General.

[4] Judge-Advocate-General.

[5] The two Russells were Lord John Russell's nephew, Lord Russell, and his brother Lord Charles Russell. The motion was defeated 335–217. According to the *Annual Register* 17 members of the Government and Household voted for it and 12 against.

[6] As an additional sop to the Radicals the Government in the same session put into effect the recommendations of Warburton's committee on penny postage (*Life of Campbell*, ii. 116). Though the actual recommendation of the committee was for a twopenny postage, their arguments and evidence indicated that in fact a penny postage would entail less loss to the revenue and this was accepted by Spring Rice, the Chancellor of the Exchequer.

[7] Vol. 71, pp. 515–16 (July 1840).

[8] Walpole, *Russell*, i. 331 (Tavistock to Russell, 13 Apr. 1839, in the course of an outspoken fraternal letter in which he told his brother that 'in my opinion you can never again become a great popular leader').

Chartist disorder, what many unphilosophic people wanted was strong government, not weak; and supporters of the Ministry would have found the insertion of a fresh propellent more edifying than the spectacle of a declining parabola. What damaged the Whigs more than their failure on any one issue was the growing impression of ineptitude and compromise on almost every aspect of policy and administration. Despite the lift given to the ballot question, the general interest—even in the towns—was now probably less in organic constitutional reform than in bread-and-butter questions. The harsher social and economic climate of the closing years of the decade threw into greater relief the shortcomings of the Government in finance and fiscal policy. It was an additional misfortune of the Whigs that their general parliamentary weakness from 1837 onwards coincided with the start of a series of budgetary deficiencies, bad harvests, and trade depression. Since the ignominious wrecking of Althorp's Budget in 1831, the hand-to-mouth financial policy of the Government had merely resulted in a reduction of direct taxation, with greater reliance on indirect taxation and consequent vulnerability in time of industrial slump. After 1837, with mounting expenditure on colonies and defence, the days of reckoning arrived. There was no surplus for tax reduction in 1837, a deficit in 1838. In 1839, on top of an existing deficit of nearly £1½ millions, the political concession of a penny post was earned at the expense of a loss of over a million in Post Office revenue. The almost literal bankruptcy of conventional Whig finance was demonstrated in 1840 when Baring, the new Chancellor of the Exchequer, faced with the prospective deficit of nearly £2 millions, reversed the popular trend towards 'cheap government' with a 5 per cent. increase in Customs and Excise and a 10 per cent. increase in Assessed Taxes.[1]

But danger creates opportunity, and this was the last opportunity for the Whigs to demonstrate that they still had reserves of administrative creativeness. The ideas which fed the new policy of 1841 came characteristically from the power-house of Radical thought. In 1839 the Government had lost their best economist, Poulett Thomson, the President of the Board of

[1] For a general account of Whig budgetary policy see Lucy Brown, *The Board of Trade and the Free Trade Movement 1830–42*, chs. 3–4, 13.

Trade. He had refused the Exchequer in succession to Spring
Rice, because he had no confidence in his colleagues.[1] Instead
he went as Governor-General to Canada and the post was taken
by the timid and conventional Francis Baring. It was his and
the more amateurish hand of John Russell that together con-
cocted the Whig Free Trade Budget of 1841. The ingredients
were twofold and not entirely congruous. With the renewed
prospect of a deficit in 1841, despite the additional taxation of
the previous year, Baring fell back on the doctrinaire theories[2]
of Hume's 1840 Committee on Import Duties. He proposed to
lower the duties on timber and sugar on the assumption that the
resultant increase in trade would not only make up the reduction but provide an actual surplus. Russell's contribution was to
insist that to the attack on the great monopolies of timber and
sugar should be added an attack on the third monopoly of corn.

[1] Poulett Thomson was a merchant's son with early business experience in the
family concern of Thomson, Bonar & Co. In the 1820's he was one of the Bentham,
Mill, Bowring, Hume, Warburton circle and a member of the Economy Club.
In 1826 he entered the House of Commons as Liberal Free Trade member for
Dover and became Vice-President of the Board of Trade in the Whig Ministry
of 1830. There he was regarded as the successor to Huskisson in matters of trade
and finance, was generally believed to have been Althorp's adviser in the 1831
Budget policy, and was promoted to the presidency of the Board of Trade in 1834.
When Spring Rice went to the House of Lords in 1839, Poulett Thomson had his
choice of the Exchequer or Canada and chose the latter as the sphere in which 'he
could make his abilities and energies most useful'. Though clearly perplexed and
doubtful as to the wisdom of his choice, he recorded in his journal three or four
days after leaving England that 'as I could not well have got out of the government,
I should have shared in the disgrace next session. . . . In England there is little to
be done by me. At the Exchequer all that can be hoped is to get through some
BAD TAX. There is no chance of carrying the House with one for any great commercial reforms, *timber, corn, sugar* etc.; party and private interests will prevent it.
If Peel were in, he might do this, as he could muzzle or keep away his Tory allies,
and we should support him.' He did not, however, live to see Peel in action. While
still in Canada he was thrown from his horse, smashed a leg, and died a fortnight
later in Sept. 1841 (*Memoir of Lord Sydenham*, ed. G. Poulett Scrope (1843), esp.
pp. 98–102).

[2] The report of the 1840 Committee argued strongly that the revenue would gain
by a reduction in the preferential duties on sugar, coffee, and timber; but in so
doing it also encouraged the belief that it would not be necessary to find additional
forms of taxation to compensate for the reduction. It took its evidence from a narrow
field of selected witnesses; the Board of Trade's statistical evidence was patchy
and not always sound; and there was a strong social bias in the testimony of the
chief witnesses, especially the Board's own officials, as well as an economic doctrinaire bias. The whole Committee was largely secured and stage-managed by the
Free Trade Radicals and their allies (Deacon Hume and MacGregor) among the
permanent officials (cf. Brown, *Board of Trade*, pp. 211–12).

His proposal was the old Radical one of a moderate fixed duty in place of the existing sliding scale.[1] As an economic experiment the 1841 Budget was something of a curiosity. For the Cabinet, the principle of Free Trade was incidental; the main object was to find some painless way of raising revenue and balancing the Budget.[2] It was a gamble, since it reduced indirect taxation without the security of any new form of revenue.[3] The ministers rested their financial reputation on the single hope that Hume's Committee was right in its economic theories. For that they were prepared to risk the disapproval of the anti-slavery school, the hostility of the colonial timber and sugar interests, and the discomfort of their few remaining agricultural representatives.[4] It is hardly surprising that Macaulay called it playing double or quits;[5] or that Melbourne's cheerful and irreverent brother, Lord Beauvale, described it as 'suicide at the foot of the gallows'.[6]

But the 1841 Budget was intended also, perhaps primarily, as a political weapon. Constitutional reform was exhausted and

[1] A fixed duty had been proposed by the Radicals in 1828 in opposition to Huskisson's sliding scale; Grote advocated it in his election compaign in the City in 1832; and Hume made a motion in its favour in 1834. As early as 1838-9 there were rumours that the Government would concede the principle in response to Radical pressure.

[2] Cf. Palmerston 'We intend to supply the deficiency of the revenue by striking a blow at some of the great monopolies which have hitherto retarded the prosperity of the country' (quoted in *Annual Reg.* 1841, p. 112); Melbourne, in a reply to an address on his retirement from office: 'The measures which we proposed . . . were calculated at once to supply the pecuniary deficiency and to relieve the commercial embarrassment' (Torrens, *Melbourne*, p. 527); Russell, who in a letter to his constituents after the election said that the additional taxation imposed in 1840 had proved insufficient to supply the deficiency of the revenue; that army and navy estimates could not be reduced; but the Government had decided it could simultaneously replenish the Treasury and lower the cost of the 'necessaries of life' (Walpole, *Russell*, i. 391-2). Baring thought that lowering the duties on sugar and timber would produce an additional revenue of £1·3 millions, leaving a deficit of £400,000 which the change in the duties on corn &c., would more than cover. In this way, by the simple expedient of lowering duties, the Budget deficit of £1·84 millions would be absorbed by the resultant buoyant revenue.

[3] Though a Free Trader and opposed to the Corn Laws, Baring was a uniform opponent of the income-tax as a source of revenue in time of peace. He placed before Melbourne three possible courses (1) a loan, (2) an income-tax, and (3) a reduction of duties. But he was clearly not prepared to concede the second course, and the alternative to (3) in his view was (1) (Brown, *Board of Trade*, pp. 221-2).

[4] Baring proposed to reduce the duty on foreign (i.e. slave-grown) sugar; reduce the duty on foreign, and slightly raise the duty on colonial, timber.

[5] Trevelyan, *Macaulay*, ii. 87.

[6] Countess of Airlie, *Lady Palmerston and Her Times* (1922), ii. 82.

any fresh impetus must come in another field of Government activity. As Baring himself pointed out to Lord Melbourne, on political issues 'all cards have been played and played in vain'.[1] Poulett Thomson in Canada wrote home in praise not only of the boldness of the Budget but also of its electioneering value. 'It does *not* meddle with religious prejudices; it does *not* relate to Ireland; it does *not* touch on any of the theoretical questions of government on which parties have so long been involved. It *is* a new flag to fight under.'[2] It was not only a new flag; it was also a Radical flag,[3] even if quartered with the Whig coat of arms. Corn Laws and Free Trade were part of a general pattern, and it had been for some years a stock Radical argument that the Corn Laws, shutting out continental grain, were primarily responsible for the stagnation of British industrial exports to Europe.[4] A fixed duty might mean both protection and revenue to the Cabinet; but to Free Traders it meant a relaxation of a monopolistic tariff. With the Anti-Corn Law League now at work in Poulett Thomson's old constituency of Manchester, this was of considerable electoral importance. Russell's sharp political nose had already scented the change. At the start of 1839 he had come out publicly in support of a moderate fixed duty. Though Melbourne deprecated a conflict on the issue, he reluctantly allowed the question to be an open one, if only to ascertain what the feeling in the party really was.[5] When Villiers brought up his annual repeal motion in

---

[1] Brown, *Board of Trade*, p. 221.

[2] To Baring, 25 May 1841. He had previously told Baring that it was no use trying to patch up an economic policy. Either he must go to work in earnest on commercial reforms (sugar, timber, corn) and obtain a revenue 'by throwing over (*if he can*) landlords, merchants, West Indians and Buxton & Co.; or he may come to a property tax' (*Memoir of Lord Sydenham*, pp. 88–89).

[3] At the 1837 election C. P. Villiers had pledged himself to work for the total repeal of the Corn Laws. This was the result of a meeting at Molesworth's house when Grote, Warburton, Hume, James Mill, and Buller had urged Villiers to make his special line in the House of Commons the campaign for the repeal of the Corn Laws (Villiers, *Free Trade Speeches*, i. xvi).

[4] This argument had been a basic ingredient in the debate on Villiers's Corn Law motion of Apr. 1840 which resulted in the appointment (at the instigation of Deacon Hume and MacGregor) of Hume's Select Committee on Import Duties in May 1840, before Baring had announced the Budget. Villiers had also been pressing Hume to move in the matter; he became chairman of the Committee and played a leading part in getting witnesses (Brown, *Board of Trade*, pp. 70–73; Villiers, *Speeches*, i. 239 n.).

[5] *Melbourne Papers*, pp. 388–90. Melbourne refused to lead a movement for

1839, he doubled the support he had received the previous year, and on a motion of inquiry into the operation of the Corn Laws, he secured 195 votes, including those of an impressive number of Ministerial Whigs.[1] The ground was therefore prepared for the decision of 1841; and the political repercussions were obvious.[2] To add corn to sugar and timber might, as some of the Cabinet thought, involve certain parliamentary defeat. It might also mean salvation if the Whigs had to go to the country.[3] By 7 May, when the full intentions of the Government were made known to Parliament, Russell had in his possession the considered opinion of the party's electoral expert, Joseph Parkes, who advised unhesitatingly on an appeal to the electorate. Half the 44 English and Welsh county seats held by the Whigs were already written off as lost in any case; and

repeal. 'I doubt whether the property or the institutions of this country can stand it.' But opinion was shifting even in his own aristocratic circle. Lord Spencer had told him privately in Feb. 1839 that he was against the Corn Laws altogether (ibid. 394). William Russell, the Ambassador in Berlin, wrote to Lord John the previous month that the Corn Laws were founded on 'error, injustice and avarice' and echoed the argument of Deacon Hume and MacGregor when he added that 'the manufacturers of Germany which are now pushing us out of the Levant and the American Markets have been forced into existence by our Corn Laws' (Russell, *Early Corr.* ii. 244). Another Whig diplomat coming under Free Trade influence was Melbourne's brother, Lord Beauvale (Ambassador in Vienna), who had met MacGregor in 1838 when he was working in Vienna on the Anglo-Austrian Commercial Treaty (Brown, *Board of Trade*, p. 68).

[1] Lord John Russell, Palmerston, Howick, Morpeth, Spring Rice, Hobhouse, Labouchere, Baring, Sir George Grey, and C. Wood.

[2] At the start of 1841 Ward told Russell that the one thing they were asking was whether the Government would deal with the Corn Law question (Walpole, *Russell*, i. 383).

[3] On 8 May, the day after Russell's speech on the whole Budget plan, Hobhouse asked him why measures were brought forward if they were sure to be defeated. Russel said he had not been sure that they would be defeated. Baring, for his side of the scheme, said that he thought he might have carried a reduction of timber and sugar duties. 'No', retorted Hobhouse, 'not if you added Repeal of the Corn Laws to them' (Broughton, *Recollections*, vi. 19–20). The curious bipartite nature of the Budget was revealed in the division of duties in the Commons. Baring made his financial statement on timber and sugar on 31 Apr., but before the House went into Committee of Ways and Means, Russell announced that on 31 May he would move for a committee of the whole House to consider the Corn Laws. Under pressure from the Opposition he disclosed on 7 May that he intended to propose a fixed duty of 8s. a quarter on wheat, and lesser amounts on other cereals. Thus the whole plan was known before the debate on Baring's separate budgetary proposals took place. The fact that the Government included a revision of the Corn Laws in their general Free Trade policy undoubtedly affected the attitude of some Whig agriculturists when they came to consider first of all the issues of timber and corn (see Appendix B).

though the corn question might adversely affect the small boroughs, a genuine Free Trade policy would aid the party in the large constituencies. On balance, Parkes did not think that the corn question would do the party much '*electoral* good or harm' but combined with a general Free Trade policy, it would justify a dissolution, and 'much enspirit the Constituencies'. A dissolution by the Whigs, he concluded, would at least preserve their strength; resignation followed by a Conservative dissolution would reduce the Liberal Opposition to between 250 and 260.[1]

The effectiveness of the Whig Budget was never tested; the appeal to the feeling in the country was. Melbourne's instinct —'Lord Melbourne,' recorded Victoria on 19 May, 'don't think so much of the feeling in the country'—was proved right and the calculations of the party's electioneering experts wrong. But even in defeat there was some comfort; it might have been worse. As Ellice wrote to Grey when it was all over, the party had been steadily sinking in strength and popularity for the past two years.

In this state of things the budget came to re-unite and consolidate the party and I easily believe, if it were not for the proposition to reform the corn laws, the popular party would have been scattered to the winds and we should have lost 150 instead of half the number, in the elections. . . . I cannot conceive, therefore, any greater good fortune than that which has fallen to the lot of Lord Melbourne and Lord John or to the Whig party, in having been enabled to effect their retreat before the increasing power of the Tory party, on measures not only right and just in themselves, and which must ultimately prevail, but which have united and satisfied their friends.[2]

Whether, without the Budget, the Whigs would have suffered

---

[1] For the text of this letter see Appendix A. After the disclosure of the whole Government plan on 7 May, feeling began to harden in the Cabinet during the next two weeks that if they were defeated on the Budget, support for their policy in the country would justify a dissolution. It is clear that much was expected of the anti Corn Law movement in Yorkshire, Lancashire, and the larger towns. The decisive Cabinet was on 19 May, by which time all but Melbourne and Normanby favoured dissolution, though Lansdowne, Minto, and Labouchere had some doubts (Broughton, *Recollections*, vi. 23, 26–29; *Victoria Letters*, i. 281).

[2] Grey MS., 14 July 1841. Lord Cottenham, in writing to Russell on the question of the Budget and dissolution, had made much the same sort of reflection. 'If the liberal party cannot govern the country, the real object is to keep the party together' (Russell MS., 12 May 1841, P.R.O. 30/22/4).

even worse defeat in 1841 is not easy to calculate; but its significance in the party's evolution was obliterated for the next four years by Peel's own successful measures. The Liberal bid for popularity had come too late.

III

The erosion and defeat of a Government through the electoral process was a sufficiently novel phenomenon in 1841 to attract various explanations of the 'failure of the Whigs'. After eleven years of office and a remarkable record of fundamental legislation, 'failure' is a relative word. But the Whigs had been struggling against a general atmosphere of weakness and decline ever since 1837; and this perhaps calls for more explanation than the actual verdict of the polls. Campbell methodically analysed the causes of that decline: the extravagant hopes raised by the Reform Act; the foolish conduct of the ultra-Radicals; Peel's skilful creation of Conservatism as an attractive political alternative; the absence of a consistent Whig policy; the listless leadership of Melbourne; the impression that the Whigs were made of 'squeezable materials', reluctantly and belatedly giving way to any popular pressure—all resulting in a steady decline of public confidence.[1] Lord Beauvale had already in 1839 offered a more fundamental diagnosis.

The country's mad fit being passed, they feel that the agitation consequent upon reforms has promoted attack upon property and they hate the Govt. as the stirrers of the system. This added to the sinking of dissent and the rise of the Church account for the feeling of the Country, and if this be so it cannot long be resisted.

But he added a more revealing criticism.

The truth is that the whole of the Whig doctrines rest on an unsound basis. Their doctrine is to govern by means of the masses, whereas in practice the Govt. must come from above, and be conducted in the interest of the masses but not depending upon them for support. To think of governing by the agency of that which is to be governed is nonsense, and from this simple principle may be derived the contradictions and difficulties in which the Whig Govt. has found itself.[2]

[1] *Life of Campbell*, ii. 151–8.
[2] *Lady Palmerston and Her Times*, ii. 37–38.

What Beauvale is here enunciating was the old Whig theory; his criticism was levelled at the modification of that theory made after 1834. Yet the classic role of the Whigs as an eccentric liberal element in an aristocratic governing caste was already outmoded by the rapid development of Victorian society. The historic formula of 'civil and religious liberty' had by 1841 been emptied of much of its practical content; and what the Liberal masses in the country wanted was not occasional emergency prescriptions but continuous leadership. This implied as large a readjustment for aristocratic Whig concepts as Peelite Conservatism implied for landed Toryism. The fundamental defect of the Whigs was that they could not make up their minds after 1832 whether to be an oligarchic or popular party.

Either way offered difficulties, for the political constitution itself was an uneasy compromise between aristocratic and popular forces. Whatever policy the Whigs adopted, they still had to govern through a constitution, mixed rather than popular, which had many oligarchic characteristics. The Crown, the House of Lords, the anomalies and defects of the electoral structure, were political realities which heavily circumscribed the effectiveness of a Liberal executive. The Whig Cabinet, even the House of Commons, was far from being the seat of practical political sovereignty. To this extent the Radicals were right in arguing that a completely Liberal policy was impossible until the deficiencies of the constitutional machinery were made good. Cobden spoke in 1852 of the elective system as 'ingeniously contrived to prevent the majority in parliament from reflecting with ease and accuracy the opinions of the majority of the nation'.[1] He could have extended his comment to the whole constitutional structure. As soon as the Whigs were confronted with an organized Conservative Opposition, led by the most sagacious politician of the day, they could retain momentum only by becoming a popular party. Yet the nature of the representative system made it difficult for them to translate popular support into equivalent parliamentary strength. The Whigs in consequence were caught between the pressure of public opinion and the limitations of a narrow parliamentary constitution; and the resultant room for manœuvre was small.

[1] *Address to the Electors of the West Riding of Yorkshire*, June 1852 (*Reminiscences of R. Cobden* ed. Mrs. Schwabe, pp. 183–4).

Any criticism which does not take into account this fundamental handicap is unrealistic. 'By one set of people', observed Melbourne in 1839,' we are told that we are ruining ourselves and losing support by allying ourselves with the Radicals and Roman Catholics; by another that we are producing the same effect by leaning too much to the Tories and Conservatives'; and, he added, with his usual engaging equability, 'probably both statements are true'.[1] To walk successfully the narrow path between these twin dangers needed outstanding political leadership and a united parliamentary party.

Of the two conditions for success, it was not the party which failed the Whigs. What is striking about the Liberal party between 1835 and 1841 is not its superficial discontents and disagreements but its substantial unity and support for the Ministers. The reduction of their majority from 25 to 5 on the Jamaica vote which caused their resignation in 1839 was not a party split; merely the defection of ten ultra-Radicals. Even so, it was an indication of a high level of party discipline that Melbourne could justify the resignation on 'the relative numbers upon this vote, joined to the consideration of no less than nine members of those who have hitherto invariably supported the Government have gone against it now'.[2] The Government was brought down at last in 1841 not so much in the House of Commons as at the polling booths; the party was solid to the last. The Free Trade Budget certainly caused a wavering in the diminished ranks of the Whig county members. Nine of the fifteen Whigs who voted against their party on the sugar resolutions were representatives of agricultural constituencies, as indeed were half of the eighteen absentees. But nearly all the rebels, and most of the absentees, rallied to the Government on the no-confidence motion in June.[3] If there was a weakness in

---

[1] *Melbourne Papers*, p. 402 (to Russell).

[2] *Victoria Letters*, i. 154.

[3] The defeat on the sugar duties in May 1841 was on an issue notoriously apt to trip up Governments (as it did Peel in 1844) largely because of the intertwining of three separate issues—Free Trade, the colonial sugar interest, and the religious anti-slavery group. Several Whig agricultural members in 1841 took the view that sugar, timber, and corn were all part of the same question and that they could not support the Government on any of them. Stephen Lushington, on the other hand, said he could not vote for the sugar resolution because of the encouragement it would give to slavery. For an analysis of the Government vote on the sugar resolutions (18 May) and no-confidence motion (4 June) see Appendix B.

the party in 1841, it was in a quarter where the Whigs had little to expect in any case. But as a Liberal party it remained unbroken. Not defections among Government supporters so much as superb whipping among the Conservatives, who had not a single absentee as compared with eight Ministerialists, produced the hair-line decision of 1841.

The deficiencies were elsewhere, in policy and leadership. Their policy, especially after 1837, showed an absence of principle and objective. Strong measures were put forward, only to be abandoned or compromised; liberal concessions designed to rally support came tardily or piecemeal. Organic reform was carried on too long; financial and commercial questions neglected till too late. Much of what was said or proposed seemed contradictory shifts and expedients rather than the results of reflection and preparation. The 1841 Budget was suspect for this reason, and not without justice. In April, only a month before Russell announced his fixed-duty plan to the Commons, Lansdowne could write that the corn question, though important, 'has been the subject of less discussion amongst ourselves than far less important questions'.[1] What particularly discredited the Whigs was the visible lack of firm and incisive leadership. To make two such fundamental issues as the ballot and corn open questions was not so much policy as the abandonment of policy.[2] This defect of leadership ran back to the immediate post-Reform years. Neither Grey nor Melbourne was fitted to be leader of a Liberal party, and Russell suffered from both temperamental flaws and lack of sufficient authority. At the same time the Ministry as a whole was open to the charge of being too eager to return to office in 1835 and too reluctant to part with it in 1839. Neither Appropriation nor the Bedchamber proved to be very durable principles on which to regain power; and Russell was to continue the series in 1846 with the Irish Coercion Bill. Avidity for office with not much

[1] Russell MS., Lansdowne to Russell, 6 Apr. 1841, P.R.O. 30/22/4).

[2] It came in for some sharp criticism from Peel (the last Prime Minister likely to permit open questions in his Cabinet), during the debate on the no-confidence motion in Jan. 1840. 'There is a new resource for an incompetent administration; there is the ingenious device of "open questions", the cunning scheme of adding to the strength of a weak government by proclaiming its disunion. It will be a fatal policy indeed, if that which has hitherto been an exception—and always an unfortunate exception in recent times, is hereafter to constitute the rule of government' (*Speeches*, iii. 691).

idea of how to use it when obtained was not the best public image.[1]

It was this infirmity of policy and leadership that was the basic reason for the weakness of the Liberal Opposition in the years 1841–5. It was true that they were faced with one of the most efficient Governments of the century, following a liberal policy with rather greater courage than they themselves had exhibited when in power. But this does not in itself explain the apathy and fragmentation which descended on the Whig–Liberal ranks immediately after the general election. A small and fractious section of the Whigs—Howick, Wood, Buller, and Hawes—looked enviously at Peel's Liberal-Conservatism and played with the notion of a regrouping which would allow the centre wings of the two parties to be united;[2] O'Connell's reversion to an active Repeal policy underlined the end of the 1835 alliance;[3] while the growth of the Anti-Corn Law League soon began to attract parliamentary Radicalism into its orbit. There was no clear agreement among the Opposition on what to advocate or oppose. Russell and Palmerston were inclined to attack the Government on foreign policy, especially the Ashburton Treaty and India. But they found themselves faced

---

[1] For the disillusioned reflections of an unpolitical liberal, cf. Haydon in June 1838. 'Every great question they [the Whigs] have messed or imperfectly accomplished. . . . All they want is *place* . . . with a Bankrupt Income! an entangled Foreign Diplomacy, an insulted Country, an irritated population, an apprehensive Church, a starving poor, proposing laws they can't carry & passing them after enduring Tory castration, eating their own words, swallowing their own Vomit, and when Nature can no longer swallow more, allowing their noses to be rubbed in their own filth, as they do to dogs when they dung a drawing Room.' He added afterwards that this was 'written in a passion, but it is true to the Bone . . . I am in a devil of a rage with the Whigs for the want of decision they display in everything but keeping their places. Surely they ought to be called the *Poultice* Administration' (*Diary*, iv. 492–3).

[2] Cf. Wood to Howick (12 Jan. 1843). 'The liberal party *per se* cannot govern the country and if we are to govern it at all, we must look to support from the liberal Tories'; Howick to Lady Howick (9 Apr. 1844): 'I do not look in public life to returning to office but to exercising a useful influence in Parliament and the country by establishing a character for acting honestly and independently. . . . If I ever should return to office it would hardly be otherwise than in consequence of a great breaking up of existing parties and their re-arrangement in some new way' (Grey MS.). Both Grey and C. Wood and also Buller would probably have been ready to join Peel when he reformed his Ministry in Dec. 1845.

[3] Russell declared in Nov. 1841 that 'party concert' was now impossible with O'Connell since he had declared for an extension of the Reform Act and making Repeal of the Union an open question (Russell, *Later Corr.* i. 50).

with opposition both from leading Whig peers—Lansdowne, Spencer, Fitzwilliam, and Bedford—and from many Free Trade Liberals and Radicals, who particularly welcomed peaceful relations with the U.S.A.[1] In vindication of their own 1841 proposals the Whigs felt obliged to oppose the 1842 Budget, but the bold expedient of the income-tax confounded their expectations,[2] and its proved efficacy in succeeding years steadily removed any prospect that they would abolish it if they ever returned to office.[3] Even on corn the Whigs were irresolute. Not many wanted total repeal, and whatever the theoretical arguments for a fixed duty, some were prepared to give the reduced sliding scale of 1842 a reasonable trial.[4]

[1] Buller had talked to Lord Ashburton before he went to America and had led him to expect that the Liberal party would support any settlement of the boundary dispute. When the treaty was concluded, it was strongly endorsed by Buller, Hawes, and Ellice, who used the columns of the *Examiner* and the *Globe* to express their views. Buller wrote to Russell in Oct. 1842 in vindication of his articles in the *Globe* (under the pseudonym of *Pacificus*) and told him that 'the treaty is approved by the great mass of the Liberal party. All our free trading friends desire to be on good terms with America.' Palmerston, who was using the *Morning Chronicle* to attack the treaty, was extremely annoyed at the attitude of 'some of our party, Radicals and old Whigs' (Russell MS., Buller to Russell, 23 Oct.; Fitzwilliam to Russell, 3 Nov.; Palmerston to Russell, 24 Sept., 24 Oct., 14 Nov. 1842, P.R.O. 30/22/4). Bedford and Fitzwilliam on the other hand deplored Palmerston's Press attacks and the attempts to stir up anti-American feeling. Bedford told his brother that Palmerston would 'disgust the best of the old Whig party' (Russell, *Later Corr.* i. 56, 58–62, Aug.–Nov. 1842).

[2] The leading Whigs—Melbourne, Russell, Palmerston, Baring, and Wood—had agreed to oppose any new tax to supply the deficiency in the revenue, but Melbourne wisely felt that if Peel brought forward any 'general and comprehensive scheme for a revision of our fiscal system', it would require fresh consideration. Palmerston wrote to Russell in Jan. 1842, 'I agree with you that it is unlikely that Peel should propose an Income Tax' (Russell, *Later Corr.* i. 53). Cf. Greville, (13 Mar. 1842) after Peel's Budget speech. 'Hitherto the Opposition have been talking very big about opposing all taxes, but they have quite altered their tone.'

[3] John Doyle (H.B.) neatly summed up the position in a cartoon showing Peel reclining luxuriously on a couch labelled *Income Tax*, watched enviously by Russell and Baring. To Russell's reproaches that 'such indulgences are bad for the constitution, and were only meant for extreme cases', Peel is retorting, 'No doubt! If any thing were to remove me, you would, I dare say, have no objection to find such a comfortable *shake-down* ready prepared for yourselves'. Baring is answering, 'No! If other people allow it, there it may remain for us'.

[4] Lord Spencer, though not departing from his view that agriculture would never be steady until the Corn Laws were repealed, thought that the alarm among agriculturists over Peel's 1842 Act was unfounded, and that it would work a good deal better than the previous Corn Law. He disliked a fixed duty because it could not be upheld when prices were high (Russell, *Later Corr.* i. 60–61). Similarly Melbourne told Russell in Aug. 1842 that the Whigs would be able to condemn Peel's Corn Law with more advantage 'after we had seen the working of the new

Russell himself, though by 1844 looking forward to eventual repeal, thought it could only be accomplished if all the county rate and half the malt tax were taken off as compensation. Moreover, while he admitted that the League had a real principle, he disliked the appearance of great manufacturers trying to increase their profits at the expense of the landowners.[1] Hence the years of opposition were years of stagnation for the Liberal party and the temporary rally of 1841 hardly survived the election year. When in January 1844 Campbell gave a dinner to the Whig leaders with the idea of co-ordinating tactics, he recorded that 'we parted without anything being determined. Our party never was in a more dilapidated or ruinous condition'.[2]

By 1845 the Liberals were in need of a policy and a leader. It was this which created the psychological importance of Russell's Edinburgh Letter at the start of the Corn Law crisis. Lord Cottenham, when congratulating Russell on its admirable timing and substance, added that it was 'most destructive of the proposals of the one party, and most wanted by the other'.[3] Le Marchant reported that the Free Traders of the party threw up their hats at the receipt of the news and even the moderates cautiously approved, though fearing agricultural reaction. Buller, referring both to the Edinburgh Letter and to Morpeth's simultaneous adherence to the League, told Lord Grey that 'it is almost impossible to over-estimate the importance of their once more rallying the whole Liberal party round the Whigs';[4] and H. G. Ward wrote to thank Russell 'for making us a *Party* again, which we certainly have not been for the last four years, and never could have been, while you differed with so many of your old followers upon what we all felt to be the vital question of the day. We shall now act with you again

---

Act, which has certainly hitherto operated differently from the old' (*Melbourne Papers*, p. 514). In 1844 at a dinner-party at Campbell's, Melbourne 'rather defended the sliding scale and the general conduct of the present government' (*Life of Campbell*, ii. 184).

[1] P.R.O. 30/22/4, 4 Apr. 1844, Russell to Parkes (wrongly given as Parker in Russell, *Later Corr*. i. 72).

[2] *Life of Campbell*, ii. 184. He had previously described the Liberal Opposition in 1842 as 'a once powerful and respectable party melting away, without concert, without spirit, and without a leader' (ibid., p. 62).

[3] Russell, *Later Corr*. i. 85.

[4] Grey MS., 1 Dec. 1845.

frankly and heartily as we did upon the Reform bill and in 1835.'[1]

If this was the Liberal reaction, however, feeling among many Whigs was more reserved. Not for the first time Russell had committed himself without foreseeing all the consequences. He had announced a policy before he had formed a Ministry; without indeed reckoning on the possibility of being invited to form one. He had not consulted his colleagues; and the Whigs were still not agreed on the corn question. Not surprisingly he encountered 'reluctance and apathy' on the part of many official Whigs[2] when he undertook to form an Administration in December 1845. The hazards of minority government, coupled with internal differences on policy and personnel, rapidly destroyed any real will on Russell's part to carry through the dangerous commission he had accepted. Peel's general assurances of support were regarded as adequate by the majority of Russell's colleagues; the fundamental difficulties were internal. Most of those whom he consulted still favoured a fixed duty, and Russell first envisaged gradual repeal with an adjustment of the burdens on the land. But it seemed clear that the rank and file preferred the Cobdenite solution of total and immediate repeal, and under pressure from the radical-minded and cantankerous Lord Grey,[3] Russell finally came down in favour of the more extreme policy.[4] This was accepted, but with the subsequent drastic and possibly unworkable condition

---

[1] Russell, *Later Corr*. i. 84 (29 Nov. 1845).

[2] The description is Ellice's (Russell, *Later Corr*. i. 88, 13 Dec. 1845), and not unfair. Lord Minto accepted the Admiralty on the discouraging grounds that 'I do not think it will endure long enough to produce any serious wear and tear of health and constitution'. Lord Clarendon told Russell that he had no desire to promote 'the hazardous enterprise which they [Peel and Graham] want you to undertake'. Lord Grey wrote, 'I am far from wishing to see an attempt at a liberal government till there is a prospect of its being able really to maintain itself' (ibid., pp. 86–87, 89, 93).

[3] The Howick of the 1830's, who succeeded his father as 3rd Earl Grey in July 1845.

[4] Russell told his colleagues on 16 Dec. that the idea of gradual repeal originated in an attempt to concert policy with Peel, but as the latter would not commit himself on details, the only practicable course was to adopt immediate repeal (Grey MS., Lord Grey to Lady Grey, 16 Dec. 1845). At a subsequent meeting on 18 Dec., attended by Russell, Lansdowne, Clarendon, Grey, Auckland, Monteagle, Baring, Ellice, Palmerston, Hobhouse, Macaulay, Labouchere, Cottenham, Sir G. Grey, and Bedford, all but five accepted Peel's written assurances of general support as sufficient foundation to form a Ministry (Russell, *Later Corr*. i. 105–6, 'Record of the Crisis').

by Lord Lansdowne that £1,000,000 should be set aside as compensation for the landed interest, but without increasing taxation.[1] When, on top of this, came Grey's objections to Palmerston's tenure of the Foreign Office, Russell threw up the game without further serious attempt to resolve the difficulties.[2] So the great chance was missed. It had undoubted risks, but it also offered a great reward. But the old Whig vices of vagueness on policy and weakness of leadership once more reasserted themselves, and it was left for Peel and not Russell to be remembered 'with expressions of good will in the abodes of those whose lot it is to labour, and to earn their daily bread by the sweat of their brow'.[3]

As an opportunity for the Whigs to rehabilitate themselves as a popular party by a striking act of national policy, December 1845 had many parallels with November 1830; with a very different sequel.[4] Despite their parliamentary inferiority, the

[1] Lansdowne was supported by Clarendon and Auckland, and his stipulation was accepted at a meeting at Chesham Place on 19 Dec. attended by Russell, Clarendon, Grey, Baring, Palmerston, Ellice, Auckland, and Labouchere. It was decided that repeal should be accompanied by relief 'in a mode hereafter to be agreed upon' to occupiers of land and payers of local rates to the extent of not less than £700,000 in the first instance, to be extended to £1 million as soon as the state of the revenue permitted. No increase in taxation for this purpose was envisaged (Russell, *Later Corr.* i. 94–95).

[2] 'I propose', Russell explained to Lansdowne on 19 Dec., 'to write to the Queen to say that we found this morning the financial question very difficult and unsatisfactory, and that on proceeding to the arrangements of offices, I had found such a difference between two of the principal persons who were proposed for the cabinet that I must decline proceeding any further' (*Later Corr.* i. 95). The 19th was the day on which Russell had first offered the Foreign Office to Palmerston at 11.30 a.m.; then at 12 held a meeting to consider Lansdowne's insistence on compensation for the agriculturists; and after the meeting saw Grey about office and heard his objections to Palmerston. Auckland subsequently told him that they could not go on in the House of Lords without Grey, and Russell therefore sent Ellice to tell Grey that he could not proceed without him. Ellice returned and said that Grey would not yield (a possibly exaggerated version of what Grey actually said) and Russell made no further attempt to see Grey himself—a remarkable omission if Russell at that stage had any real determination to form a Ministry. The Old Whigs—Lansdowne, Bedford, Minto, Fox Maule, and Bessborough—were all glad that the attempt was abandoned, though some were sorry at the way in which it had happened. But Lansdowne was probably speaking for many when he told Russell 'it is good for you and for all to be out of the mess this time on any terms' (Russell, *Later Corr.* i. 99).

[3] Peel's resignation speech, 29 June 1846.

[4] The *Westminster Review* expressed the opinion that a snap dissolution by Russell in Jan. 1846 'might have secured not only a large majority of free traders, but a good working Whig majority in a new parliament' (vol. 45, p. 233).

Whigs took office after all six months later, as the result of a factious and momentary combination over the Irish Coercion Bill, and without the credit of repealing the Corn Laws. Their solid support in both Houses had enabled Peel to carry through his last dramatic act of major legislation, while they endured all the consequences of taking over the government for the next six years, with divided counsels, no clear policy, and a disrupted House of Commons. The general election of 1847 was the prelude not to a fresh start but to an unhappy recapitulation of the late 1830's with much the same men and much the same problems. The immediate context for their difficulties was provided by the new House of Commons. Though the theoretical Liberal majority just outnumbered Protectionists and Peelites combined, the extreme and independent Radicals had increased their strength at the expense of the good party men. Tufnell, the Chief Whip, estimated the total Liberal strength at 336, of whom 40 were doubtful, though half might be expected to vote with them, leaving a dependable strength of only 316, or less than a majority of the whole House.[1]

It was not an impossible position, given the divisions among Protectionists and the goodwill of the Peelites. But it asked for higher political qualities than Russell's Cabinet was likely to afford. In 1846 Clarendon had written a trenchant memorandum on the need to reform Whiggery itself—'as a political party it is thought to be nearly effete, and as the means of governing, a matter of history rather than of fact'. His solution was to reconstruct an Administration on a broader basis by incorporating Peelites and Free Trade Radicals, and so 'constitute a government fairly representing the industrial mind and

---

[1] Dod, *Parliamentary Companion 1847*, estimated the divisions of the 1847 House of Commons as:

Liberals	324
Protectionists	199
Peelites	117

a total of   640 in a full House of 656
(Sudbury had been disfranchised in 1844).

Tufnell's analysis was:

Liberals 336 (doubtful 40)
Peelites 85–90
Protectionists the rest (i.e. 225–230)
    (Hobhouse Diary, 8 Sept. 1847, Add. MS. 43751).

conservative progress of the country'. Any attempt to conciliate, as distinct from avoiding offence to the aristocratic and landed interest, he thought, would fail; unless the Whigs fell back on a standstill or retrograde policy which would infallibly alienate those classes on which all future Governments must inevitably depend.[1] The history of the next six years was little more than a commentary on this text. Russell himself was not insensitive to the matter of recruitment. But he tended to think in terms of Ministerial reinforcement rather than an enlargement of the party basis. He told Lansdowne in January 1848 that a Whig Ministry with Peelites or a Peelite Ministry with Whigs would offer the best chance of strength and stability. Yet he felt, not unnaturally, that as the Whigs furnished the numbers, it was for the Peelites to come over to them.[2] Clearly a great deal would have been accomplished had he been able, in Wood's phrase, to 'get the House of Commons into two parties'. An admixture of Peelites would have strengthened the Government's prestige, and a solidification of the Opposition would have united the Liberals.

On the question of Peelite recruitment Russell was certainly sincere, and the failure was not his fault. But there was perhaps a deeper significance in the fact that the only non-Whig politicians whom he made serious and repeated efforts to bring into the higher reaches of the Administration were the Peelites. The explanation is perhaps seen in a letter written by Russell to Bessborough in April 1846. In it he was arguing against an alliance with Liberal Protectionists, but in the argument he betrayed a more revealing attitude. 'I should not like', he observed, 'to embark on a government which rested on the support of any extreme party. This has been the case too much both with our Ministry of 1835 and Peel's of '41.'[3] If in fact Russell was turning back from the evolution of Liberalism as adumbrated in the late thirties, and pinning his hopes on a centre bloc of conservative Liberals—or liberal Conservatives—he was both abandoning the notion of a forward policy and making the future depend on his ability to forge a Whig–Peelite coalition; and such a union required mutual consent. The consent was not forthcoming; and in many respects the independent

---

[1] Maxwell, *Clarendon*, i. 265–7.   [2] Russell, *Later Corr.* i. 185.
[3] Russell MS., 11 Apr. 1846, P.R.O. 30/22/5.

role of the Peelites between 1846 and 1852 paralysed the Whigs. Behind the genuine desire to recruit some of their outstanding members, there was a more ambivalent attitude. There was a fear that the Peelites were the real rivals to the Whigs as aristocratic exponents of a popular policy; and a contradictory fear that any radical Government policy would reunite Peelites and Protectionists in a formidable Conservative Opposition.[1] It was a dilemma that was never resolved. When in the winter of 1850–1 Russell tried to enlist Cabinet support for a fresh effort at parliamentary reform, it represented little more than a despairing tactical expedient in which Russell himself only half believed, and his colleagues not at all.[2] Collectively the Whigs were never sure who were their best allies and who their real enemies.

It was this ambivalence on a crucial issue that explains the cardinal failure to bring Cobden into the Cabinet. Russell himself was not illiberal in this respect; and some of the Liberal-Radicals—Buller, Ward, Hawes, and Milner Gibson— were appointed to junior office. But the omission of Cobden outweighed these minor concessions. He could only be given cabinet rank, and to this there was obstruction from some of the Whig grandees and also from the Queen. Clarendon and Horsman emphasized the tactical advantage of detaching Cobden from a possible Peelite confederation; others thought that his accession to office would cement a combined Conservative Opposition. The decisive role was played by Russell, and his curiously vague overtures to Cobden in 1846 and 1847 betrayed the basic uncertainty of his own attitude. If he really wanted to appoint Cobden, he did not impose his will; and

[1] Cf. Charles Wood's argument to Russell in Aug. 1847 that though the Peelites were destroyed as a party, and the Protectionists thoroughly beaten, yet the Whigs must avoid mistakes that would play into Peelite hands. 'They and we are the rivals for the lead of the great popular party' and this was a compelling reason for recruiting some of their best men. Open warfare would be with the Protectionists, but 'I am afraid of the force on our flank' who would get credit and popularity whenever the Whigs tripped up (Russell, *Later Corr.* i. 179–81).

[2] When Russell broached his reform plans in Cabinet during the winter of 1850–1, they had a very cool reception. Any reform would necessarily involve more direct representation of a wider electorate, and hardly any of his colleagues wanted that. When asked by Hobhouse in Jan. what was the point of making a change, Russell replied that 'it would give satisfaction and show we were not afraid of introducing more of the popular element into the constitution' (Hobhouse Diary, Add. MS. 43755, pp. 33–34, 50–51).

there is no evidence that he seriously tried to impose it.[1] Either way, it was the first major error of the new Ministry, and it left Russell with a Cabinet which was little more than a reshuffle of Melbourne's team of 1841.

The consequences were immediate. In April 1848 some fifty or sixty Radicals under Cobden and Hume formally constituted themselves as a separate party with a general programme of governmental retrenchment and parliamentary reform; and though the endemic Radical vices of quarrelsomeness and individualism soon asserted themselves,[2] the breach between them and the Whigs was a running sore for the remainder of Russell's Administration. The split was not so catastrophic as that in the Conservative party in 1846, since the majority of the Liberals stayed with their official leaders. Nevertheless, with a slender Government majority, the declared independence of such a sizeable group of Radicals, coming after the strains inside the Liberal party revealed by the election of 1847, meant that the Whigs had lost control of the House of Commons. The first clear evidence of this had already come in February 1848 over the Budget, when criticism from Protectionists and Radicals forced the Cabinet to withdraw its proposal to increase the Income Tax from 7d. to 1s. in the pound in order to meet defence expenditure. From that point the Government was in a state of permanent weakness which could only be redeemed by resolute and consistent leadership.

It was precisely this which the Russell Administration was unable to supply. The policy of the Government in financial and fiscal matters was Peelite—or rather Peel and water; in ecclesiastical matters Low Church Anglican; in foreign policy Palmerstonian. It was not necessarily bad because eclectic; but

---

[1] Walpole, *Russell*, i. 442; Morley, *Cobden*, p. 403; *Victoria Letters*, ii. 131.

[2] A meeting over dinner of leading Radicals (Joshua Walmsley, Hume, Roebuck, Milner Gibson, Villiers, Cobden, Bright, and Fox) in July 1849 with the idea of concerting action, broke down on an inability to agree on either a leader or a policy. The main division was between those like Cobden who sought primarily retrenchment in Government spending, and others like Bright who wished to destroy the aristocratic monopoly of government by further parliamentary reform. In Dec. 1848 Cobden had launched a public campaign to compel the Government to effect reductions of £8 millions in the service estimates for 1849, but he remained sceptical of the advantages of any extension of the suffrage (Leader, *Roebuck*, p. 230; Morley, *Cobden*, pp. 487–8, 498, 500–1). For the Radical secession of Apr. 1848 see Grey MS., Grey's Diary for 17 Apr. 1848; Clarendon MS., Lewis to Clarendon, 17 Apr. 1848; Russell MS., P.R.O. 30/22/7, Hume to Gibson, 20 Apr. 1848.

in the circumstances of the parliamentary situation from 1847 to 1852 each section of the House outside the official following was bound at some point to be alienated. The Peelites disliked Palmerston's handling of foreign, and Russell's handling of religious affairs; Protectionists disliked Free Trade, income-tax, and Palmerston; Dissenters disliked the abandonment of Irish Church reform and the Government's educational policy; Radicals disliked the apparent aristocratic desire to conciliate the landed interest and the maintenance of heavy taxation to finance what they regarded as unnecessarily large expenditure on defençe and colonies. From one point of view this fragmentation of opinion enabled the Whigs to play off one side against the other; but in the long run it reduced Government policy to a series of shifts and compromises, and steadily eroded party loyalty among the mass of the Liberals themselves.[1] When tactics are elevated above strategy, there is always a danger that they become ends in themselves. Russell's Cabinet had no strategy, and the attempt to conciliate all the great interests earned the steady support of none. By 1850 the end was in sight. Bentinck's death in 1848, while it left leadership problems, was probably an advantage to the Protectionists; Peel's death in 1850 removed the one solid external prop of the Administration. The agricultural depression which started in the previous year created a sharper hostility among agriculturists and an increasing reaction against Free Trade.[2] At the end of 1850 Russell's

---

[1] Cf. *Greville*, 18 Mar. 1851. 'The Government is now so weak and powerless that its feebleness is openly talked of in Parliament, as well as derided in the Press. . . . Nothing is more extraordinary than the conduct of many of their friends, and the levity with which almost everybody follows his own particular inclination or opinion, regardless of the condition of the Government and of the grave questions which are looming in the distance.'

[2] In Dec. 1849 Russell told the Duke of Bedford, when discussing the Government's policy for the following session, that the imposition of a fixed duty would be 'foolish and even perilous. It would revive the Corn Law League and its agitation combined with projects for the destruction of the Church immediately and of the throne prospectively.' On the other hand he denounced the retrenchment campaign of Hume and Cobden, who seemed to wish to disarm the country and simultaneously expose it to war (*Later Corr.* i. 197–8). But not everyone had been sure that the Government would stand firm. Peel and Graham had received warning hints from Ellice in Nov. 1849 about the revival of the notion of a fixed duty. In consequence Peel wrote a calculated letter which Graham showed to Ellice, expressing his view that Russell could not possibly revert to a food tax and indicating strongly that he would be bound to oppose the Government if it did. It is fairly clear that Ellice passed the warning on. A month later, the Whig Chancellor of the

conduct in the Papal Aggression crisis provoked the simultaneous antagonism of High Church Peelites and the Roman Catholic Irish. From then on the Government went from chance victory to chance defeat in a kind of parliamentary medley which rapidly destroyed its inner cohesion and Russell's personal prestige.

Not the least consequence of the disintegration of Liberal policy and morale in these closing years was the steady decline of Lord John Russell's credit as a party leader. He had never systematically imposed his will on either the Cabinet or the House of Commons, and though not without liberal impulses, he had never evolved a coherent liberal policy. For all his talents as a parliamentarian, he was neither a good administrator nor an efficient Prime Minister.[1] It was perhaps a consciousness of this personal ineffectiveness that led to the increasing petulance of behaviour witnessed during the last years of his Ministry. In March 1850 he annoyed many Liberals by threatening to resign if defeated over Hutt's motion to withdraw the African squadron; and though the motion was in fact rejected, it was by a composite and almost casual majority of official Liberals, Peelites, and Protectionists.[2] Next year he gave an even worse exhibition over Locke King's motion for the extension of the county franchise. A similar motion in 1850 had been defeated with the aid of Peelites and Protectionists. In 1851 most of these independent allies marked their displeasure

Exchequer, Charles Wood, when travelling with Peel's son-in-law, Lord Villiers, said to him: 'Tell Sir Robert that we had six Cabinets, and the Corn Laws never once mentioned in one of them.' Peel had also spoken privately to the Duke of Bedford on the matter. Parker, *Graham*, ii. 87–90, does not make it clear that Peel wrote a separate letter, to be shown to Ellice, but for obvious reasons not mentioning him (see Graham MS., Graham to Peel, 14 Nov., Peel to Graham (two letters), 17 Nov. 1849).

[1] 'Lord John is not effective as a minister over the different departments. He positively exerts no control. Even in the Treasury his existence is scarcely known. I suspect that as a leader and a manager of a Cabinet he is not very successful. But as a leader of the House of Commons he is *facile princeps*' (G. C. Lewis to Clarendon, 7 Jan. 1852, Clarendon MS.).

[2] Cf. Greville, 20 Mar. 1850, for an account of the Liberal party meeting which preceded the vote. 'People came away furious and indignant, and several came into my room complaining of the hardship of being compelled to vote against their conscientious opinions on such a question, and on the unjustifiable conduct of the Government in threatening to resign at it. It seems to me that John Russel is demented at taking this violent course in reference to so unpopular a question. ... He has given deep offence and prepared great difficulties for himself hereafter.'

or indifference by abstaining from the division. Mustering only a miserable handful of official men, the Ministry was defeated by 100–52. It was a scarcely more significant issue than the African squadron, and indeed in the course of the debate Russell had promised to bring forward an equivalent motion himself at some future date. But over Disraeli's agricultural motion only a week earlier, which received the support of twenty discontented Irish Liberal M.P.s, the Government had been pushed to within fourteen votes of defeat, and Russell had had enough. The abrupt resignation of the Cabinet took most people by surprise, not least the Government supporters, and evoked severe criticism.[1] It was not only the back-benchers who were aggrieved. Russell's advocacy of parliamentary reform in the Cabinet had been coolly received; and his precipitate pledge of reform in the Locke King debate annoyed many of his colleagues. The decision to resign was impolitic and in the event rather ludicrous. The attempt to form an alliance with the Peelites failed, as it was almost bound to fail in the year of the Ecclesiastical Titles Bill; and Stanley was equally unwilling or unable to form an Administration. The Russell Cabinet resumed in a more shaken and provisional state than ever.

The last stroke was provided by the dismissal of Palmerston. If anything had been proved by the Don Pacifico debate in 1850, it was that Palmerston was henceforward an indispensable part of any Liberal Government. In seeking to consolidate their position in Parliament, the Russell Cabinet had in effect nailed the Palmerstonian flag to their masthead. His departure in December 1851 removed the last element of popular strength and the collapse of the government over the Militia Bill[2] early

---

[1] Charles Grey (Prince Albert's Private Secretary) wrote to Lord Grey on 9 Jan. 1852 a bitter criticism of the Government's 'parliamentary cowardice'; the apparently greater importance which the Whigs attached to concessions and management rather than boldly meeting their opponents in the House of Commons; and the ineptitude of introducing hasty measures to conciliate one party, only to drop them to please another. 'It will not do to allow the House of Commons to run riot at pleasure and then to turn suddenly upon them and on some defeat from your own friends in a small house, to throw the government up without previous warning as Lord John did last year' (Grey MS.).

[2] The majority against the Government (136–125) was mainly composed of Protectionists, Peelites, and about two dozen Liberals. The effect of Russell's Ecclesiastical Titles Bill was seen in the adverse vote of 15 Irish Radicals, who thus turned the scales against the Ministry. Apart from this disastrous defection, however, the significance of the division lay in the small numbers who took the trouble

in 1852 was merely the long-delayed bankruptcy of an insolvent Administration. It was a telling feature of Russell's period of power that without any major achievement or major crisis it left the Liberal party in 1852 more disintegrated and purposeless than it had been six or even twelve years earlier; and that his capacity for leadership was now seriously doubted by a large and influential section of his own party.[1] Faced in 1846 with a difficult but not desperate parliamentary situation, he had allowed it to deteriorate still further in the half-dozen years of his Premiership. His position of isolation in the Aberdeen coalition was a measure of the disrepute into which he had fallen.[2]

The nature of Russell's failure is clear enough. He had failed, not altogether through his own fault, in constructing a strong centre party. He had failed in the only possible alternative policy; that of building up a Liberal party with some momentum and principle. The wider responsibility for this is clearly shared by the leading Whigs as a whole. They did not lack realistic critics in their own ranks; but as a group they seemed psychologically incapable of acting on those criticisms. They did not throw up any commanding personality—for that perhaps their own essentially oligarchic temper was partly to blame —and they were unable to evolve a continuous and consistent policy which would harness and yet satisfy the aspirations of the

to vote—a characteristic of most of the divisions of the preceding sessions (with the notable exception of the Don Pacifico debate) and a clear mark of the breakdown of party discipline among the Liberals. It is possible that inefficient whipping by the inexperienced Hayter, who had succeeded Tufnell as Liberal Chief Whip, contributed to the result; but Russell perhaps rightly construed the defeat as a deliberate withdrawal of confidence.

[1] In July 1852 Roebuck asked Graham to lead a Liberal party in the House of Commons. Tufnell, the former Liberal Whip, whose resignation in Nov. 1851 had been one of the many signs of the disintegration of the official cadre of the party, told Graham about the same time that a great portion of the old Whig party would not support or serve in a government headed by Russell (Parker, *Graham*, ii. 161, 169). Aberdeen told the Queen in Dec. 1852 that the Peelites would not serve under Russell and that 'a great many Whigs even objected to Lord John' (*Victoria Letters*, ii. 415).

[2] Palmerston had been working in the autumn for a coalition of Whigs under Lansdowne with Peelites and moderate Conservatives; and when the Derby Administration resigned, the Queen sent not for Russell but for Lansdowne and Aberdeen. Though Russell formally took his party into the Aberdeen coalition, he became in effect merely an individual and when he retired two years later, he did so alone.

Left. Most of them perhaps did not wish to do so; for these the Age of Reform was already over. 'I am afraid', wrote Charles Wood to Grey in November 1852, 'that in the nature of things the Whig position is gone. We have carried nearly all that we contended for as leaders of the Liberal party. On 9 points out of 10 which remain to be argued and fought for we disagree with Cobden and Bright and the more active school of liberal politicians.'[1] It was a confession of bankruptcy; but perhaps a gratuitous one. There were other ways to lead the Liberal party than to swallow wholesale the conflicting schemes of Cobden and Bright. As the Don Pacifico debate had demonstrated, these two prominent parliamentary Radicals did not necessarily speak for middle-class Liberalism. Palmerston and Gladstone were to show that there were other means of eliciting national support. There was no substitute for leadership, however, and this neither Russell nor the Whigs had been able to provide.

Yet the material was there to be led. In a sense indeed the Liberal party between 1832 and 1867 was the residuary Government of the country: always a large and usually the majority party in the House of Commons. Only Peel's remarkable personal achievement in 1841, and a few transient and powerless Conservative minority Governments thereafter, broke their monopoly of office. Even in 1841 their defeat had not been catastrophic. At all other times the Whig–Liberal politicians at least governed the country, if they did nothing else. The formation of the Aberdeen coalition made no real alteration to this pattern. It marked the weakness of the Whig oligarchy rather than the disappearance of their following. There was a future for Liberalism, but none for Whiggery; and the man who ultimately climbed to power from the chaos of the 1846–52 period was not Russell but Palmerston, the veteran politician who had served his apprenticeship under Perceval, Liverpool, Canning, and Wellington.

[1] Grey MS., 5 Nov. 1852.

APPENDIX A

Electoral Prospects, 1840–1:
Two Rival Party Agents and Their Leaders

THE two letters reproduced below,

(*a*) Bonham to Peel, 4 Jan. 1840,
(*b*) Parkes to Russell, 7 May 1841,

from the central election agents of the Conservative and Liberal parties to their respective chiefs in the House of Commons, illustrate the kind of detailed advice party leaders sought and received from their electoral experts in this critical phase of the politics of the post-Reform era. Parkes's letter is self-explanatory; Bonham's is in reply to a letter from Peel (2 or 3 Jan. 1840?) which cannot now be traced and was probably destroyed by Lord Stanhope when the trustees of the Peel Papers purchased the Bonham correspondence in 1863. But Peel clearly put to Bonham a number of specific queries, the nature of which may be inferred from the answers:

(1) the probable result of a direct trial of strength in the House of Commons;

? (2) the likelihood of any defections from the Liberal party in the event of a Conservative Ministry;

(3) the probable strength of the Conservatives in a new Parliament following a dissolution at the hands of a Whig Government;

(4) *ditto* in the case of a dissolution by a Conservative Government.

The immediate background to this exchange was the question, then being privately discussed by the Conservative leaders, whether the relative equality of party strength in the Commons and the growing impatience of their followers did not call for an immediate attack on the position of the Government. But though early in the session the opposition beat the Ministers on the reduction of Prince Albert's Civil List allowance (by 158–262), on Yarde Buller's no-confidence motion of 28 Jan. the Government won by the comfortable margin of 21 votes (308–287). Parkes's letter sixteen months later was written at an even more critical juncture: when a governmental resignation was expected, when negotiations between Anson and Peel were about to start, and on the day when Russell announced the details of his fixed duty on corn in the Commons.

Apart from various illuminating *obiter dicta* on the practical work-ing of the electoral system, the primary interest of both letters is in the contrasting views they take of the probable result of a general election following a Whig dissolution. Bonham had been out in his forecast of a trial of strength in the Commons in Jan. 1840, but on this fundamental issue he proved more accurate than Parkes. On a subordinate point it is worth noting that if Parkes's 'dozen seats' included Irish constituencies, both experts were agreed in their estimate that about twelve seats were directly influenced by the Ministry of the day; but Parkes obviously expected the general circumstances of the political situation in May 1841 to work more pervasively in favour of the Government than they did.

(a) F. R. Bonham to Sir Robert Peel

(Add. MS. 40428, ff. 13–16)

31 U(pper) G(rosvenor) Street. Jany 4th (1840)

My dear Sir Robert. I have received by this mornings Post your letter together with that forwarded by Fremantle and shall proceed to answer both as far as I am able. To your first question I enclose a detail on which you will be able to form your own conclusion. *Prime* is, that on a direct vote of want of confidence we should have a certain majority. The eight doubtfuls would probably absent them-selves; or at least *not* predominate in favor of Ministers.

Of the eight Radicals I think we should have the first six; and the other two, with *many others* on all general questions against us, would not on *this* question directly vote with them, nor *on this point* do I see that Howick & C Wood could vote confidence in them without impugning their own course as selfish & factious. *Absence* would be their only kindness to them. On any Corn Law Question *they* would have the 8 Rads., *we* the 8 Doubtful, and a large number of their *uniform* supporters also.

On the Church or Education question again we should have nearly all the doubtful and some few others against the 8 Rads. But *at this moment* I doubt its being a very politic point to *raise*. Altogether then without troubling you with further detail I think on casting your eye over the list, you will agree with me that they have abso-lutely *no majority*. And as to the six seats to be *immediately* filled up, we are not unlikely to have one half. The other two are remote. To the 2^d question I answer the first *five* or *six* on the list. To the 3^d & 4th, my conviction is that in *England* and *Scotland* the result would be nearly the same tho' in *Ireland, your* Election might make a difference of five or six Seats in our favor.

There are about six Seats *at most in England* which would depend on the Minister of the day. *At this moment* I doubt whether there are so many.

On the other hand, if *they* dissolve *now*, you would find in many Towns the radical Constituencies (*far more radical than their Representatives*) prepared to make common cause with us against the Whigs, while at *your* Dissolution they will instantly reunite against the Tory ministerialist, and tho' on the first blush it may appear extravagant, yet when you have the probable results of a Dissolution *in detail before you* I think myself prepared to prove as far as such matters admit of actual demonstration the soundness of my conviction that excluding Ireland, *their* Dissolution will be no injury to us. I do not of course refer to *the only positive inconvenience* in compelling your friends to vacate on accepting office. Even in this evil however there is one advantage, that if your officials are distinctly apprized that in losing their Seats, they must also lose their offices, you will be less besieged with applications than you might otherwise be. But does it not occur to you that if the Whigs seek *under Court influence* their return to power in more favourable times when the present tide of unpopularity ceases to flow, they would more wisely follow *in all its parts* the policy of George the 3rd in 1806 and 1807? *They know* that a dissolution *now* would be utterly ruinous to them, but *if tried*, with what face could they at no distant day again dissolve *their own* Parl^t. Whereas it would be a *justifiable & necessary* step towards *yours*. As to the probable numbers in a new Parl^t it is of course absolutely necessary that you should be in possession of the details before the 16th, and I have worked at them with the utmost care and rather in the spirit of distrust, but they are so *very favourable* that I would rather decline laying them before you till they have been *thoroughly investigated* and *checked* by Granville Somerset & Graham who are entirely au fait on the subject, with the aid that Fremantle & Clerk may afford. I will however say generally that the result will be beyond what the most sanguine who had not gone minutely into the subject *could* have anticipated. *So entirely too are we prepared* (some elections will always *regulate themselves* at the last moment) that I should *relatively to their preparation* be glad Parl^t was dissolved next week.

I am too well aware of the mischief that *is brewing* in Scotland. At present it would be comparatively slight, and none of our *energetic* friends there take the popular side, but it is manifestly on the increase and with me would form *absolutely the strongest ground for an immediate Dissolution*. I can hardly think that *Melbourne* at least could go to the country on an Anti-Corn Law Cry, but many people think that *he* is about to retire. Again this question would produce the greatest majority against them, and it would hardly be good policy on their part to go to the Country with the greatest majority against them. The moral effect on *wavering* Electors would not be *convenient*. In a word then without presuming to give an opinion as to PARLIA-MENTARY convenience, tho' with reference to the *Mutiny Act*, I presume the earliest Dissolution is the most convenient; *as to our Election arrangements it is clearly so*. And I have also explained my reasons, quantum valeant, for my almost indifference as to the party dissolving *so far as the Returns are concerned*.

I cannot in justice to myself, or you, conclude without assuring you of the very general desire even *among those who have hitherto held a very different opinion* to turn out these *Ministers*. Every letter and every individual that I have seen breathes the same spirit. Forgive me *now* for intruding this fact on your attention which tho' pressed by many I should certainly have continued to avoid, as unbecoming and in me presumptuous, if I had not felt that your letter could not have been *faithfully* answered without some allusion to that on which Fremantle could doubtless give you fuller information.

Ever my dear Sir Robert,
yours most truly,
F. R. Bonham.

(On 5 Jan. 1840 Peel wrote to Wellington enclosing an account of the state of the House of Commons he had received from Bonham 'who is the best authority probably on this particular point'. The enclosure is clearly the 'detail' to which Bonham refers in his letter to Peel. It was as follows.)

Present State of the House of Commons Jan. 4

Conservatives	317	a.	Sir G. Heathcote
Doubtful[a]	8		G. Heathcote
Radicals[b]	8		Bennet
Vacant seats[c]	8		Chetwynd
Speaker	1		Goring
	——		Ingham
	342		Sir R. Howard
	——		B. Wall
		b.	J. Fielden
			Leader
			Molesworth

From   658
Take   342
    316 the maximum
of the ministerialists.

The attendance on both sides
I presume to be equal but I
presume we shall have the
advantage. However, *that*
Fremantle will report in
due time.

J. Jervis
W. Williams
Grote
Hume
Wakley

c. Ludlow
    Totnes
    Southwark
    Edinburgh
    Devonport
    Falmouth
    Newark
    Birmingham

(Apsley House MS.)

NOTES

Bonham was over-sanguine in his calculations of the result of a trial of party strength in the Commons, especially on the extent to which there were likely to be Ministerial defections. The division on Yarde Buller's no-confidence motion which took place after four nights of debate on 31 Jan. 1840 produced the following results.

Of the doubtfuls (a), there was in fact a predominance in favour of the Ministers. Five voted for and only three (Bennett, Sir R. Howard, and Goring) absented themselves.

Of the Radicals (b), only Fielden voted for the Opposition; Grote and Jervis were absent; the rest voted with the Government. So for that matter did Howick and C. Wood.

Of the six pending by-elections (c) decided before the division took place (Ludlow and Totnes remained vacant till a later date), all resulted in the return of a Liberal candidate.

The Government strength was increased therefore to that extent from the 316 estimated by Bonham.

Of the absentees from the division listed in Hansard, nine were Conservatives, and eight Ministerialists.

No-Confidence Motion (31 Jan. 1840): *Division Lists*

	Tabular Result	(from figures in *Hansard*, vol. 51, 1073)
Opposition		*Ministerialists*
287	voted	308
2	tellers	2
19	pairs	19
308	total vote	329
9	absent	8
317		337

Ministerialists	337
Opposition	317
Speaker	1
Vacancies	2
Unaccounted for	1
total strength of H. of C.	658

Comparison with Bonham's calculations

Opposition		*Ministerialists*
317	estimated party strength	316
0	doubtful	5
1	radicals	5
0	by-elections concluded	6
318	theoretical strength	332
9	absent	8
309	nominal strength	324
308	actual vote (incl. pairs & tellers)	329

(b) J. Parkes to Lord John Russell

(P.R.O. 30/22/4/A)

(Endorsed 'Jo. Parkes, May 7, 1841

    Question of Resignation   Westminster.
       or Dissolution')   21 Great George St.
                                         7 May 1841

Private

The Question of RESIGNATION *or* DISSOLUTION in my mind is one of no difficult solution. I form my opinion from much practical knowledge of the Representative System, & from some weeks mature reflection on the state of Parties; and from discussions of the question with many well judging & practical public men of the common Liberal Party. Moreover, I hear some shrewd opinions of the *Tories* on the subject,—opinions of opponents always worth some weight as comparison with our own.

I am decided for a Dissolution of the Parliament before resignation of office, and for the following reasons:—

I assume that *a* Dissolution, by one party or the other, is *inevitable*; and as to *time* that neither party could possibly many weeks defer it.—Even if Sir Robert Peel, succeeding the Whigs on their resignation this month, deferred dissolution till next Session—a most improbable event—the delay of course would only be to aid & better his own chances at the Elections. Dissolution by Sir Robert Peel, & especially the delay of it some weeks or months by him would be deeply injurious to the Liberal interest. His dissolution would be a great *rout.* Many present M.P.'s representing *Liberal* Constituences would, as always on a counter party dissolution, retire & not recontest their counties & boroughs. New Candidates in the *Liberal* interest would be fewer in a dissolution by Peel. Moreover, the liberal constituences in the entire Kingdom would be correspondingly dispirited by the Court & a Peel Government making the dissolution against them. Further, I consider the Government influence still most materially affects the returns of a dozen seats, if not more. It cannot be doubted that six or eight boroughs (Cinque Ports & other port towns) are much influenced by the Government of the day.—

The abandonment of office by the Cabinet *before* dissolution would particularly dispirit the Liberal Constituences, in as much as throughout the Provinces it would be deemed a *Political Suicide* in the Whigs and an act of *treachery* towards the Reformers.—

I am well aware of the temporary difficulties of the Liberal Constituences & Candidates, in respect of Poor Law prejudices (greatly *over*rated I think as the 1837 dissolution *proved*), in respect of Chartism,—& now in the Budget duties affecting sinister interests; and on the new turn of the Corn Laws question. But I am confident these difficulties are unavoidable; that is to say, that they cannot be avoided by Resignation before Dissolution. They are difficulties that will equally beset the Liberals on a PEEL DISSOLUTION: indeed I think they would be aggravated then, and much increased by Peel's craft and pretences on his dissolution. I admit the present position presents only a choice of evils, but for the above & other reasons I can see no difficulty in the election.—

I do not think the Corn Law question, after Lord John Russell this evening declares the particulars, will do us much *electoral* good or harm; but it will, with the Free Trade policy of Ministers, not only justify resort to the Royal Prerogative but much enspirit the Constituencies. When I say that these questions will not do us 'much electoral good or harm' I mean that I think the new policy & above questions will not much alter the comparative party returns.—

I assume, as the general opinion of both parties, that Scotland & Ireland will return about the present relative number of Party Representatives. I only qualify this opinion as to Scotland, doubtful till it is seen how the Scotch returns will be influenced by the *Kirk* questions. On this I am not competent to offer an opinion.

We have now only 43 or 44 Liberal *County* English & Welch M.P.'s. Apart from the Corn Law & Free Trade questions we long since well knew that nearly half this class of the Liberal Representation was lost to us on the next Dissolution, be it when or by whom made. Going over the *County* Lists I think we shall save half *our* present number at least; and indeed I think that liberal members such as Lord Worsley, Sir R. Price, Hodges, Handley etc. will be favoured by their opposition to the Government propositions. I see also by the Registration Returns subsequent to 1837 a *great* increase in the Constituencies of some of the more commercial Counties. This increase may perhaps aid the retention or gain of a few county seats.—I believe the greater part of this increase is in the franchises not Tenants. I need not set out these increases. They appear particularly in the Parliamentary Return ordered last Session, no. 579. (Abstract Returns of Registered Electors, ordered 1 August 1840)—

The real contest of Parties therefore will be for the 323 Borough Seats of *England*, and the 14 ditto in *Wales*.

The data on this department of the subject—involving only about half the entire Representation of the United Kingdom—is therefore the chief matter for consideration.—

Experience of 16 years active work in all classes of the Representation, and especially experience behind the Party scenes of the two last dissolutions, has convinced me—first; that the action of *political* principle & particular Cabinet policies on the English Borough Constituencies is much overrated: secondly; that the returns are much more influenced by particular *local* circumstances and the particular personal relations of *Candidates* than generally imagined: thirdly; that the returns are greatly influenced by the *sufficiency* & *purse weight* of *Candidates*: fourthly, that the Borough results in England generally much baffle previous calculations of both parties. I have noted those calculations on 2 Dissolutions; & I have been struck by the *unexpected* gains and losses of *both* Parties.—I know Mr. Holmes holds the same opinion.

The Gains & Losses in 1837 proved this fact, and were nearly balanced in number—contrary to the calculations of most of the managing men of both Parties. I believe I stood nearly alone in 1837 in the pre-estimate of the boroughs netting no material gain or loss, & in the estimate of a heavier loss in the English Counties; & which the results proved.—

The Corn Law Question I calculate may affect us adversely in some of the small *agricultural* Borough constituences of England; but not I think to the degree some anticipate; whereas it will (with Free Trade policy) aid us in the larger constituences. The effect may be seen by the analysis of the division on Mr. Villier's motion on Corn Laws, 19th Feb. 1839; and that division (the analysis shewing also the numbers of the Constituencies represented,) does not alarm me for the effect of Corn Laws on the smaller Boros. Also, it is observable that Corn Law is only *one* question and on that question Liberal Members will trim & keep their seats.

I am therefore disposed to consider exact and perhaps fallacious estimates of 'gain & loss' not so material in the decision of the Question of *Resignation* or *Dissolution*.—I view the question rather generally, & as a whole; on the above general grounds.

The County losses I apprehend most are

Bedfordshire	1.
Cheshire	1 if not 2.
Cornwall	1.
Dorsetshire	1.
E. Gloucester	1.
Herefordshire	1. { Hoskins I deem safe. Price *may* succeed.
Hertfordshire	1.
West Kent	1.
Somersetshire	1. [*sic*, but ? E. Somerset]
W. Sussex	2.
North Hants	1.
W. Somerset	1.
N. Stafford	1.
E. Sussex	1.
W. Worcester	1.

But several other County seats I think very critical if *all* are systematically contested by the Tories. Still, I cannot help thinking that the Corn Law votes of several present Liberal Members will aid the retention of seats that would otherwise have gone adversely at a Dissolution.

We may counterbalance some County losses by gains in W. Gloucester, S. Derby, W. Norfolk, S. Somerset [*sic* but ? W. Somerset], Middlesex & Flintshire. I fear the county of Cumberland on the votes of the present members. If *pro* Corn Law but nevertheless a Tory opposition there might not be a hearty support in the Cumberland towns of the Liberal Candidates.[1]

With Candidates in sufficient NUMBER to contest *all* assailable English Boroughs, and with ADEQUATE FUNDS, I think we might gain sufficient or nearly so to counterbalance loss in the English Counties.—

We shall lose or risk loss particularly in

1. Worcester
2. Leeds
1. Bedford
1. Bolton
1. Buckingham
1. Cambridge
1. Clithero
1. Exeter
1. Gloucester
1. Halifax
1. Hull
2. Knaresboro.
1. Lincoln

1. London *note* I think
     not 2.
1. Ludlow
1. Newark
1. Oxford
1. Petersfield
1. Pontefract
1. Reading
1. Shrewsbury
1. Wigan
1. Warwick (if Lord
         Brooke stands)
1. Scarboro.

and Bristol, Honiton, Norwich, Southampton, Tynemouth, York, Taunton I think doubtful.—

We shall gain or much chance gain in the following Boroughs particularly:—

1. Barnstaple
2. Bath
1. Beverley
1. Boston
1. Bridgnorth
1. Bridgewater
1. Brighton[2]
1. Colchester
1. Cricklade
1. Dover
1. Evesham

1. Lancaster
1. Liverpool
1. Marylebone
2. Nottingham Lord Rancliffe
         standing:
1. St. Ives.
1. Shaftesbury
1. Stockport
1. Wallingford
1. Wells
1. Weymouth
     Preston we might gain 1.

[1] I allude to James, ignorant of his vote on C. Laws.
[2] If local feud appeased.

1. Greenwich	Lymington & Lynn may be
1. Harwich	chance fought.—
1. Hereford	
2. Ipswich	
1. Kidderminster	

I omit 12 or 15 seats in notorious rotten Boros procurable. Last Dissolution most of these seats were left entirely to the Tories. Some I think—such as Norwich, Sudbury, Bridgewater, Berwick, etc.— might be expediently compromised 'one & one'.

Leeds well planted may now be saved. Indeed several seats I have entered as risk *losses* may & would be safe for good men.

I should consider it very expedient to fight 'dry elections' in several counties for obvious advantage in occupying & punishing adversaries and I would endeavour to contest every English Borough possible.

A Parliament of equal numbers in Party strength would not surprise me. I feel confident that the dissolution would array full 300 opposition members. On a Dissolution by Peel I should not be surprised if the Liberal Opposition did not exceed 250 or 260.

Joseph Parkes.

> P.S. From observation out of doors & in private Tory quarters I am confident that a Ministerial Dissolution is terror to the Tories. This fact speaks volumes on our policy.

NOTES

The results of the general election of 1841 showed that Parkes was generally more reliable in his estimate of probable Liberal losses than in his estimate of probable Liberal gains.

Anticipated losses in English & Welsh counties

Here Parkes was almost completely accurate. Of the 17 seats he listed, all but two were duly lost. The exceptions were E. Somerset and N. Hants (where the Speaker, Shaw Lefevre, was returned unopposed with a Conservative colleague). Moreover, not one but two Liberal seats were lost in Cornwall, so that of 17 anticipated losses, 16 were realized.

Anticipated gains in English & Welsh counties

Of the six possible gains he mentioned, only one occurred— Flintshire (where, however, the Conservative candidate, Sir Stephen

Glynne, was subsequently seated on petition, *vice* Mr. Edward Mostyn).

Anticipated losses in English boroughs

Of the 26 seats, the Liberals held those at Worcester, Bolton, Clitheroe (subsequently lost on petition, E. Cardwell being seated *vice* M. Wilson), Exeter, Gloucester, Halifax, Oxford, and Warwick (where Lord Brooke did not stand). They lost not only one but two seats in London, Reading, and Wigan (where, however, they recovered one seat later on petition, C. Standish being seated *vice* T. B. Crosse); but lost only one seat at Leeds. On the other hand they gained a seat at both Bolton and Gloucester.

Summary (excluding changes on petition)

anticipated losses	26
actual losses	17
additional losses	3
gained	2
held	9
net loss of	18 Liberal seats

Doubtful Boroughs

The Liberals lost one seat at Honiton and one at Southampton; no change in the other five boroughs.

Anticipated Gains in English Boroughs

The 32 seats listed by Parkes (i.e. including Preston, Lynn, and Lymington) must be reduced to 31, as the Liberals already held one of the two Nottingham seats. Of these anticipated gains, the Liberals realized fourteen:

Bath (2)	Greenwich	Nottingham
Beverley	Hereford	Shaftesbury
Brighton	Ipswich (2)	Stockport
Cricklade	Marylebone	Preston

On the other hand they lost former Liberal-held seats at Barnstaple and Harwich to the Conservatives.

There was no contest at Lynn; Lymington was contested without success by a single Liberal candidate; at Weymouth the two unsuccessful Liberal candidates, F. Bernal and W. D. Christie, were subsequently seated on petition *vice* Viscount Villiers and G. W. Hope.

Summary (excluding changes on petition)

anticipated gains	31
actual gains	14
losses	2
net gain of	12 Liberal seats

APPENDIX B

The Defeat of the Liberals, May–June 1841

THE following comparison of the Government vote on the sugar resolutions (18 May) and the no-confidence motion (4 June) is based on the division lists and the analysis of the sugar division in *Hansard* (vol. 58, 668–73, 1241–6), and the analysis of the no-confidence division in the *Westminster Review* (vol. 36, 232). The Government was defeated by 317–281 on sugar and by 312–311 on the no-confidence motion. It is worth noting that, in contrast to the division on Yarde Buller's no-confidence motion of Jan. 1840, there was only one recorded Conservative absentee from the sugar division and none on the no-confidence motion.

Nominal Liberal Party Strength and actual Government
Vote, May–June 1841

Sugar		No-confidence
281	voted	311
2	tellers	2
18	paired	11
301	total vote	324
1	deduct W. S. Lascelles (1)	
300	effective party vote	324
15 (3)	Liberals voted against	2 (2)
18 (4)	Liberals absent	8
		334
	deduct Bassett (5)	1
333	nominal party strength	333

NOTES

(1) A Conservative Free-Trade Member who voted for the Government on the sugar resolutions (see his speech in the debate 10 May, *Hansard*, vol. 58, 107).

(2) Long and Bennett (see below, note 3).

(3) 9 county M.P.s and 6 borough M.P.s voted against their Party on sugar, namely,

Co. M.P.s	Borough M.P.s
Townly (Cambs.)	H. Berkeley (Bristol)
Moreton (Gloucester E.)	Ingham (S. Shields)
Ld. Worsley (N. Lincs.)	Lushington (Tower Hamlets)
Handley (S. Lincs.)	Stewart (Honiton)
G. J. Heathcote (S. Lincs.)	Sir T. Styles (Scarborough)
Cavendish (E. Sussex)	Heneage (Grimsby)
Long (N. Wilts.)	(Of these, Lushington voted
Bennett (S. Wilts.)	on slavery grounds and it is
Cayley (N. Riding)	perhaps significant that four
	of the others sat for seaports)

(4) Of the 18 absentees on sugar, 9 were county M.P.s.

(5) Though J. Bassett (Helston) is listed as a Liberal, he was regarded as hardly an opponent by the Conservative Whips, and Dod, *Electoral Facts*, subsequently listed him as Conservative. He had in fact voted against the Government on sugar.

Summary

Of the 9 rebel county M.P.s on sugar, 6 voted for the Government on the no-confidence motion; one was absent (Heathcote); and 2 voted *against* (Long and Bennett). All the borough rebels voted for the Government on no-confidence. Both Long and Bennett were returned as Protectionists in 1841 and 1847, so that in fact their vote on 4 June marked their secession from the Liberal party.

Of the 18 absentees on sugar, 14 voted for the Government on the no-confidence motion and none against.

Of the 46 English and Welsh Liberal county M.P.s in June 1841, two may be omitted (Byng for Middlesex, which was hardly a true county constituency, and the Speaker, who sat for N. Hants). Of the 44 remainder, 30 voted (including 1 pair) for the government on sugar, 9 voted against, and 5 were absent; on no-confidence, 40 (including one teller and one presumed pair, K. Hoskins) voted for the Government, 2 voted against, and 2 were absent.

The analysis given by the *Westminster Review* for the no-confidence division was:

Majority for (including tellers)	314
Minority against ,, ,,	313
Pairs (11)	22
Absent (Ministerialists)	8
Absent (opposition)	0
Speaker	1
Total	658

The absent Ministerialists were: J. Bassett (Helston); J. Fielden (Oldham); R. Fitzgibbon (Limerick co.); W. C. Harland (Durham city); Sir G. Heathcote (Rutland); G. J. Heathcote (S. Lincs.); Sir R. Howard (Wicklow co.); General Johnson (Oldham).

APPENDIX C

Party Voting Patterns, 1841–7

PROFESSOR W. O. Aydelotte's analysis of party voting patterns from the division lists of the House of Commons 1841–7 (see his article 'Voting Patterns in the British House of Commons in the 1840s', *Comparative Studies in Society and History*, vol. v, no. 2, Jan. 1963) shows that a substantial number of divisions on different subjects—including Free Trade, political reform, income-tax, Irish questions, and ecclesiastical questions—fall into a single cumulative scale in the sense that almost all those voting positively in a given division prove to have voted positively in all divisions lower in the scale, while almost all those voting negatively in a given division prove to have voted negatively in all divisions higher in the scale. On this large group of issues, which occupied a principal share of the attention of the House of Commons, the voting patterns were 'relatively simple, regular, and comprehensive'. It is true that party voting on the issues in this scale was by no means always unanimous. Of the five divisions in the illustration below, only one—on the income-tax in 1842—was subject to almost a straight party vote. In a broader sense, however, a clear pattern of party voting is visible, since within the ideological spectrum defined by the scale, Liberals appear almost exclusively in the upper range and Conservatives almost exclusively in the lower range. Thus, in the table below, Liberals were almost unanimously positive on the third, fourth, and fifth items, while Conservatives were almost unanimously negative on the first, second, and third items. Despite disagreements within each party, the general area of opinion represented by each was unmistakable. The results suggest, therefore, that party attitudes on issues in the 1840's showed a considerable degree of consistency and that ideological differences were much more closely related to party in this period than has always been acknowledged. It may be observed that not all issues fit the scale just described. Divisions on factory legislation do not; they turn out, on the contrary, to form a separate little scale by themselves, quite unrelated to the first, and on issues in this second scale neither party took a clearly defined position. The following illustration shows party voting on a sample of the divisions in the first scale. It should be emphasized that the divisions chosen for this table are a selection only, and that many others could be added to or substituted for them without changing the pattern.

	Liberals		Conservatives	
	for	*against*	*for*	*against*
Chartist petition, 3 May 1842	51	68	0	221
Motion for repeal of the Corn Laws, 15 May 1843	127	52	0	331
Opposition to Income Tax Bill, 18 April 1842	186	6	4	279
Repeal of Corn Laws, 15 May 1846	235	10	114	241
Rejection of proposal that duty on imported livestock be taken by weight, 23 May 1842	169	29	213	86

It will be seen that a feature of the issues which can be fitted into this scale is that those which divide one party do not substantially divide the other. In other words, there were some issues on which voting followed almost exactly party lines and others which divided Liberals but not Conservatives, or Conservatives but not Liberals. As Dr. Aydelotte puts it, 'the break between Liberals and Conservatives comes at a clearly defined point on the scale, and the ideological gamuts of opinion in each party radiate away from this central point: the Liberals in one direction, and the Conservatives in the other'.

The article itself should be referred to for a discussion of the complex question of the proper interpretation of these scales. This brief account merely cites a few points from it which seem to throw some light on the nature of party in these years.

(I am indebted to Dr. Aydelotte and to the Editor of *Comparative Studies in Society and History* for permission to print this table and for other quotations from the text of the article.)

BIBLIOGRAPHICAL NOTE

PRINTED SOURCES

(*a*) Dates of editions of printed books are usually given in the footnote reference when first cited.

(*b*) All references to Hansard's *Parliamentary Debates* are to the
third series.

MANUSCRIPT SOURCES

(*a*) *British Museum* (*Additional Manuscripts*)
    Aberdeen Papers, Add. MSS. 43061–5.
    Broughton Papers, Add. MSS. 43748–57.
    Gladstone Papers, Add. MSS. 44275, 44777–8.
    Peel Papers, Add. MSS. 40181–617.

(*b*) *Public Record Office*
    Ellenborough Papers, P.R.O. 30/12/4–37.
    Russell Papers, P.R.O. 30/22/3–10.

(*c*) *Other Collections*
    Clarendon Papers, Bodleian Library, Oxford.
    Goulburn Papers, Surrey Record Office.
    Graham Papers, Netherby.
    Grey Papers, Priors Kitchen, Durham.
    Wellington Papers, Apsley House.

INDEX